# ARE YOU MOVING FORWARD WITH JESUS?

## HOW TO EXCEL IN YOUR IDENTITY IN CHRIST

Practical Applications For Your Growth:
Ideal for New and Seasoned Christians

## BY DR. RUTH TANYI

*Are You Moving Forward with Jesus? | How to Excel In Your Identity in Christ*
Copyright © 2017 by Dr Ruth Tanyi.
Published by     Dr Ruth Tanyi Ministries, Inc
                 P O BOX 1806
                 Loma Linda, CA, 92354, USA.
                 www.DrRuthtanyi.org

Cover design and Interior layout by: AJ Design

Additional copies of this book can be obtained from:
          Online: www.DrRuthtanyi.org
          Email: Info@DrRuthtanyi.org

All Scripture quotations, unless otherwise indicated, are taken from the *Holy Bible, New International-al Version®, NIV®.* Copyright ©1973, 1978, 1984, 2011 by Biblica, Inc.™ Used by permission of Zondervan. All rights reserved worldwide.

Scripture quotations marked NLT are taken from the Holy Bible, New Living Translation, copyright ©1996, 2004, 2007, 2013, 2015 by Tyndale House Foundation. Used by permission of Tyndale House Publishers, Inc., Carol Stream, Illinois 60188. All rights reserved.

Scripture quotations marked (AMP) are taken from the Amplified Bible, Copyright © 1954, 1958, 1962, 1964, 1965, 1987 by The Lockman Foundation. Used by permission.

**We want to hear from you. Please send your comments and/or testimonies about this book to: Info@DrRuthTanyi.org  or  write to:**

          Dr. Ruth Tanyi Ministries, Inc
          P O BOX 1806
          Loma Linda, CA, 92354, USA.

If you find any error in the citation of Scripture anywhere in this book, kindly contact us so we can make the necessary corrections, thank you.

ISBN 978-0-9986689-0-1
Library of Congress Control Number: 2017907052

All rights Reserved. No part of this book may be reproduced in any form without written permission from Dr. Ruth Tanyi Ministries Inc.
**Printed in the Unites States of America.**

# CONTENTS

| | | |
|---|---|---|
| 1 | Just In Case! | 11 |
| 2 | Know Your Identity in Christ | 27 |
| 3 | Know Who the Holy Spirit Is | 47 |
| 4 | Know the Basic Nature of the Bible | 65 |
| 5 | How to Harmonize the Testaments | 85 |
| 6 | Trust the Bible as God's Word to You | 103 |
| 7 | How to Study & Meditate on the Scripture | 117 |
| 8 | How to Practice What the Word Teaches | 137 |
| 9 | How to Pray the Word of God | 163 |
| 10 | Know the Basic Tenets of the Church | 207 |
| 11 | How to Become a Living Sacrifice | 243 |
| 12 | How to Develop an Intimate Relationship with God | 259 |
| 13 | How to Avoid Extremes in Your Relationship with God | 281 |
| 14 | How to Grow in Your Relationship with God | 299 |
| 15 | How to Be an Effective Witness for Christ | 317 |
| Conclusion | | 331 |
| Bibliography | | 335 |
| Ministry Resources | | 338 |
| About the Author | | 342 |

# Introduction

As a Bible teacher since 2006, I have taught and ministered to countless individuals, Christians and non Christians alike. What I find the most disturbing is when I encounter Christians, new converts and those who profess to know the Lord for over 5, 10 or more years, who are still unaware of what happened to them at the moment they accepted to follow Jesus Christ as their Lord and Savior. I wish I could tell you otherwise, but in my experience, many Christians are ignorant about their true identity in Christ. And it is unfortunate that many of my colleagues who are Ministers have expressed the same sad tale about their experience with many godly Christians who do not have a true revelation of what Christ did for them on the cross. This is rather heartbreaking, because this ignorance will prevent them from enjoying the many benefits of their salvation in this present life.

The Bible teaches that God's people perish due to a lack of knowledge, this is pitiful. In my view, one of the worst things that can happen to a Christian is to accept to follow Jesus Christ, and then walk away without any understanding of how to proceed in their relationship with Him. I liken this to allowing an infant child to feed themselves; that child will certainly not survive, they will die, because he or she will not be equipped to do so. Likewise, anyone who becomes a Christian and has not been discipled (i.e., taught about the Truths of the faith) is at a "crossroads", at risk of (1) remaining a "baby Christian;" (2) falling away; and (3) becoming an easy target for the enemy, Satan, who will definitely deceive the individual. Hence, discipleship is critical.

Discipleship is not just critical, it is mandatory. In Matthew 28:19, the Lord Jesus commanded us to make disciples. Being grounded in the Word of God is the antidote for overcoming the lies from our enemy, Satan, and in living godly lives. Thus, this book serves as a handy resource to disciple new and seasoned Christians alike. It provides practical recommendations to enable your growth as a child of God. To the new Christian, this book will help you to understand what took place the moment you became a Christian, and teach you how to proceed in your faith. To the seasoned Christian, this book is an excellent resource as it will bring to the forefront the unfathomable benefits and blessings you have in Christ. You will be edified and strengthened, as you will be reminded once more, of God's unconditional love and grace.

Furthermore, you will find that this book is easy to read, and packed with simple and practical daily recommendations that will propel your pilgrimage. As you enjoy its simplicity, you will want to recommend it to others who desire to grow in their relationship with God. For the non-Christian who is curious about the spiritual blessings Christians have inherited in Christ, this book provides the answers.

As you flip through the pages of this practical book, you will better understand your inherited position in Christ Jesus; the ministry of the Holy Spirit; the nature and trustworthiness of the Bible as God's inspired Word; and how to study and meditate on the Holy Scripture and apply it into your life daily. Additionally, you will learn how to harmonize the Old and New Testaments; the importance of the Church; how to pray God's Word into your life; how to develop an intimate relationship with God; how to effectively witness for Christ; and how to continuously grow in your journey as a Christian, plus much more.

It is my prayer that this book will bless you, as much as it has blessed me during the writing process. And I pray for you to open your heart, and by faith, allow God to speak directly to you, as He imparts His wisdom and guidance in your heart.

Sincerely,

Dr Ruth Tanyi

A very special and inexpressible gratitude to my beloved mother, Mercy T. Tanyi, for her unshakeable faith in Christ in spite of insurmountable challenges, including the recent unexpected death of her youngest son, my younger brother. I am blessed to be a witness of how the Lord is strengthening you through this very difficult journey. And I thank you, for all those formative years of my life when you took me to church; I will be forever grateful.

And to my beloved brother, Bedolf Tanyi, whose spirit is alive in the presence of the Lord, I will see you soon!

# Other Teaching Materials by Dr Tanyi to help you Grow with God through Christ

## BOOKS BY DR TANYI:

- *Answers to the Toughest 25 Questions about the Real Jesus.*
- *Can I trust the Bible as God's Word? How do I Know? What Is the Evidence?*

## COMING SOON!

- *13 Reasons Why People Get Sick! A Biblical Perspective & Remedies.*
- *Did God Really Say that? How to Overcome Doubt and Receive God's Promises: 10 Life-Changing Lessons Learned from Overcoming Metastasis Colon Cancer.*
- *A True Story of God's Unconditional Grace and Love: Healed by the Stripes of Jesus: My Story! My Miracle! How I Overcame Metastasis Colon Cancer.*

## AUDIO CD TEACHING LIBRARY:

- *The Heart of True Christianity: The Gospel Message of Jesus Christ: Answers to 10 Major Questions Pertaining to Your Salvation in Christ Jesus.*
- *What Are the Gifts of the Spirit?*
- *Holy Spirit-Led Healthy Emotions: The Fruit of the Spirit and Your Health.*
- *How to Overcome Doubt and Receive God's Promises.*
- *13 Reasons Why People Get Sick: A Biblical Perspective & Remedies.*
- *Unforgiveness and Other Toxic Emotions: How to Walk in Forgiveness.*
- *Live Above Your Fears & Overcome Sicknesses and Diseases.*
- *Be Anxious No More.*
- *Daily Habits For Your Soul.*

Grow in the Word of God and Receive His blessings through our Discipleship Bible Teaching Series.

The **Audio Podcast Series**, titled *"Biblical Principles for a Blessed Life,"* is an in-depth teaching through the entire Bible, from Genesis to the book of Revelation, focusing on major biblical principles, and teaching you how to apply those principles daily and receive God's blessings.

**Biblical Preventive Health with Dr Ruth®**
*Biblical Preventive Health with Dr Ruth®* is an educational magazine, which will educate individuals on how to integrate Bible-based principles into their lives, thereby preventing and overcoming sicknesses and diseases. You have heard what Medicine has to say! But do you know what the Bible says about a host of diseases plaguing people today? This magazine will teach you how to view your health from a godly perspective, and it offers practical recommendations to take care of God's temple.

**13 Reasons Why True Christianity is Different: A Wall Mount Poster**
This wall mount poster answers the question many individuals often ask: What makes Christianity different? This evangelistic poster will remind you daily of your unique relationship with God through Christ, and provide answers to confidently educate others and defend your faith. You will never be dumbfounded when asked to explain why your faith in Christ is unique, compared to other religions.

**Obtaining Ministry Resources**
To obtain additional copies of this book, or to get more information about the above ministry resources, please visit our Website:

www.DrRuthTanyi.org. You can also email, write or call us:

Dr. Ruth Tanyi Ministries, Inc
P O BOX 1806 I Loma Linda, CA, 92354, USA.
Email: Info@DrRuthtanyi.org
Phone: (909) 383-7978

# Chapter 1

# JUST IN CASE

This book is written for those individuals who have already made a genuine commitment to follow Christ Jesus as their Lord and Savior, and have denounced their sins, other gods or idols in their lives. However, if you have not made that commitment, or you just attend church and other Christian events, and have never made an honest commitment to follow the Lord Jesus, this chapter is specifically written for you, so that you may benefit from the teachings in the subsequent chapters.

Proverbs 14 verse 12 teaches that there is a way that may appear to be right, but the end will lead to destruction and death. With the many mundane daily decisions that we have to make, choosing the wrong way may lead to certain levels of destruction or even the death of an idea or a plan that could be remedied. For example, a bad business decision could lead to the destruction or death of a company, but this can be remedied or revitalized given a different circumstance. But in regards to your salvation (i.e., being delivered from the Sinful Nature of Mankind; the kingdom of darkness, and given a new life in Christ Jesus), and your eternity (i.e., life after physical death), making the right decision and choosing the right path is a matter of ending up either in hell or heaven once you die; this decision is entirely your choice.

Physical death is guaranteed. We are all living on borrowed time. Thus, we will all die someday. Currently, we are all dying at different rates; hence, preparing to meet God someday is the wisest decision we will ever make in this life. God does not only want us to be prepared to meet Him once we die, He also wants us to be delivered from the bondage of sin and from the

Kingdom of darkness in this life, which is ruled by Satan and his angels (Galatians 1:4). God wants us to come into the Kingdom of light, which is His Kingdom, because of His unconditional and unfathomable love for His creation, human beings.

### Each Human Being is Born Into this World as a Sinner

The Bible teaches that by nature human beings are sinners. Some of you may claim to have never sinned. But that is not true, because, all of us were born as sinners, and as such, have sinned before God, and we can never meet His holy and righteous (perfect) standard on our own (Romans 3:23) without a Savior. In order for you to fully understand why the entire human race sinned against God, we have to go back to the beginning of creation to find out what God tells us. Thus, a brief introduction to the first three chapters of the book of Genesis is warranted.

In the beginning, God created a perfect world as recorded in Genesis chapters one and two, and He created the first human beings on earth: Adam and Eve in His image, and placed them in the Garden of Eden to care for it. He gave them a choice (i.e., a Free Will, which is the ability to independently decide), and instructed them not to eat from a particular tree in the middle of the garden, which contained the knowledge of good and evil, lest they would die. The death in this context was not physical death, but rather, a spiritual death or darkness in the spirit of Mankind (see Genesis chapters 1 and 2). A person who is spiritually dead cannot have a relationship with the living God, and as such is lost (i.e., spiritually), without the assistance from his or her Creator, God. Such a person will also be separated from the presence of God, in all eternity, once he or she dies (i.e., the individual will end up in hell).

Adam and Eve were created as tripartite beings, consisting of a mind, body and a spirit, bound together as one. As such, all human beings born of a woman are born as tripartite beings, since Adam and Eve are considered to be the original ancestors of the entire human race. The Lord Jesus said the spirit part of a person is

*Just in Case*

what gives life (John 6:63), thus if the spiritual part of a person is darkened, and as such without life, the soul (i.e., the person's emotions, will, personality or temperament), and the physical body of such an individual, will not function as designed by God. This is because the life generated from the spirit gives meaning to the soul, which in turn enables the physical body to function.

Unfortunately, Adam and Eve were deceived by Satan, and they willfully disobeyed God and ate from the forbidden tree (see Genesis chapter 3). When this transgression (i.e., a willful action against God's command) took place, the spirit part of Adam and Eve was darkened, and as a consequence, sin and death entered God's perfect world and creation (see Genesis chapter 3). Since this transgression and subsequent "Fall from Grace," every human being ever born of a woman into this world, regardless of the culture, race, ethnicity or gender, is born as a sinner (Romans 5:12); because at birth, each individual automatically inherits this Sinful Nature from our common ancestors: Adam and Eve. By Sinful Nature, I am referring to that tendency or propensity that drives people to commit and practice sins.

Since all human beings can be traced back to one family: Adam and Eve, this explains why at the core, we are the same, although our exterior (i.e., skin color, language, etc) may be different. All humans have the need to be loved, accepted, respected, and the tendency to experience fear, loneliness, sadness, restlessness, practice sins, etc, regardless of our varied geographical regions, culture, language barriers, etc.

## Only Through Christ Jesus

God is 100% holy, with no darkness, deceit, sin or evil in Him (Isaiah 6:1-3; Psalm 99:9; 1 Peter 1:16; Revelation 4:8, etc). As such, in His view, a sinner is anyone born of a woman into this world, because of that inherited Sinful Nature from Adam and Eve. You do not have to commit a particular sin to be considered a sinner; just being born into this world by a woman qualifies you as a sinner. In Psalm 51 verse 5, King David acknowledged his Sinful Nature when he wrote that he was sinful at birth, and sinful from the time his mother conceived him; this applies to all of us.

I have actually heard some people say that in spite of their Sinful Nature, they have not sinned against God. In my view, that is not a wise perspective because at times we commit sins everyday without even knowing it, such as sins of omission, whereby we may ignore someone who needs help, or we may not exercise love and mercy towards others, or we even might harbor ungodly thoughts towards others, etc. Besides, not acknowledging your own Sinful Nature, believing and exalting your own goodness and holiness is an affront against Holy God, who calls your self-righteousness as filthy rags (Isaiah 64:6).

Because of God's unfathomable and unconditional love, grace, and deep desire to have a relationship with His creation, human beings, He had to deal with the sin and death issue, in order to reconcile us to Himself. As such, He became one of us, a human being, through the supernatural conception of Mary, by the Holy Spirit (I discuss more about the Holy Spirit in chapter 3). God became a Man, in the person of Christ Jesus, lived in time and space in this world over 2000 years ago, had a life-changing ministry, was crucified and died on the cross, but raised from the dead on the third day.

Through the death and resurrection of the Lord Jesus, He overcame death, and has delivered us from the Sinful Nature inherited from Adam and Eve. Christ Jesus died in place of each of us. Had He not died, each of us would have had to die for our individual sins, plus pay the penalty for each sin, which is impossible, given God's perfect standard. This sacrificial death of the Lord has made it possible, for each one who desires, to have a direct relationship with God, but you must come to Him through Christ Jesus only. This is the eternal Gospel message (that God became a human being like one of us, in the person of Christ Jesus, died for our sins because of His unfathomable love, and now we can have a relationship with Him).

You may wonder: Why was death the only way for the Lord Jesus to meet God's perfect standard? Great question! According to God's Law, a blood sacrifice had to be offered for sins to be forgiven. During the Old Testament era, animal sacrifice was the only way the people could appease God for their sins, and the New Testament teachings agree that without the shedding of blood, there is no forgiveness of sin (Hebrews 9:22). The Old Testament people had to perform the 10 commandments, plus over 600 other Jewish Laws in order to satisfy God's perfect standard of holiness (see the books of Exodus through Deuteronomy), but they were unable to do so, because they needed a Messiah (Christ Jesus, the anointed One, Savior of the world).

Many of the Old Testament Saints lived and died in great anticipation of the coming Messiah who would deliver them from their Sinful Nature, because of their inability to deliver themselves. But, Christ Jesus is the only person in the history of the world who lived a sinless life, and fulfilled God's standard of holiness perfectly (see the Gospels; 1 Peter 2:22; Hebrews 4:15; 2 Corinthians 5:21).

Because of God's perfect standard of holiness, His standard for a relationship with us, "Fallen and Sinful human beings", is the Lord Jesus, who met His criteria of holiness 100%. So no matter how perfect you may be in your actions and goodness towards others, without going through Christ Jesus, who was God Himself in the flesh, God the Father sees you as a sinner, period! Some of you may be wondering why I am referring to the Lord Jesus as God? It is a valid question, which demands and answer.

### Christ Jesus: 100% God and 100% Human

The Bible teaches that Christ Jesus was God incarnate, meaning, He was supernaturally conceived in Mary's womb by the Holy Spirit, then Mary gave birth to Him. Jesus was fully human (100%), and fully God or Divine (100%), and existed even before the creation of the world (Colossians 1:15-17; John 1:1-14; John 8:58). True Christianity is a monotheistic (i.e., worship of one God) faith; One God in three unique or distinct persons: God the Father, God the Son (referring to Christ Jesus), and God the Holy Spirit, equal in divinity and power, usually called the Triune Godhead, which is referring to the teaching of the Trinity.

The mystery of the Trinity is such that we accept it by faith, because that is how the God of the Bible has revealed Himself to us in His Word. The God of the Bible condemns Polytheism (i.e., the practice of multiple gods), and has revealed that we should worship Him as One God (Deuteronomy 6:4; Isaiah 45:21; Mark 12:29 ). Although the word Trinity is not found in the Bible, the teaching is taught throughout the Old and New Testaments. Some examples include, but are not limited to: Genesis 1: 26; Matthew 28:19; 2 Corinthians 13:14; 1 Peter 1:2; Luke 3: 22, etc.

Throughout His ministry, Jesus called Himself God, and explicitly stated that He is the Only way to eternal life. Today many people erroneously call Jesus a "good person or a teacher," but He was more than that: He was God Himself who came to teach and to reveal the goodness of God the Father to us. Others outright reject Christ Jesus as the only hope of the world, but He is. In the Gospel of John chapter 14, Jesus Himself said, *"I am the way and the truth and the life. No one comes to the Father except through me"* (v. 6) (emphasis author's). The Lord Jesus is not just a way. **He is <u>THE ONLY WAY to the Only One True God of the Bible</u>, and your Only ticket to eternity.**

> *The Lord Jesus is not just a way. He is THE ONLY WAY to the Only One True God of the Bible, and your Only ticket to eternity.*

Below are just a few of Jesus' claims to be God:

John 10:30:    *"...I and the Father are one."* Jesus made no apologies about this matter, He categorically called Himself God;

John 5:21:     *"...For just as the Father raises the dead and gives them life, even so the Son gives life to whom he is pleased to give it,"* Jesus verbalized His equal authority with God the Father;

John 6:35 *"... I am the bread of life. Whoever comes to me will never go hungry, and whoever believes in me will never be thirsty."* Jesus claims He is the Only source to quench our innate spiritual quest for the living God;

Mark 2:10 *"... But I want you to know that the Son of Man has authority on earth to forgive sins..."* Jesus is claiming equal authority with God the Father to forgive all of the sins of Mankind;

John 14:6 *"... Jesus said to him, "I am the way, the truth, and the life. No one can come to the Father except through me."* In order to have a relationship with the Only True God, Jesus is claiming that you must come through Him only;

John 10:9 *"... I am the gate; whoever enters through me will be saved. They will come in and go out, and find pasture."* There is only One true gate into eternity, a narrow gate, and Jesus is claiming that He holds the key to that gate: You must go through Him first, in order to get in and spend eternity with God;

John 15:1 *" I am the true vine..."* Using an allegory to describe the relationship between a vine (plant ) and its branches, Jesus is claiming that He is the Only source of True power, just like God the Father, and without abiding in Him by faith, we, the branches, cannot bear good fruits;

John 8:58 *"Very truly I tell you,"* Jesus answered, *"before Abraham was born, I am!"* Jesus claimed to be God by using the same name: I AM, that God Himself used when He appeared to Moses in the burning bush (see Exodus 3:14);

John 11:25  "... *Jesus said to her, "I am the resurrection and the life. The one who believes in me will live, even though they die..."* Jesus is claiming that He has the power to raise anyone from the dead and give them eternal life, just like God the Father;

John 8:12  "... *When Jesus spoke again to the people, he said, "I am the light of the world. Whoever follows me will never walk in darkness, but will have the light of life."* Jesus called Himself God by describing Himself as light, one of the characteristics used to describe God the Father throughout the Bible.

The above claims by the Lord Jesus were not just mere words, He backed them up by displaying supernatural power and control over nature. He performed hundreds of miracles: He raised the dead; calmed the storm; walked on water; fed the multitudes; healed the sick; displayed unconditional love and care for the poor and destitute. He Himself was raised from the dead exactly as He prophesied, plus much more as recorded in the four Gospels. You may wonder why I am so convinced that Christ Jesus was God Himself. The answer is simple: **No other self-proclaimed religious leader in the history of the world has ever claimed to be God as the Lord did, and then backed it up 100% with validated, verifiable, and historical documented evidence, except Jesus.**

> *No other self-proclaimed religious leader in the history of the world has ever claimed to be God as the Lord did, and then backed it up 100% with validated, verifiable, and historical documented evidence, except Jesus.*

With regards to the humanity of Christ, there are many Scriptural references that teach how Christ Jesus was also 100% man (i.e., a human being like one of us). The Holy Scripture teaches that Jesus grew physically in stature and in wisdom (Luke 2:52); He experienced hunger, thirst, fatigue, and pain, just like we do (see John 19:28; I Peter 2:23; Matthew 4:2); He was tempted (see Hebrews 4:15; I Corinthians 10:9); He represented the head of humanity, just

*Just in Case*

like Adam did in the Old Testament (1 Corinthians 15:45, 47); Jesus called Himself the Son of Man (see the Gospels); after His resurrection, He ascended into heaven in bodily form; and even now, Jesus still identifies Himself with man (see Revelation 1:13, 16). Based on the few Scriptural examples above, it is obvious that Jesus Christ lived and operated on this earth like one of us: a human being, even though He was also God 100% in His essence (I am not referring to the physical form of Jesus, because God is a Spirit. Rather to His mannerisms, such as His unconditional love, compassionate, meekness, forgiving nature, etc). The identity of Jesus as 100% God and 100% man is something that is difficult for many people to "swallow." But, this is how God chose to reveal Himself to us, and we have to, by faith accept it, in order to experience His peace and comfort about the matter.

**Christ Jesus is Either God or He is Not: There is No In-between**

Christ Jesus is God's free gift to Mankind, but He has left us with only two choices: (1) accept His claims in faith and experience His presence, confirmation and transformation in your life; or (2) deny and reject Him, and live your life without Him and spend eternity in hell (i.e., separation from God's presence). It is as simple as this: You must decide. By the way, not deciding is a choice, against Him. It is either Jesus is who He said He was, or He was a liar and a mentally deranged individual. He leaves us with no in-between choices; we either accept His claims or reject them by faith, period! In Revelation 3:20, Jesus said He is at the door knocking (i.e., He wants to reveal Himself to us), if we will allow Him in. And if a person says yes, He will send His Spirit to indwell them.

What are you going to do with the claims of Jesus? They cannot be ignored! These are some serious claims that each one of us has to deal with at some point in this life. Also, ignoring these claims is actually a decision against the Lord. Besides the Bible, there are numerous accounts from first Century historians such as Flavius Josephus, and other sources such as the Jewish Talmut (collection of extra biblical Jewish writings, customs and traditions) that documented the existence of the Lord Jesus in time and space in this earth. In fact, did you know that there are more extra biblical evidence (i.e., historical accounts) of the existence of Christ Jesus than there are about other noted individuals, such as Plato, Julius Caesar, etc? Many people are shocked to know this simple truth about the existence of our Lord.

Over 2000 years ago, the Lord Jesus asked His disciples a simple question as recorded in Matthew 16:13: *"Who do people say the Son of Man is?"* (emphasis author's). His disciples had to answer for themselves. Likewise, this is a question that each one of us must independently answer. Today, I am asking you the same simple question: **"Who do you say Jesus is?"** Hopefully, God has been speaking to you, and you have come to the conclusion that Jesus is who He claimed to be. The Bible teaches that there is no other name given to man by which salvation must come, except through the Lord Jesus (Acts 4:12), and God will only accept those individuals who accept His Son Jesus (Matthew 10:33). I hope you are in agreement.

*Although Jesus died for the sins of the entire world, each individual has to make a choice to accept Him by faith. He died for a "whosoever" that believes, meaning anyone, including you, and not just for a pre-selected group of people like some people erroneously proclaim.*

Christ Jesus loves you unconditionally. If you were the only one in this planet earth, He would have still died for you, because His deepest desire is to have fellowship with you, whom He created. For God so loved the world that He gave His One and Only Son, the Lord Jesus, that whoever believes in Him shall not perish but have eternal life (John 3:16). **Although Jesus died for the sins of the entire world, each individual has to make a choice to accept Him by faith. He died for a "whosoever" that believes, meaning anyone, including you, and not just for a pre-selected group of people like some people erroneously proclaim.**

*Just in Case*

# PRACTICAL APPLICATION

God wants to lead you through the right path that leads to a life of peace and assurance about your destiny after you die. Do you know what happens to you the moment you die? You can know for sure today, right now! The Lord Jesus is the answer! Christ Jesus is the only human being who came from the other side (i.e., heaven), and can directly take you there once you take your last breath here on the earth. Why would you not want to trust such a person? Do you know anyone who has been on the other side and back?

Satan's primary goal is to steal, destroy and ultimately kill you, but the Lord wants to give you abundant life, in this life, and to deliver you from yourself and from the Kingdom of darkness, belonging to Satan. The Lord wants to give you a supernatural peace and joy that can only come from God (John 10:10). You may think your life is perfect now, but you will be surprised what a difference Christ Jesus will make in your life.

Now that you know the Truth why Jesus died for you, only one thing is required. An honest decision to follow Him as your Lord and Savior. Accept to follow the Lord today and start experiencing a supernatural dimension of joy and peace, which only true Christianity can offer. The world will offer you "happiness," which is primarily based on the circumstances in your life, which fluctuates daily. But Christ Jesus will give you joy, peace, hope, stability, etc, that cannot be affected by your circumstances, because He is the same yesterday, today and forever (Hebrews 13:8).

## Accepting to Follow Christ Jesus is Simply Making a Heartfelt Decision

You do not have to change your lifestyle before accepting to follow Jesus— come exactly as you are, right now; He loves you as you are. It is a decision of the heart. You do not have to figure it out before following Him, just accept Him, then things will start making sense. It is a step of faith, and the moment you take that step, God will reveal the next step to you, then you will start gaining understanding. It is amazing how this works out; trust God, and you will not regret it.

If you are considering what I have been teaching thus far, and you are reluctant to make a decision to follow Christ, do not do that, because that is probably Satan, trying to prevent you from turning away from his Kingdom. Do not postpone this decision: Salvation is now, tomorrow is not guaranteed. Before going to bed tonight, you want to be absolutely certain about what will happen to you the moment you die.

Once you make the decision to follow Christ, He will instantly shine His light into your darkened spirit, and you will be instantly "born again," meaning you will experience a spiritual rebirth or become twice born (John 3:3). Your first birth was when you were physically born into this world. Accepting to follow the Lord will be a second birth, except it will be a spiritual birth, in the spiritual realm. Once you become born again and your darkened spirit becomes illuminated or regenerated, you will be instantly given a brand new spiritual identity (2 Corinthians 5:17), and you will become a true Christian.

You may ask: What do I have to do to be born again? It is simple: Accept you are a sinner, then ask God to forgive all of your sins, then believe in your heart in all of the claims and works of Christ Jesus, and confess with your mouth that God raised Him from the dead after three days, that is all. Once you do that, according to the Bible, you will be saved and instantly experience this new birth (Romans 10:9-10; 2 Corinthians 5:17).

I have used the phraseology "true Christian" throughout this book because many people are deceived into thinking they are Christians, because they attend church and other various Christian functions regularly, or are raised in a Christian home, or their parents are ministers or pastors, or because they live in the United States of America (USA), which is predominately considered to be a Christian nation. Unfortunately, these external things do not mean a person is a true Christian, because it is impossible for anyone to

*Just in Case*

earn their way into eternity: You must be born again.

In the Parable of the Wheat and the Tares, the Lord teaches how in the world, which obviously includes the Universal Church (i.e., all Christian churches globally), since the Church (i.e., the Universal Church) is in the world, genuine and "counterfeit Christians" coexist (Matthew 13:24-30). And at times, it might be difficult to tell the difference between the two. But at His second coming, He will separate them, and the counterfeit ones will end up in hell. This is a very scary teaching, because it implies that there are thousands of people who attend church regularly, but they are deceived, thinking that church attendance will grant them salvation and eternal security.

My personal testimony is that I was raised by godly Christian parents, and I attended church regularly, but I did not experience the spiritual life the Lord died for me to enjoy. I was faithful in reading the Bible, but I had no revelation of God's Word, and I was unable to overcome the basic challenges in life. Then one faithful day, after watching a Television (TV) show by Evangelist Billy Graham, he posed a question that caused me to seriously consider my life. After he finished proclaiming the Gospel message, he simply said something like this: "I don't care if you attend church, or if you are a minister or elder in your church! Do you have a personal relationship with Jesus?" When he said that, I realized that I had never, personally asked Jesus to come into my life, even though I was very involved in church activities. So I went on my knees and asked Jesus to come into my life, and He did. So, there are many of you who attend church, and are falsely thinking that you are a true Christian, but you are not: You must be born again

Just in case you are wondering, the following is a description of a true Christian according to the Bible: **A true Christian is an individual who has denounced their sins and has accepted Jesus Christ as their Lord and Savior. This individual believes in their heart by faith, and has confessed with their mouth that Jesus is God (the Only One and True God), who was crucified, died and resurrected on the third day by God the Father. Such an individual has been "born again," their past sins, and** the penalties of the sins completely paid for and forgiven by the blood of Christ Jesus. A true Christian has also been sealed with the Holy Spirit, and is destined for heaven upon death (**Romans 10:9; Ephesians 1:13; 2 Corinthians 5:7**).

Does the above description apply to you? If not, you can change that today. The Bible teaches in Ephesians 2:8 that: *"by grace you have been saved, through faith—and this is not from yourselves, it is the gift of God— not by works, so that no one can boast* (emphasis author's). No godly activity will ever make you a genuine Christian, and household salvation is not a choice either, you must decide individually. So if you are unsure whether or not you have made a sincere commitment to follow the Lord, it is time to evaluate your heart and consider making that commitment today! Right Now!

If you are ready to receive God's forgiveness and to follow Jesus as your personal Lord and Savior, or if you want to rededicate your life to the Lord , say this simple prayer, if you are sincere:

*Dear God, I thank you for sending your Only Son, Christ Jesus to die for all of my sins and to wipe out all of the penalties for my sins. I acknowledge I am a sinner. Please, I ask you to forgive all of my sins knowingly and unknowingly. Forgive me for not acknowledging this Truth before. Today, I believe in my heart in Your Son Christ Jesus, and in all of His claims and works. I believe He died on the cross for my sins and was raised from the dead after three days. Today, I am asking you, Jesus, to come into my life as my personal Lord and Savior and change me. From this day forward, I denounce all other false gods and idols in my life, and I have chosen you, the Only True living God. I declare by faith, that I am now a true Christian. Thank you God, in Jesus name, Amen*

If you genuinely said that prayer from your heart, based on the authority of the infallible Holy Scriptures, you are a true Christian, and your destiny has automatically changed. You have changed positions from the Kingdom of darkness (belonging to Satan) and now you are in the Kingdom of light (belonging to God). I welcome you into the family of God: The body of Christ (i.e., the collection of all true Christians globally, regardless of gender, race, ethnicity, church or denominational affiliation, who have personally placed their faith in the Lord Jesus and have a relationship with God).

In conclusion, now that you are a true Christian, the immediate changes that just took place in your spirit are enough to empower you to want to learn more about your brand new identity in Christ. In the remainder of this book, I will use the words "believer(s)", "brethren", or Christian(s) interchangeably, to refer to true Christians. Now proceed to chapter 2 to learn what just happened to you in the spiritual realm. Or, if you are a "seasoned" Christian, proceed to the next chapter to learn more about "excelling" in your identity in Christ and experience God's best for you.

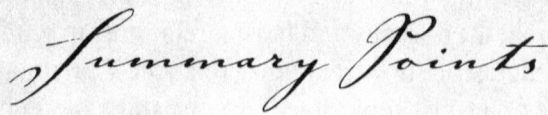

- Sin and death entered God's perfect creation because of the transgression from our common ancestors: Adam and Eve;

- All human beings are born into this world with a Sinful Nature inherited at birth because of the transgression of Adam and Eve, and are in need of a Savior to redeem them;

- Because God is perfectly righteous and holy, He had to deal with the sin issue before restoring fellowship with fallen human beings;

- Christ Jesus, the Savior of the world, whose death and resurrection overcame sin and death, has paved the way for "fallen" human beings to have a personal relationship with God, who is holy. But this relationship is only possible through Christ Jesus, who is The Only way to the Only True living God of the heavens and the earth: the God of the Bible;

- Although Christ Jesus died for the sins of the world, God has given each one of us the choice to personally accept His sacrificial death, and to follow Him as our Lord and Savior;

- Accepting to follow Christ Jesus is simply a heartfelt genuine decision by faith, with no extra "works" needed from you, and God will accept your decision 100%.

# Chapter 2

# KNOW YOUR IDENTITY IN CHRIST

Many of us who live in the United Sates have seen those make-over TV shows, where a person is completely transformed into a new person outwardly. At times, the transformation involves a slender physique, a new hair-do, new makeup, etc. Such transformations are always amazing and exciting to watch, as the transformed individual would walk around with much confidence and boldness. Usually, they would make comments such as: "I can now take on the world," or "I am now confident to date," etc.

When I watch such make-over TV shows, I am often concerned because such external transformations only provide temporary assurance, because any lasting change must come from within and through God only, and not without. Well, the best news is that, as Christians, God has blessed us with a brand new "DNA" in the spiritual realm, which I believe will empower us with much stability, confidence, boldness, assurance, and the ability to experience the permanent transformation that God designed for His children.

Whether or not you just accepted to follow the Lord today, right now, or you have been a Christian for some time, according to the Bible, numerous instantaneous changes took place in the spiritual realm the moment you made that genuine confession of faith. In brief, these Truths (see the next section) include but are not limited to the eternal fact that you have been redeemed; reconciled with God; justified; sealed with the Holy Spirit; made righteous; have direct access to God; adopted into God's Kingdom; baptized into the body of Christ; already glorified and sanctified in God's eyes (although the continuous process towards perfect sanctification and glorification are still underway); your eternity is secured; you will be resurrected after you die; and God sees you through Christ as a Saint. These instantaneous blessings represent your new position in God's Kingdom, and they are often referred to as positional Truths.

## Positional versus Experiential Truths
**You Cannot Change Your Position or Standing**

The true Christian's "position" in Christ, sometimes referred to as positional Truths or standing, has to do with the way God sees you right now in this world, because of your relationship and union with Christ Jesus, regardless of your present "state" (i.e., the way you live out the Christian faith or the way you view yourself). This union with Christ is so real that the Bible says once we become Christians, we actually become partakers of Jesus' death, burial and resurrection (Colossians 2; Romans 6:4).

Before I delve into much discussion, below are a few things you must keep in mind about these positional Truths, which are solely based on your decision to become a Christian:

1. It is 100% based on God's grace because of your acceptance of Christ Jesus' sacrificial death, burial and resurrection. None of us is worthy of this, and we do not deserve this; it is 100% because of God's love. It is a FREE gift, which cannot be earned through any sort of diligent prayer, church attendance, godly service, etc ( Romans 5:2).

2. We must accept it primarily by faith, because God tells us so in His Word. We cannot "feel these Truths" before accepting them. For we live out the Christian life by faith, in accordance with God's Word and not based on what we see or feel (2 Corinthians 5:7).

3. These Truths are perfect. It is the best it will ever be. We cannot add or delete from these Truths, and there is absolutely nothing we can do to make them better or improve on them. For example, you have complete forgiveness of all of your sins at the time you genuinely accepted Christ Jesus, period, whether or not you

accept it ( Romans 5:2; Hebrews 10:14).

4. These Truths are identically the same for every true Christian. All true Christians have an equal position, standing and status with God, regardless of their present state. For example, the weakest and most "Carnal" Christian today (i.e., one who is attempting to live out his or her Christian faith primarily based on emotions, worldly standards or from his or her own efforts, rather than from biblical teachings and Truths), and the greatest godliest Saints of the faith, such as the apostles Paul, Peter, or John, etc, whom God used mightily, all have an equal standing with God (1 Corinthians 12:12-13; 2 Corinthians 5:17).

However, when it comes to receiving the abundant blessings and rewards from God in this life and in eternity, the godly Christian living in obedience will prosper and "shine." Such a Christian will be better equipped to handle and overcome the trials and tribulations in this life, compared to the carnal Christian, who will have nothing to show, and be subject to defeat and torture from the enemy, Satan. Even if you have been a Christian for some time and your present "state" does not glorify God due to your poor choices, that does not change these positional truths about your salvation, which are permanent and eternal.

Compared to our positional Truths, the Christian's present "state," condition or experience as a follower of the Lord is a completely different matter, because it solely depends on his or her decisions after the initial confession of faith is made. For clarification, your "state" as a Christian, refers to your actual spiritual experience with the Lord Jesus as you live out your faith, at any given point in this life. Many Christians often refer to this experience as "their walk" with the Lord Jesus, referring to the way the Christian lives and conducts him or herself daily.

This notion of the believer's experience or "state" is where many godly Christians become very frustrated and are easily deceived by Satan that this "Christian thing" is not real, and that it does not work. But that is a lie, because it is as real as what God says you are, as expressed throughout His Word, the Bible. And for the unbelievers, they cannot even fathom or reconcile a believer's position in Christ Jesus, with some of their actions, which unfortunately, can be a turn off to them. Nonetheless, the primary reason for the frustration is because your experience primarily depends on your decisions, whether or not you (1) entirely trust the Lord to guide your life daily; (2) abide in Him daily; (3) obey His Word; and (4) obey the inner promptings of the Holy Spirit in your heart (I discuss all of these in subsequent chapters).

## You Can Change Your State or Experience

Since God has given each of us a Free Will, it is up to us to live in accordance with His will or reject it. This principle is the same even after you accept to follow Christ Jesus as your Lord and savior. Thus, your decisions will greatly affect your experience as a Christian. Below are a few things about the Christian's "state" or experience to keep in mind:

1. Your "state" or experience as a Christian falls short of perfection, and you will never attain perfection no matter how hard you try. We are still finite beings living in a fallen world. Even the greatest Saints of the faith, such as the apostle Paul, who wrote over 50% of the New Testament under the inspiration of the Holy Spirit, expressed how he had not yet attained the goal of his walk with the Lord, after almost 25 years in ministry (Philippians 3:12). This is not intended to be discouraging, but to enable you to maintain a healthier perspective about your walk. Of course, this is not an excuse to live an ungodly lifestyle either, as doing so will place a heavy burden on your walk.

2. Depending on your choices and subsequent decisions, your "state" may improve or get worse. We have some examples in the Bible of true Christians whose experience actually got worse, such as the Christians in the church in Galatia and in Corinth (see the books of Galatians; 1 & 2 Corinthians).

Likewise, your decisions to obey Satan, disobey God, or refuse to abide in Christ and His instructions as expressed in the Bible, will make you either an exemplary or disgraceful Christian. This is not up to God, it is your responsibility.

3. Your "state" or experience will be completely different from other believers. Some Christians are constantly walking in the Spirit (I discuss more of this in the next chapter) and solely trusting God, while others are walking in the flesh (i.e., trusting their own self- serving carnal desires) or worldly experts with their daily decisions. As such, because of our choices, some Christians are experiencing the fullness of their salvation and are mightily blessed, and serve as excellent "advertisement" for God, as their lifestyles are drawing many into God's Kingdom. But unfortunately, other Christians are experiencing defeat in every area of life, and are unable to appropriate the multiple blessings of God because of their poor choices and ignorance.

With the above distinction between your "position" and "state," I now proceed to examine each of these positional Truths separately, although they happen concurrently in the spiritual realm at the time a person accepts to follow the Lord.

## Your Current Standing [Position] in Christ

### You Have Been Sealed with the Holy Spirit

Now that you have accepted to follow Jesus, you have been sealed with the Holy Spirit, and the Triune God is supernaturally dwelling (living) on the inside of you until eternity (Ephesians 1:13; 2 Corinthians 1:21-22). As an example, think of a seal, like a penny jar with a permanent plastic seal around it to protect the pennies from being stolen or snatched away if someone breaks the seal. Only the owner can break that seal when the time comes, in order to claim the pennies. Likewise, no one will ever snatch you from God because of that permanent mark of the seal placed on you

(John 10: 28-29). The Holy Spirit inside of you will also confirm and attest in your heart that you are a Christian, and He will give you supernatural peace about your salvation.

Your life is no longer yours, and God owns you now. You have been purchased with the blood of Jesus from the hands of Satan, and you have been set free from yourself, and from the demonic powers that rule in this world. Because God Himself is living on the inside of you, you can now begin to hear His voice ( John 10: 27). I am not referring to an audible voice, but rather His desires in your heart. And as you study God's Word and gain a better understating of His true nature, you will become mature at discerning His voice and in living in a manner that will glorify Christ (I discuss more about the Word of God in upcoming chapters).

You now have a best friend on the inside of you who sticks closer than a brother (Proverbs 18:24); a friend who will never leave or forsake you (Deuteronomy 31:6); a friend whom you can talk to at anytime, and is available to help you through this life, and to enable you to make godly decisions (John 14:26). God, who created you in His very image loves you. He knows you personally, and even knows the number of hairs on your head (Luke 12:7). Indeed you are blessed! So rejoice in this unshakeable relationship that no one can steal from you.

Having the Holy Spirit indwelling you also means you have been blessed with the necessary power needed to live the Christian life daily, if you choose to activate that power by faith, in accordance with God's Word. And as you obey God's Word, His fruit, meaning the Fruit of the Spirit: love, joy, peace, forbearance, kindness, goodness, faithfulness, gentleness and self-control will begin to manifest in your life (Galatians 5:22-23), and others will take notice of it. This Fruit of the Spirit, referred to as singular, rather than plural, represents the qualities of the Triune God indwelling every Christian. Although you are immediately sealed with the Holy Spirit at the time of your salvation, you do not automatically manifest His Fruit in your life, because you have a role to play, depending on your choices ( I discuss more about this later in this chapter).

## You Have been Justified

To be justified means you have been absolved (totally forgiven; cleansed) from All of your sins committed knowingly and unknowingly, because of your decision to accept Christ Jesus. For example, imagine committing a heinous crime that you have been sentenced for, to a long time in prison, but because your biological or adopted father loves you dearly, he asked the judge to place the charges on him instead. Surprisingly, the judge agrees and completely removes all of the charges against you, including the consequences or penalties of that crime, and you are set free to live as a brand new person, and are given a new start in life. For just a moment, think how much of a sacrifice your earthly father would have made for you because of his great love! If you are an appreciative person, hopefully you are, you would definitely love your father much more, and do everything within your power to honor and serve him because of such a sacrifice, right?

Well, the above example is what your heavenly Father, God, did for you, except He took it one step further, and actually died in your place, and as a result, He has forgiven All of your sins: past, present and future sins. All sorts of sins exist today, such as murder, homosexuality, rape, pornography, lies, thievery, jealousy, etc. Other sins that would be committed knowingly and unknowingly in the future were all placed on the sinless body of the Lord Jesus on the cross, who took upon the judgment of the entire world.

Because you have been justified, God will never judge you because of your sins, if you are a true Christian. Who would not want to love and serve such a good and loving God? You get the picture, right? God has not only forgiven your sins, He has released or freed you from the guilt, consequences, punishment or judgment attached to the sins, because of your relationship with Jesus Christ (Romans 5:9-11; 8:1-2; 1 Corinthians 6:11). God is no longer angry with you; His wrath has been appeased by Jesus, and you **have been reconciled** to Him (2 Corinthians 5:20-21).

Some of you may be wondering how and why your past, present and future sins can be forgiven? Indeed, they have! They have been completely cleansed by the precious blood of the Lord Jesus, who died once, and will never go through that humiliation again. Think about it this way: Jesus died on the cross for your sins over 2000 years ago before you were born, right? He only died once, and He will never go through that public shame and disgrace again (Hebrews 9: 27-28; Romans 6:10; 1 Peter 3:18). And you were born as a sinner into the word with a Sinful Nature and committed acts of sins unknowingly and knowingly, before becoming a Christian, right?

The moment you became a Christian was not when Christ died for you! He had already died for you before you even heard of Him the first time, and He was patiently waiting for one of His coworkers here on the earth to proclaim this good news to you, so that you will believe and accept His sacrifice and unfathomable love. This is such awesome news that it should draw you closer to God, and further away from sin. No wonder the Bible teaches that it is the grace (i.e., undeserved favor) of God towards us that leads individuals to repent and accept Him (Romans 2:4).

Much more, God does not even remember your sins anymore (Psalms 103:12), so do not bring your past to Him, He sees you as "white as snow" through Christ Jesus. Some of you may be wondering: "How is this possible for God not to remember my past?" It is possible because of God's acceptance of Christ Jesus who fulfilled All of His perfect Laws in your place, the sinner. And since the Lord Jesus has permanently dealt with the sin issue, God has given you a second chance in life, except this time, He will be on your side. This is the supernatural and unfathomable love of God, to you.

In spite of this good news, many Christians are still tortured by the guilt and condemnation of their past transgressions before they accepted to follow Jesus, and they are mistaken into thinking that God has not forgiven them. That is a lie from your enemy, Satan, whose primary purpose is to plant doubts in your heart about your salvation. The Bible is clear that even when you were still a sinner, God loved you and died for you, and since you have been justified (Romans 5:8-10; 8:1-2), accept this Truth by faith, and start enjoying your new freedom in Christ. Additionally, because of this justification, God also sees you as righteous.

## You Have Been Made Righteous

Because of your justification, God sees you as personally righteous, meaning in right standing with Him because of Christ. God is dealing with you through Christ who has taken your place in front of God the Father: Whao! How awesome! This righteousness or right standing is imputed (i.e., credited to you) as a FREE gift the moment you become born again ( 2 Corinthians 5:21; Romans 3:22; Philippians 3:8-9). This Justification and imputed righteousness are not excuses to practice sin. The Lord has permanently set us free from the bondage of sin, thus we can no longer be ruled or dominated by sin, through the enabling of the Holy Spirit, if we choose to obey (Romans 8: 1-17).

*Sin will damage your relationship with God, limit His presence, protection and power in your life, thereby allowing Satan to come into your life to kill, steal and destroy you.*

Practicing sin will not cause God to judge you, but He will be displeased. And sin will not prevent you from going to heaven, because only one thing prevents a person from going into heaven: blasphemy against the Holy Spirit (i.e., a complete rejection of the Lord's Jesus sacrificial death and God's FREE gift), to Mankind (Mark 3:29). **But sin will damage your relationship with God, limit His presence, protection and power in your life, thereby allowing Satan to come into your life to kill, steal and destroy you** (Romans 6:16; John 10:10).

The effects of sin are deadly, so do not practice sin. Any true Christian at any given time in their journey may struggle with overcoming certain sins, while allowing the Holy Spirit to work through them for deliverance. Anyone who professes to be a Christian, but has no conviction when practicing sin, but are actually enjoying it, causes me to wonder if they are genuinely saved. This is because the Holy Spirit convicts, chastises and corrects us when we disobey Him (Hebrews 12:6). This conviction and chastisement is out of love and gentleness, as He would speak to your heart, or even put others in your path to warn you to stop the sin. Such a loving conviction will lead to true repentance and obedience.

On the other hand, condemnation (which brings shame and guilt) is never from God, it is always from Satan, so keep this difference in mind. With that distinction made, I want to emphasize again, that, if an individual is not willing to repent and stop practicing sin, but are enjoying it instead, it is highly probable that they do not have the Spirit of God indwelling them, or they have completely quenched the convictions from the Holy Spirit. Thus, if you profess to be a Christian, and are practicing sin without any conviction, I suggest you search your heart, whether or not your conversion to Christianity was genuine. This is not meant to hurt you, but to help you to overcome and be victorious.

Besides, as sincere Christians, our desire should be to live holy lives. The Bible teaches that anyone whose hope is in God purifies him or herself (1 John 3:3), so it is the goal for every Christian to maintain purity and holiness (i.e., abstain from any sort of sin). This brings me to the notion of **practical righteousness**, which in its simplistic description, refers to "righteousness in practice." That is to say, your daily actions of practicing holiness or living righteously in accordance with God's standards as instructed in His Word.

*Being blessed with imputed righteousness in the spiritual realm does not mean that your lifestyle will automatically reflect this practical righteousness, you have to deliberately choose to live holy, through the power of the Holy Spirit.*

**Being blessed with imputed righteousness in the spiritual realm does not mean that your lifestyle will automatically reflect this practical righteousness, you have to deliberately choose to live holy, through the power of the Holy Spirit.** The Bible teaches that we should work out our own salvation with fear and trembling. This is referring to a holy fear of God, abstinence from sin and allowing the Holy Spirit to enable and guide us (Philippians 2:12). Furthermore, as part of your new identity, you have been adopted into God's Kingdom.

## You Have Been Adopted into God's Kingdom

As a Christian, God has not only justified you, but He has made you righteous, sealed and adopted you into His Kingdom. You are now a citizen of God's dwelling place, heaven, and you are on a lifelong pilgrimage to your final destination (1 Peter 2:11). Many of you are probably familiar with the concept of adoption, especially if you reside here in the USA, where adoption is a common practice. As an example, imagine an adult lady who is a slave girl to her master ( in this example, we will call this slave Master, Satan), and the slave girl will represent our former life before Christ. The slave girl's Master dominates and controls her life. She is in bondage and has no freedom to make her own decisions, because all of her choices are subconsciously, and at times, consciously influenced and directed by her Master, Satan.

She is so involved in the ways and practices of her Master, that she does not even realize there is any other way to live. She is miserable, unhappy, yet trapped because on her own, she is unable to break free from the bondage. Then one day, a wealthy son (i.e., representing the Lord Jesus), whose father is extremely wealthy (i.e., representing God the Father), and who is the heir of his father's estate purchases (i.e., redeems or buys) her with an indescribable amount of money, including precious fine gold (i.e., representing the precious blood of Christ Jesus that redeems), thus permanently setting her free from the slave Master. Once she is redeemed, the wealthy son takes her to the house of his extremely wealthy father, who then adopts her as one of his own precious children, and makes her a joint heir (i.e., joint owner) with his son, of his estate. As a result, she is instantly given a new life and identity in her adopted father's kingdom.

The above example is a similar depiction of what happens when we accept to follow Christ. **God instantly redeems us from the demonic influences in this world, and from our Sinful Nature with the perfect and precious blood of Christ, then He adopts us as His children.** Then by faith, we are supernaturally joined with Christ as one, and thus positioned to inherit all of the blessings and promises of God (Romans 8:17; 2 Corinthians 1:20). God takes this adoption so seriously that we are told in Galatians 4:6 that because we are His children, "... *God has sent the Spirit of his Son into our hearts, the Spirit who calls out, "Abba, Father"*(emphasis author's). And He told us again in Romans 8:15 that: *"...the Spirit you received does not make you slaves, so that you live in fear again; rather, the Spirit you received brought about your adoption to sonship. And by him we cry, "Abba, Father"* (emphasis author's).

The phrase "Abba," is an endearment, meaning Father, which expresses an intimate relationship with God. During the Old Testament period, the Jews could not call God "Abba", because they did not have such a close relationship with Him, like we do today. This was one of the reasons why the Pharisees (i.e., religious leaders during Jesus' ministry) accused Him of blasphemy because He called God His father. Thus, it is quite an honor that we, New Testament believers, have the privilege, because of Christ, to call God our Father: What a blessed position we have with God!

Because you have been adopted, God treats you as a child, and is always available to direct your life as you allow Him. You now have direct access to Him, so go boldly to Him in the name of Jesus with all of your care and concerns; He wants to hear directly from you. Unlike the Old Testament Jews who could only hear from God through the prophets and not directly themselves, we are blessed, with a direct access to Him; so pause, and thank the Lord for this blessing.

Much more, because of this adoption, God sees you as: "... *a chosen people, a royal priesthood, a holy nation, God's special possession, that you may declare the praises of him who called you out of darkness into his wonderful light*" (1 Peter 2:9), (emphasis author's). And as His child, God will continuously correct and discipline you, in love, when you are wrong (Hebrews 12:6-11), in order to ultimately mold and shape you into the image of Christ Jesus (Romans 8:28-29). This process of molding and shaping, is referred to as sanctification.

## You Have Been Sanctified

Positional sanctification means God has set you apart for Himself, and for His use presently, and in all eternity. As such, He sees you as a Saint (i.e., one who is set apart, made holy, sanctified) because you are a joint heir with Christ in His Kingdom (1 Corinthians 1:2, 30; Hebrews 10:10; 13:12). On the other hand, **practical sanctification** is the process whereby you allow the indwelling Holy Spirit to teach you how to live out your Christian life, like the Saint that you are, in God's eyes. The Bible teaches that we should have evidence of this sanctification in our lives (1 Thessalonians 4:3). In yourself, you are unable to walk in this type of holiness, but as you obey God and allow the Holy Spirit to assist you, you will be sanctified, moment -by- moment, day- by -day.

## You Have Been Glorified

God sees every believer as already glorified (i.e., as perfect), because He has already predestined each of us to be conformed into the image of Christ (Romans 8:28-29). He sees us as we will be — complete and perfect in Christ ( Colossians 2:9-10), although no Christian can ever reach perfect sanctification and glorification in this lifetime. Perfection will only happen once we die and are reunited with the Lord, or if He comes back to the earth before we die (1 John 3:2). So **glorification as a process** is underway in your life right now!

## Your Eternity is Secured

Another positional Truth is that once you die, you will definitely spend eternity with God, in heaven. I am aware that some Christians believe that a person could lose their Salvation in Christ. I absolutely disagree and do not even believe that line of reasoning is Scriptural. Because, **if you have genuinely placed your faith in Christ Jesus as your Lord and Savior, you can never lose your salvation — it is a free gift which is guaranteed.**

> *... if you have genuinely placed your faith in Christ Jesus as your Lord and Savior, you can never lose your salvation — it is a free gift which is guaranteed.*

Nothing, even sin and disobedience, which dishonors God, will keep you out of heaven—Hallelujah! As I have already explained, the Lord Jesus died for your past, present and future sins. Again, a genuine Christian will abhor sin, and desire to glorify God through their actions. Thus God's grace is never an excuse to practice sin (I discuss more on this in chapter 13). Due to space limitations in this book, I am unable to expound on the issue of eternal security, but suffice it to say, below are some major reasons why a genuine believer cannot lose their salvation in Christ Jesus:

1. Firstly, there was nothing you did to be saved, as such, you cannot lose it, because salvation is based solely on your faith in the finished work of Christ on the cross and not on your works. Thus, your salvation is not fickle or dependent on your actions or works (Ephesians 2:8). Therefore, since there is nothing you did to receive it, except believe by faith (i.e., saving faith from God), then there is absolutely nothing you can do to lose it, if you are genuinely saved;

2. Secondly, you are sealed with the Holy Spirit, and that seal cannot be broken by your actions, if you have genuinely

accepted Christ (Ephesians 1:13);

3. Thirdly, Jesus said no one can snatch you from His hands, once you choose to follow Him (John 10: 27-29).

Many people have incorrectly interpreted Hebrews 6:4-6 and concluded that it is possible for an individual to lose their salvation. But if you study the totality of Scripture regarding salvation, it will become readily apparent that, it is impossible for anyone to lose a genuine salvation. Moreover, according to the epistle of First John, those who claim to have lost their salvation, or those who later denounced their faith in Christ, were never true converts in the first place. Under the inspiration of the Holy Spirit, the apostle John noted in First John 2:19:

*"They went out from us, but they did not really belong to us. For if they had belonged to us, they would have remained with us; but their going showed that none of them belonged to us "* (emphasis author's).

Instead of worrying about your salvation, if you are unsure, I recommend that you repent and accept to follow Christ, right now! But if you have sincerely and confidently placed your faith in Christ, relax, as you are safe in His hands.

## You will be Resurrected

Because of your decision to follow the Lord Jesus, you will never die spiritually. Even when you experience physical death, your spirit and soul lives forever in God's presence. Then on the second coming of the Lord, you will be resurrected and given a glorified physical body, just like the Lord Jesus' resurrected body (John 6:44). Much more, you will be reunited with all loved ones: family members and friends who died as Christians— what a reunion to look forward to!

## PRACTICAL APPLICATION

If these positional Truths do not make you want to shout "Hallelujah," then I recommend you meditate on them for some time. Knowing these Truths in your heart makes a major difference on how to approach your Christian pilgrimage, because everything you need to live a victorious life is already available to you. Your job is to learn how to manifest these spiritual blessings into the physical realm, and in turn experience the abundant life the Lord Jesus died for you to enjoy.

The Bible teaches that we are made up of a mind, body and a spirit (1 Thessalonians 5:23), and in the spiritual realm, God sees us as perfect, right now, in this world, just as He sees Jesus (1 John 4:17). Since you are therefore complete in the spiritual realm, it means that, only your soul and the physical realms are incomplete. Which is why the Bible teaches the necessity to renew our minds in accordance with who we are in Christ, in order for the life we already have in the spirit, to manifest in our souls and physical bodies (Romans 12:2).

The Lord Jesus taught that life is in the spirit (John 6:63). But, your actions of sin and disobedience can quench the Holy Spirit in such a way that, the life in your spirit will not manifest in your soul and physical body. Hence, you will end up being a very miserable Christian, dying prematurely, all the while, missing out on the abundant and blessed life God has already made provision for you to enjoy. Below are some recommendations for applying these Truths into your life daily and appropriating God's blessings.

1. Firstly, be diligent in studying the Scriptures to learn more, and to grow in these Truths (I discuss more about the Bible in upcoming chapters).
2. Secondly, accept these Truths as absolute Truths, by faith, because God says so, and accept that they are not based on your emotions. Thus, never wait to experience these

Truths through your emotions before believing them; rather, believe and act on them, then your emotions will adjust. If you choose to wait to experience God's best, you will die waiting. God's best is NOW! For example, God sees you through Christ as holy, thus view yourself as holy, and refuse to practice sin.

3. Thirdly, change your inward perspective of yourself. Start to perceive and accept yourself exactly as God sees you in Christ (i.e., loved by God, a winner, the head and not the tail, victorious, etc), rather than how your family, friends, employer, society, etc, sees you. **As an example, the notion of "self-esteem," which is very popular in the USA is not Scriptural. As Christians, we are to uphold "Christ-esteem," and not "self-esteem."** You never want to esteem the self, instead, you want to learn to die to yourself by denying it, its ungodly and selfish desires. Therefore, learn to esteem Christ in you; this is the attitude that gives life to your soul and body.

As another example, whether you feel it or not, God loves you unconditionally, even if your family members do not love you. God is always with you, even when you feel abandoned by your loved ones. Do not allow anyone to cause you to doubt your salvation because you do not appear "holy" in their eyes. God does not esteem some Christians higher than others; He is no respecter of persons (Acts 10:34; Romans 2:11). He views you equally in Christ with everyone else, so do not waste your efforts to impress others or manipulate people into accepting you. You are already accepted by God and adopted by Him. Additionally, refuse to allow Satan or anyone else to deceive you that God has not forgiven your past sins; He has, so move on.

4. Fourthly, make it a daily effort to "cast down" imaginations in your thoughts that are inconsistent with what God says about you. Refuse to think any other way, and gain a godly perspective in every area of your life. It is challenging to do,

but with the Holy Spirit on your side, you can do it.

5. Fifthly, have a solid understanding about the differences between positional Truths and your "state." Keep this in the forefront of your mind, and take full responsibility for your practical experience, and live out your faith in accordance with the positional Truths in Christ. You are now a new creature in Christ (2 Corinthians 5:17), and old things are gone, and the new has come, it is here, right now! So live up to it! You have been blessed with a new " Spiritual DNA," and as such, you have no business living a lifestyle like you did in your past? Why would you want to go back and taste your vomit (Proverbs 26:11)? No wise person will do such a foolish thing.

Live a life worthy of your new identity: Stop the gossiping, chronic complaining, frustration, strife, cheating, stealing, lying, hoarding money and refusing to give, laziness, etc. Also, stop making excuses and take responsibility for your spiritual maturity. **Bottom Line**: Avoid sin, and give the Holy Spirit preeminence in your life.

6. Sixthly, you have not received a Spirit that causes you to be in bondage or a slave to fear (Romans 8:15), but you have been blessed with a Spirit of freedom in Christ (I discuss more of your freedom in Christ in chapter 13). Therefore, perceive yourself as dead to the Sinful Nature, and in boldness, allow Christ Jesus who lives in you, to live through you.

7. Seventhly, since you have been raised up with Christ in His resurrection, walk with your head up like a victor, and set your mind and heart on your heavenly blessings. And as you do that, you will be renewing your mind, and the change will slowly, but surely begin to manifest in your actions, and it will subsequently transform your life.

In conclusion, your new identity in Christ is as real as your physical body. Never ignore or forget who you have become, because of God's grace. God's Spirit is always present, to better help you to understand your spiritual blessings. Thus, having a basic understanding of the ministry of the Holy Spirit is essential, in enabling you to experience these Truths daily. Let us now proceed to chapter 3, where I begin a discussion of who the Holy Spirit is.

## Summary Points

- Although your individual actions cannot change your positional Truths in Christ, your decisions to obey or disobey God will determine the effectiveness of your Christian walk;

- Through disobedience, you will impede your relationship with God, which will definitely prevent you from enjoying the abundant blessings He has already predestined for you. So the determining factor is you, not God, because He has given you a Free Will;

- Obeying God will enable you to better experience these positional Truths;

- Learn to view yourself as God sees you, and allow the Holy Spirit first place in your life, and you will start experiencing the life that will transform your soul and physical body.

# Chapter 3

# KNOW WHO THE HOLY SPIRIT IS

In chapter 1 you learnt that true Christianity is a monotheistic faith. We serve and worship one God in three unique persons: God the Father, God the Son, and God the Holy Spirit, commonly referred to as the Triune Godhead. In this chapter, I will focus on the third person of the Godhead, the Holy Spirit. It is impossible to live a successful Christian life without the supernatural power from the Holy Spirit. Even though He has sealed you at the time of your conversion to Christianity, He does not automatically control your life; it is up to you to activate His ministry, thereby allowing Him to direct your life.

While every Christian is sealed with the Holy Spirit, not every Christian is filled with the Spirit (i.e., walking in the Spirit), there is a big difference! Before I discuss the filling of the Holy Spirit, some basic background information about the Ministry of the Holy Spirit is necessary. For purposes of clarification, the ensuing section presents what I call the " 5Ws:" the WHO, WHAT, WHEN, WHY and WHERE, of the Holy Spirit. Please note that the expression: "5Ws," is the author's own phraseology, in order to enhance understanding of this discussion, and is not a part of who the Holy Spirit is!

### The Holy Spirit: Third Person of the Godhead

The word Holy means "pure," or "perfect," which reflects a quality of God. Depending on the Bible translation, the words Ghost and Spirit are used interchangeably, as they come from the same Greek word *pneuma,* meaning like a "wind or breeze." Thus, you may hear others refer to the Holy Spirit as the Holy Ghost.

In the Bible, the words "wind" and "breath" are used as symbols of the Holy Spirit (Genesis 2:7; Job 32:8; John 20:22. Other symbols of the Holy Spirit described in the Bible are " dove" (Mark 1:10; Matthew 3:16; John 1:32); "living water" (John 4:14; 7:37-39); and "fire" (Acts 2:3-4; Luke 3:16).

### Who Is the Holy Spirit?

The Holy Spirit is God Himself (Acts 5:3-4; 1 Corinthians 2:10; John 15:26); He is eternal (Hebrews 9:14), and is described in the Bible using attributes of a person such as the pronoun "He." This implies that the Holy Spirit is a person with emotions who can be grieved (Ephesians 4:30); lied to; tested (Acts 5:3-4, 9); blasphemed against (Matthew 12:31); and resisted (Acts 7:51). The Holy Spirit also has other attributes of a person such as a will of His own (1 Corinthians 12:11), and a mind (Romans 8:27). In addition, the Holy Spirit can speak to you ( Acts 28:25); comfort and encourage you when in distress (Acts 9:31); and help you during times of your weakness (Romans 8:26). The Holy Spirit is also your personal teacher (John 14:26). He will pray for you when you are unable to pray for yourself (Romans 8:26-27); and He will enable you to experience joy (Romans 14:17). He also loves you (Romans 15:30).

Other significant roles of the Holy Spirit include His inspiration of all Scripture (2 Peter 1:21); His involvement in the creation of the heavens and the earth, and in the creation of the first human beings: Adam and Eve (see Genesis chapters 1 and 2). The Holy Spirit is also involved in the salvation process (Ephesians 1:13), and He bears witness and confirms that you are saved (Romans 8:16). Additionally, the Holy Spirit is the one who always glorifies the Lord Jesus in your heart, and reminds you of His Words. The Holy Spirit is the Spirit of All Truths, and He will only speak to you what He hears from Heaven, and He will show you things to come in the future (John 16:12-14).

## What Does the Holy Spirit Do?

The Holy Spirit has multiple roles in the world, the church, and in your life. Let us briefly examine each of these roles.

*The Holy Spirit In the World*

In the world, the Holy Spirit is doing three things, convicting the world of (1) sin; (2) righteousness about God's standards: Christ Jesus; and (3) impending judgment of sins (John 16: 8-10). Among the unbelievers, the Holy Spirit is constantly rebuking (i.e., admonishing or warning) them in regards to their sins and their need for a Savior, Christ Jesus. He rebukes unbelievers about their rejection of Christ, thereby bringing them to repentance, if they are willing.

With regards to righteousness, the Holy Spirit is in the world revealing God's standard of righteousness: Christ Jesus to the unbeliever; thereby enabling them to perceive that their self-righteousness is as "filthy rags" ( Isaiah 64:6) in God's view. This is because none is righteous, except the sinless and perfect Son of God—the Lord Jesus. Without the enabling of the Holy Spirit, the unbeliever would be deceived into thinking that their "good morals" would grant them a ticket into heaven.

The Holy Spirit also convicts the world of impending judgment, the final judgment, for rejecting the sacrifice of Christ Jesus. In spite of what the Holy Spirit is currently doing in the world, God has given each human being a Free Will, and unfortunately, some people still reject the warnings. And the Holy Spirit will not force or coerce Himself onto anyone; each person must accept the Holy Spirit's ministry, voluntarily.

*The Holy Spirit In the Church*

In the church, the Holy Spirit is responsible for baptizing the new believers into the faith; (1 Corinthians 12:13), sanctifying and encouraging unity among the believers in the body of Christ (Romans 15:6). The moment you accept to follow the Lord Jesus, you are automatically accepted into the body of Christ collectively; this is the work of the Holy Spirit. Through His leading of various leaders, the Holy Spirit is very involved in the process of selecting and sending out gifted missionaries from various churches to proclaim the Gospel across the nations (Acts 13: 3-4), and in directing their paths (Acts 8:29). The Holy Spirit also directs and guides church leaders during the process of selecting gifted individuals called by God to oversee and manage church organization and leadership positions, such as the office of the Bishop, Deacon, Elders, etc.

The Holy Spirit is also responsible for the distribution of the different leadership gifts and positions in the local churches and in the body of Christ at large. These gifts include but are not limited to, the apostles, prophets, teachers, miracle workers, administrators, etc, for purposes of strengthening the church and making it a complete unit, so that every believer can be helped (1 Corinthians 12:27-31). In the body of Christ and in the local churches, the Holy Spirit is further involved in manifesting His various gifts, such as the word of wisdom, word of knowledge, gift of faith, healings, prophecy, discerning of spirits, etc; however He pleases, during and outside church services, for the betterment of all, in order to accomplish God's work on the earth (1 Corinthians 12: 1-11).

As an example, in any typical church service or similar gatherings, the Holy Spirit may work through any Spirit filled Christian to bring about healings of the sick in that gathering; the utterances of prophetic messages to encourage the attendees; or to impart godly wisdom and discernment to others, etc. This way, God would be meeting the needs of His children through various gifted individuals, whom He chooses to work through.

## The Holy Spirit in the Life of a Believer

In the believer's life, the Holy Spirit lives inside of you, and serves as your personal advocate, teacher, and counselor. Because He is The Spirit of Truth, He will reveal All Truths to you as you personally seek Him for advice and direction. **The Holy Spirit is a "gentleman," meaning, He is humble and loving, and will not force His decisions upon you. You would have to ask Him to lead you into all Truths and wisdom; then by faith, you would take the necessary actions required as He leads you.**

*The Holy Spirit is a "gentleman," meaning, He is humble and loving, and will not force His decisions upon you. You would have to ask Him to lead you into all Truths and wisdom; then by faith, you would take the necessary actions required as He leads you.*

The Holy Spirit is responsible for reminding you about the awesome ministry of the Lord Jesus, and to tell you of future events. He will also help you to understand Scripture, thus giving you the practical revelation of how to apply the Word of God into your life (John 14:15-31).

I remember the first two years when I was fighting metastasis colon cancer. I had memorized multiple healing Scriptures. On my way to each doctor's visit, I would be speaking aloud those Scriptures over my body. But it was amazing how when I was inside the doctor's office, and as he was "spewing" the negative blood test results and other diagnostic test results over my life, the Holy Spirit would bring to my remembrance specific Scriptures. Those specific Scriptures would serve as the buffer I needed, at that time, to overcome the negativity and "death" the doctor was telling me. It was supernatural how that comforted, encouraged and assured me. Likewise, the Holy Spirit will bring to your remembrance Scriptures or promises from God's Word, especially during crisis, in order to help you to overcome. That is His ministry: A ministry of comfort, hope and exhortation.

Furthermore, the Holy Spirit will abide in you until death, and then He will transition you into God's presence, eternity. He is the source of the supernatural power you need to live the Christian life. In the Greek language, the word **"dunamis,"** is translated to mean power, in the English language. The Holy Spirit will give you the power to face trials, persecutions, hardships, and to overcome the lies and deception from Satan. He will also give you the power to witness (i.e., share the Gospel of Christ to others; tell others about your testimony in Christ) in the name of Jesus, and enable you to enjoy the victorious life He died for you to have (Acts 1:8; Galatians 1:4; John 10:10). Additionally, the Holy Spirit is responsible for shaping and molding you into the image of Christ as you obey Him (Romans 8: 28-29), and He is constantly involved in the process of sanctifying you, for God's purposes (1 Thessalonians 4:3-8).

In ministering to people, I have discovered that many Christians often ignore or forget about the awesome ministry of the Holy Spirit during challenging times. In whatever circumstance you are right now, speak to the Holy Spirit directly about your situation, and ask Him for help. He will help you. Or, at the very least, ask Him to lead you to others who might be able to help you, and He will; that is how much He loves you. The Holy Spirit wants you to be set free, so take advantage of His ministry and depend on Him 100%, you will not be disappointed!

## Where Is the Holy Spirit Dispensed?

The word dispensed or dispensation in regards to the Holy Spirit simply refers to a certain period of time, during which the operation or work of the Holy Spirit was evident by humans in the earth. The Holy Spirit is eternal and has always existed, even before the creation of the world (Genesis 1; Colossians 1). However, there are three major dispensations which have been noted: (1) The Old Testament dispensation; (2) The Gospel dispensation; and (3) The Day of Pentecost, through the present Church age.

During the Old Testament dispensation, the Holy Spirit did not live on the inside of individuals. Rather, He endowed certain people for a specific purpose, and thereafter, He departed from them. For instance, Samson and the Philistines ( see Judges 6:34; Judges chapter 14), Moses and the Exodus experience (see the book of Exodus, etc). The Holy Spirit was also very involved in the ministry of the Old Testament prophets, as He spoke through them to deliver His utterances to the people.

During the Gospel dispensation, as recorded in the four Gospels, the Holy Spirit was active and endowed certain people, like John the Baptist (Luke 1:15-16); Simeon (Luke 2:25-26 ); Elizabeth, who was John the Baptist's mother (Luke 1:41); Zechariah (Luke 1: 67); and the human part of Jesus Christ (see Mark 1:9-12; Luke 4:1, 14, 18; Matthew 3:16-17; John 1:32-33).

The third dispensation of the Holy Spirit was evidenced on the Day of Pentecost, as recorded in Acts chapter 2, when the Holy Spirit promised by Christ Jesus came, and He is permanently indwelling each believer. Since then, from the Day of Pentecost until currently, in what is called the "Church Age," the Holy Spirit has taken up everlasting residence inside of all those who have confessed Christ Jesus as their Lord and Savior. This is such awesome news, such that we should scream— Hallelujah!

## When Did the Holy Spirit Come?

I have already explained how the Holy Spirit is God, who is self-existent and has always existed. As such, the Holy Spirit's ministry has always existed, and He was involved in the creation of the world. But, there are many critics of the Bible who espouse that even though the Holy Spirit was involved in the creation of the world, ever since, He has handed over the control of the earth to human beings, and He is no longer involved. This is obviously wrong and incorrect, based on the different activities of the Holy Spirit as already explained in the preceding sections. As an example, we know that the Holy Spirit was involved after the creation of the world, as evidenced in His role during the Old Testament dispensation; His involvement with the supernatural conception of the Lord Jesus; and in His presence in the Lord's ministry, including His resurrection, etc.

Also, please note that the peace that the world is currently enjoying, is because the Holy Spirit is still in the world, even though many people may not perceive His presence and, may in fact, disagree that there is some degree of peace. However, a time will come, when the Universal Church (i.e., the body of Christ) will be "raptured" (i.e., caught up in the air with the Lord Jesus), and ascended into heaven, and whatever degree of peace the world is now enjoying, will no longer be present ( 1 Thessalonians 4; see the book of Revelation ). Once the Church is "raptured", unbearable pain and suffering will abound on this earth. Then, those who have purposefully rejected the Holy Spirit will have to finally deal with the consequences of their decision. So for now, be grateful for the ministry of the Holy Spirit.

## Why the Holy Spirit Came?

Jesus spoke of the Holy Spirit as His other self, and promised that a helper would come to assist us, His followers, to live the Christian life. Plus, the Holy Spirit had to come because Jesus was finished with His earthly ministry, and He knew His followers could not continue in His teachings without the Holy Spirit enduing them with supernatural revelation and power (see John chapters 14, 15, 16). Additionally, the Lord Jesus was physically limited in His human body, and was unable to be everywhere concurrently, but the Holy Spirit, who is a Spirit, can be everywhere at the same time — This is awesome! Imagine, right now, the Holy Spirit is with me as I am writing this book, and wherever you are in the world, the Holy Spirit is also with you at this very moment: Hallelujah! Let us Praise the Lord!

Earlier, I expressed how no human being can live the Christian life without the power of the Holy Spirit: It is impossible. *Attempting to live as a Christian through your own power or effort is a guaranteed recipe for disaster, discouragement and failure —you cannot do it, so do not even try!* The Christian journey is a supernatural pilgrimage as you learn to allow the Holy Spirit to lead, guide, and direct your life moment by moment, step by step, and day by day, hence He had to come. As you grow in your journey, you have to learn daily how to deny yourself of your selfish ungodly desires, and allow godly desires to take precedence in your life (Galatians 2:20). And as you delight yourself in God (i.e., take pleasure in Him and focus on the things of God), He will replace your ungodly desires with His desires (Psalm 37:4).

For those of you who may be thinking that it is difficult to deny yourself of your fleshy desires, let us briefly examine this principle with an example. The Bible teaches that we should forgive one another, whether or not they ask for forgiveness, period! Therefore, if someone offends you, you do not have to wait for them to apologize to you, before you forgive them—you forgive them whether or not they are wrong, or if they have apologized to you regardless of how you feel. By obeying this command, you would be expressing the kind of unconditional love (i.e., agape love) which is Christ-like, thereby denying yourself of the selfish desire not to forgive.

As you choose to act on the Word of God, such as forgiving when you do not feel like doing it, you will be learning to "die to your flesh," delighting yourself in the Lord, and allowing the Holy Spirit to lead you. To be led by the Spirit is a good description of a Christian who is filled with the Holy Spirit. Being constantly filled with the Holy Spirit is not an option, but a necessity, in order to live the Christ-like life that will glorify and honor God (Ephesians 5:18). Besides, according to Jesus, no one should be witnessing to others in His name without the power from the Holy Spirit, thus allowing the Holy Spirit to fill you with His power is mandatory for the submissive Christian (Acts 1:8). By submissive Christian, I am referring to the Christian who is always willingly ready to be led by the indwelling Spirit.

## PRACTICAL APPLICATION

### The Filling of the Holy Spirit

I mentioned earlier how there is a difference between being indwelt (sealed) with the Holy Spirit, and being filled with the Spirit. While all Christians are equally sealed with the Holy Spirit, not all Christians are equally filled with the Spirit. You are aware that being sealed is automatic at the time of your salvation, but being filled is dependent on your choices. In fact, some Christians are barely filled with the Spirit, period! (i.e., they are living in disobedience and are chronically carnal), yet the Bible commands us in Ephesians 5:18-20 to be filled with the Holy Spirit. This filling implies a continuous process, whereby you constantly: (1) abide in Christ or are dependent on Him daily; (2) obey and practice God's Word; and (3) submit your plans to the Triune God.

Some Christians have experienced a second baptism, usually referred to as the baptism of the Holy Spirit, as such they are filled with the Spirit. Some of you may be surprised to hear about a second baptism. Yes indeed, it exists. When you became a Christian, you were baptized by the Holy Spirit into the faith or the body of Christ ( Galatians 3:27; Ephesians 4: 4-6), but the Bible teaches about a separate experience (i.e., the baptism of the Holy Spirit) whereby, a Christian is filled with the Holy Spirit for purposes of having the supernatural ability to live the Christian life. This power becomes available, but it is still up to the individual to obey and activate it.

Being filled with the Holy Spirit is absolutely necessary, especially because Christ Jesus Himself did not perform any miracles until He was baptized and filled with the Holy Spirit (see Luke chapter 3). If you are unsure about this, here is what happened. After being baptized, the Lord Jesus was led by the Spirit into the wilderness where He was tempted. Then in Luke 4: 14, we are told how the Lord, filled with the Holy Spirit, went to the synagogue and proclaimed how the Spirit of the Lord was upon Him. Thereafter, He started His ministry, evidenced by signs and wonders (i.e., miracles). If the Lord Jesus (i.e., the human part of Him) needed to be filled with the Holy Spirit, then certainly, we, His followers, absolutely should desire this filling as well!

Besides the Lord's experience of being filled with the Spirit, His first Century disciples were born again after He breathed the Holy Spirit into them, after His resurrection ( John 20: 19-23). But in Acts chapter 1 verses 4-5 , we are told how the Lord Jesus informed them to wait for the promised Holy Spirit before they could witness to others in His name. Then on the Day of Pentecost, all of His disciples were filled with the Holy Spirit, and began to speak in other tongues (Acts 2: 1-4).

We also have other Scriptural examples how individuals who were already born again experienced a second baptism of the Holy Spirit and were endowed with power (see Acts chapter 8; 19). So based on the examples presented thus far, it is evident that the Bible teaches about a separate baptism, apart from the initial baptism into the body of Christ and the initial salvation experience of being sealed with the Holy Spirit.

A Spirit filled Christian will constantly be walking in the light as Christ is, and as a result, will experience the continuous cleansing from all unrighteousness (1 John 1:7). Because some Christians are not filled with the Holy Spirit, unfortunately, due to their choices and actions of sin, He does not have an active ministry in their lives; they have silenced, grieved and quenched Him.

## How Do I Know I Am Spirit Filled?

There are many outward evidence of a Christian who is filled with the Holy Spirit, such as speaking in tongues (i.e., an unknown language to Man, but known to God, or an unknown language to the speaker, but a known language to others); the manifestation of the Fruit of the Spirit in their lives (Galatians 5:22-23), etc. The apostle Paul lists nine Fruit of the Spirit that exhibits the presence and work of the Holy Spirit in a believer's life: love, joy, peace, patience, kindness, goodness, faithfulness, gentleness, and self-control. The singular "fruit," is used here and not the plural, to suggest unity. Every believer has this Fruit in their born-again spirit since the Triune God indwells them, although the manifestation varies among believers, as they submit to the Spirit, and are willing to adhere to His directions and work in their respective lives.

Other evidence of a Spirit filled Christian is the ability to witness for Christ Jesus with boldness and confidence, and an exemplary holy lifestyle which honors God. **Please note that living holy, which might indicate obedience to God's Word, must equally accompany good service for Christ, such as witnessing for Him.** This is because there are many unsaved individuals, whose lifestyles are exemplary, and may even appear as "holy" outwardly, but they are not Christians. Therefore as Christians, we need both in equal balance (i.e., evidence of holiness and godly service such as witnessing for Christ).

Other obvious evidence of a Spirit filled Christian is an individual whom God is flowing through to manifest His various gifts, such as healings, miracles, prophecy, etc (see 1 Corinthians 12:8-10), because God requires a submissive and obedient vessel (i.e., a Spirit filled Christian), in order for Him to work through him or her.

In spite of the various external evidence discussed above, I want to emphasize that only God knows the heart (1 Samuel 16:7). Therefore, any outward evidence of a Christian who is Spirit filled may not be 100% accurate. Rather than being concerned about the evidence of being Spirit filled, you would be wise to instead, abide in Christ, obey Him, and continuously walk in the light.

## How to Be Filled with the Holy Spirit

The Lord teaches that God will not refuse to give us any good thing, including the Holy Spirit, if we ask Him in faith, in accordance with His will (Luke 11:13). The only prerequisite is that you are a genuine Christian. If that is the case, then you must:

1. *Have the Desire to Be Filled.* This is critical because there are individuals who do not want to be led by the Spirit, even though they profess to be Christians. Also, regarding the second baptism, some Christians are ignorant about this, and as such, are uncertain, due to wrong doctrine or fear that God would cause them to do things that they do not want. Such excuses are FALSE, because God will never force you to do anything against your wish. Hopefully, this teaching is setting you free today.

2. *Be Willing to Submit to Christ 100% as Your Lord.* Even though He is your Savior, you must submit to His Lordship ( I discuss more of this in chapter 12). Many Christians accept Christ as their Lord and Savior, but submitting to Him as their Lord becomes a battle for them. But, in order to be filled with the Spirit, and be used by God and fulfill His will for your life, a complete submission is necessary. This does not mean that God will "toss you back and forth like a whip". Rather, it means that you will allow Him to guide your life daily, which is actually best for you, since He did not originally design you to rule your own life (Jeremiah 10:23). Even though God has given you a Free Will because of His love, He wants you to seek Him for guidance, because He knows best (Proverbs 3:5-7).

3. *Repent.* If you have been a Christian for some time, and you have been the "lord" of your own life, walking in disobedience knowingly or unknowingly, and you desire to now "come clean with God," then a sincere repentance is necessary. A sincere repentance requires that you stop ruling and controlling your own life and making a "mess of things," and stop grieving the Holy Spirit who loves you.

If you are now ready to be filled with the Spirit, say this simple prayer:

*Dear God, I thank you for your Holy Spirit which is available to help me at all times. I ask you to forgive me for any disobedience and sin against Your Spirit. Right now, in Jesus name, I ask that you fill me with Your Holy Spirit and enable me to live the Christian life. Your Word commands me to be filled, and You promised you will not withhold any good thing from me if I ask in accordance with your will. I desire to glorify you, so help me God. By faith, I believe I have received the answer, and I am now filled with the Holy Spirit, in Jesus name, AMEN.*

If you said that prayer genuinely, accept by faith that you are filled. You may or may not experience an emotion after that prayer, but it is okay because you meant it in your heart. And as Christians, we do not use our emotions to gauge whether or not we have received anything from God, we accept it by faith (2 Corinthians 5:7).

After that prayer, if you have the desire to pray in tongues, start moving your lips right now, as you are led by the Spirit. And as you do that, if it is inspired by God, you may start uttering some unknown words. If that is the case, do not ignore it, that is acceptable because you would be speaking your heavenly language, an unknown tongue to you, but known to God. As you are led by the Holy Spirit, continue to practice praying in that language and ask God for the interpretation ( 1 Corinthians 12). Keep in mind that the primary purpose for praying in tongues is that, you will be speaking mysteries directly to God, and it will edify, refresh, and strengthen you, especially when dealing with crisis (I Corinthians 14, Jude 20-21; Isaiah 28:11-12).

Once you are filled with the Spirit and you constantly obey Him, you will fall in love with God all over, and the inward working of the Holy Spirit in your life will be underway. Accordingly, the abundant life of God will begin to flow out of you onto others; you will be a blessing! Then, when you speak to others, your words will be filled with praise to the Lord in hymns and psalms (Ephesians 5:18-20); this is God's will for you.

**I want to conclude this section by highlighting that there are many people erroneously thinking that speaking in tongues, or being filled with the Spirit is some sort of evidence of salvation, or of being a mature Christian; these are all FALSE and not**

**Scriptural.** Firstly, I have already established that our salvation is a free gift because of the finished work of Christ on the cross, and we accept that by faith, without any external works. Secondly, being filled with the Holy Spirit does not grant a person instant maturity as a Christian. The Bible teaches how the Christians in Corinth were filled with the Spirit, yet exhibited major carnality, as they had issues with sexual immorality, lawsuits, strife, abuse of the Lord's Supper, etc, in the church (see 1 Corinthians), which revealed much immaturity.

Furthermore, being filled with the Holy Spirit does not automatically guarantee the supernatural confidence, boldness, power, or changes in your lifestyle. Rather, the power becomes available, but it is your choice to remain attached to the source of that power: Christ, and walk in obedience, thereby activating it. Thus, it is necessary to be continuously filled with the Holy Spirit, in order to avoid carnality and the quenching of His presence.

## How to Stay Continuously Filled with the Holy Spirit

The filling of the Holy Spirit is not a one-time event, but a continuous filling, as you abide in Christ daily. Each time you find yourself venturing towards carnality, stop, and ask the Holy Spirit to fill you again; Or, if you sin, stop the sin, genuinely repent, and ask the Holy Spirit to fill you again. Although I have discussed some of these already, below are some examples, as reminders, on how you can abide in Christ and be continuously filled with the Spirit:

- Diligently study, meditate and act on the Word of God by faith ( I discuss more of this in subsequent chapters);
- Obey God;
- Be steadfast in prayer ( I discuss this in chapter 9);
- Fellowship with believers who love God;
- Engage in godly activities, such as praise and worship, church attendance, etc;
- Advance the Kingdom of God through Holy Spirit led good service for Christ, such as witnessing, etc.

As you allow yourself to be filled with the Spirit daily, you will be effortlessly activating His power, which will enable you to live the supernatural life as a Christian, thereby overcoming the trials and hardships in this dark world. And as you allow the Spirit to direct every area of your life, you will experience the most fruitful, productive and blessed life, because God always blesses obedience!

In conclusion, by allowing your life to glorify God through your actions, you will live a life that many people, even professing Christians desire but cannot accomplish because of their disobedience. This godly lifestyle will attract others to God; it is worth it! Being filled with the Spirit will make it much easier for you to discern the voice of God directly from His Word. Let us now turn to chapter 4 to study about the basic nature of the Bible, which is God's instructions, specifically to you.

## Summary Points

- The Holy Spirit is God Himself, the third person in the Godhead, who can be quenched, grieved, resisted, and even rejected;

- Complete blasphemy, meaning a total rejection of the Holy Spirit, is the only unpardonable sin, that will send a person to hell;

- Without the active ministry of the Holy Spirit in a believer's life, he or she will endure unnecessary self-inflicted pain and suffering. In fact, it is impossible to live out the Christian life and glorify God without the enabling power of the Holy Spirit;

- The Bible admonishes us to be continuously filled with the Holy Spirit, in order to fulfill God's unique plan in our lives;

- A continuous filling of the Holy Spirit requires that we become diligent students of the Word of God, obey Him, abide in Christ daily, and engage in godly service;

- The manifestation of the Fruit of the Spirit in a Christian's life is one outward evidence of a Christian who is Spirit-led. Other evidences include, but are not limited to: speaking in tongues, confidence and boldness in witnessing for Christ, etc.

# Chapter 4

# Know the Basic Nature of the Bible

This chapter, and the upcoming four chapters are dedicated to different aspects of the Word of God, such as its trustworthiness, how to harmonize the testaments, meditate on the Word and apply it to your life. In my view, after our salvation, the next best thing that God has done for us, His children, is to reveal Himself to us, in His Word. It is my belief that a person cannot know God apart from His written Word. God is His Word, His Word is God—they are inseparable. Hence, the heavy emphasis on God's Word in these forthcoming chapters is not an accident. Rather, it is intentional, in order to better equip you in your journey with Him.

There is an entire discipline called Bibliology, which is the study of the theological doctrine of the Bible, such as its inerrancy (i.e., incapability of error; containing no mistakes); canonization (i.e., pertaining to the inspired books of the Bible); inspiration; revelation; interpretation, etc, of the Holy Scriptures. It is not the focus of this chapter to delve into these very relevant topics about the nature of the Bible. Rather, this chapter will present a basic overview of the nature of the Christian Bible, in order to equip you with its fundamental nature, before much discussion about its content.

## What is the True Christian Bible?

The Greek word for Bible is biblion, meaning the "book." The Bible is a collection of 66 books: 39 from the Old Testament and 27 from the New Testament, inspired by God, and considered authoritative, inerrant, and infallible (i.e., flawless) by the collective Christian Church in espousing the Christian doctrines (i.e., teachings) and beliefs. By inspired, I mean, God spoke His thoughts to the minds of over 40 different authors across different geographical locations and centuries apart, over a period of over 1000 years, and they wrote down everything, exactly as they were guided and instructed.

Although these authors wrote in different parts of the world, during different eras and in different languages, there is perfect consistency and unity about the contents each of them wrote— The revelation of the Triune God of the Bible and His plan for redemption after the transgression of Adam and Eve. This unity is no accident; the writings are supernaturally inspired by God Himself.

It is noteworthy to mention that the Roman Catholic and Orthodox branches of Christianity have extra Old Testament books, called the Apocryphal books, which the Protestant Church collectively rejects as inspired by God. It is beyond the scope of this book to address the various reasons why the Protestants reject these Apocryphal books. However, all three branches of Christianity: Orthodox, Roman Catholics, and Protestants, agree on all 27 books of the New Testament. Most importantly, all three branches of the faith accept the Bible as the infallible and inspired Word of God.

## What Does the Word Testament Mean?

The word testament itself means a "will or a covenant". A will is a person's wishes or desires, while a covenant is an agreement between two parties. With regards to the Bible, the Old and New Testaments are describing God's will for His children, those who have accepted a relationship with Him through Christ Jesus. So simply put, God has a covenant relationship with all true Christians, as expressed in His written Word encased in the Bible.

The Old Testament revealed God's initial covenant with Mankind through His relationship with Adam and Eve; that is to say, His instructions to them not to eat from the forbidden tree. God also established a covenant with other Old Testament patriarchs, such as Noah, Abraham, and with humanity, through His chosen people, the Jews (see the book of Genesis). Also, God provided details of His covenant with the descendants of Abraham, the Jews, through His various holy and righteous Laws given to the prophet Moses. These Laws, called the Mosaic Law, were given to God's chosen people, the Jews, to adhere to (see the books of Exodus, Leviticus, Numbers, Deuteronomy).

The Bible teaches that our New covenant or the New Testament is much better than the old (see the book of Hebrews), especially as it is solely based on God's grace because Christ Jesus has fulfilled all of the Old Testament Laws. This new covenant (i.e., New Testament), has therefore been established by God because of the shedding of the precious blood of the Lord Jesus (Luke 22:20; Matthew 26:28; Mark 14:24). Keep in mind that even though we currently have a better covenant with God, that does not nullify the old covenant (i.e., Old Testament), as some Christians erroneously believe ( I address this issue in the next chapter).

## What is the Purpose of the Bible?

The primary purpose of the Holy Scriptures, as found in the Bible, is to reveal God to us, His creation. The written words in the Bible tell God's story, and His plan to redeem and reconcile us to Himself, after the "Fall of Mankind", as recorded in Genesis chapter 3. It reveals God's deepest desire for His creation: A love relationship with us. In telling His story during the Old Testament period, God spoke through godly prophets, who spoke and acted on

His behalf, and in turn wrote everything down. Some examples of such prophets were Moses, Elijah, Jeremiah, Isaiah, etc.

In what is described as progressive revelation, God revealed Himself to Mankind in a progressive manner throughout the Old Testament period, as He spoke through the prophets in various ways, such as in their thoughts, dreams, visions, etc. But then, in the New Testament era, in God's perfect timing, He fully revealed Himself to us in the person of Christ Jesus (Hebrews 1:1-3). **The fact that God chose to reveal Himself to us in this progressive manner does not imply that He changed. The Scripture teaches that God is immutable in His nature** (Numbers 23:19; Malachi 3:6; Hebrews 13:8; James 1:17). In the next chapter, I discuss how to harmonize the testaments, which will enable you to see that God is the same in the Old and New Testaments.

> *The fact that God chose to reveal Himself to us in this progressive manner does not imply that He changed. The Scripture teaches that God is immutable in His nature.*

God's story as recorded in the Bible can be easily viewed into four unique stages:

1. How He created the heavens and the earth (see Genesis chapters 1 and 2);

2. The temptation, transgression, and subsequent "Fall of Mankind From Grace" (see Genesis chapter 3);

3. The plan of redemption right after the fall, as recorded in Genesis 3 verse 15, then moving forward throughout the writings in the Bible, God spoke through Old Testament prophets and Saints (i.e., those set apart as holy for God's use), until He Himself became flesh in the person of Christ Jesus to redeem His creation (John 1:1-14);

4. The final stage of God's redemptive plan is underway during

this Church age, until the consummation. This involves the second coming of Christ Jesus; the resurrection of all the believers; the Lord's 1000 years of reign on this earth with His followers as the King of Kings and Lords of Lords; the final judgment of sin and Satan; and the establishment of the New Jerusalem (see the book of Revelation).

In all, you can view the writings in the Bible as an instruction manual, with directions from God to you, on how He wants you, His child, to live your life, and what you can expect from Him.

### What are the Original Languages of the Bible?

The Bible was originally written in three different languages: Hebrew, Aramaic and Greek, but today, it has been translated into modern English and many other major languages of the world, such as French, Spanish, etc. With the Bible now available in many major languages, there are dozens of different translations or versions available. The history of how we got the English Bible is beyond the scope of this book, but suffice it to say that our contemporary English translations from the original languages can be trusted, due to much scholarship in this area.

### Are the English Translations of the Bible Accurate?

Yes. It is well acknowledged that any book which is hand copied has the potential of human errors, such as typos, spelling errors, misplaced punctuations, etc. And the Bible is no exception. The Jewish Scribes who were responsible for hand copying the biblical text from the original manuscripts were not immune from such careless errors or typos. But, the awesome news is that, an entire discipline in biblical studies called Textual Criticism, has the painstaking, tedious task of comparing and contrasting the various available manuscripts and translations of the Bible, for accuracy and consistency, thus discerning and eliminating any sort of errors or discrepancies.

Please take note that the word "criticism" used in this discipline, does not imply searching for faults. Rather, it involves a very close examination and evaluation of the text, compared to the original languages or text it was written in, in order to evaluate and address any potential errors or typos. Due to the scrupulous efforts of godly inspired scholars in their extreme evaluation of the biblical text during the translation process, we have excellent news! Evidence from Textual Criticism over hundreds of years have consistently revealed that our modern English Bible translations are extremely accurate, and are close to the original manuscripts in the Hebrew, Aramaic and Greek. **Thus, Bible scholars unanimously agree that the majority of our modern Bible translations can be trusted.**

> *There is one translation that I want you to totally avoid. It is the New World Translation (NWT), which is the Jehovah's Witnesses Translation. This translation is completely wrong, inaccurate, and falsified in its translation.*

**Research in the field of Textual Criticism also reveals that in areas where errors were found, these errors were mostly pertaining to minor things such omitting a letter or a word, writing the same thing twice, changing the order of words, misspelling of names or words, etc. But, these minor careless errors do not change the meaning or doctrinal teachings of the biblical text.** So you can absolutely trust the various translations. Much more, most modern translations will let the readers know about these minor errors or inconsistency in a footnote, thereby allowing the reader to interpret the text for themselves.

Notwithstanding, **there is one translation that I want you to totally avoid. It is the New World Translation (NWT), which is the Jehovah's Witnesses Translation. This translation**

**is completely wrong, inaccurate, and falsified in its translation.** I discuss more about the Jehovah's Witnesses and Mormons in chapter 10.

## What Are the Different Modern Translations?

There are two general basic approaches to Bible translation (i.e., from the original languages to the English language), leading to two major categories: Formal equivalence and functional equivalence. However, there is an added in-between category called: Mediating or combination versions or translations. I use the words versions or translation interchangeably to mean the same thing. Let us briefly examine these categories.

**Formal Equivalence**: This is also known as a thought-for-thought, word-for-word, or literal translation, which aims to retain the same syntax from the original Hebrew, Aramaic and Greek languages into the English language, during the translation process. This type of translation is very challenging, because some of the syntax from the original languages do not exist in the English Language. Some examples of Bible in this category include, but are not limited to the: King James Version (KJV); New King James Version (NKJV); New Revised Standard Version) NRSV, etc.

**Functional Equivalence**: This type of translation aims to reproduce the "meaning" from the original Hebrew, Aramaic and Greek, into good, natural, contemporary English. This type of translation is also referred to as a *meaning-based* translation, because words are translated based on their "meaning." Some examples of this type of Bible translation include, but are not limited to the: New Living Translation (NLT); The Message Bible (MB); Good News Bible (GNB), etc.

**Mediating Versions**: This type of translation is like the middle ground between the formal and functional equivalence, as it provides a balance between the two categories. Some examples of meditating Bible translations include, but are not limited to the: New International Version (NIV); Today's New International Version (TNIV); The Jerusalem Bible (JB), etc. However, some Bible scholars actually consider versions such as NIV and TNIV, as belonging to the functional equivalence category.

## Why So Many Translations?

This is a very relevant and fair question that demands an answer. And the most simplistic answer is that, the growth of Christianity, and its subsequent demand for God's Word by its practitioners in their respective languages warranted the translations. Secondly, and obviously, the majority of Christians do not speak Hebrew, Aramaic and/or Greek, thus the translations are necessary. Thirdly, we need the different translations because they serve different purposes, and for different groups of individuals. In fact, by the time this book goes to print, we will probably have more translations available.

For example, a person may want a study Bible, which will require a different type of version, such as the NKJV or NRSV, while someone else may require a devotional easy- to- read Bible, such as the NLT or the LB versions — you get the point? **This is the bottom line:** All of the different types of translations are necessary, and a serious student of God's Word needs at least one Bible translation from each category.

## How Do I Choose a Translation?

To answer this question, you must know why you want the Bible? Do you need a study Bible? A devotional Bible or what? The answer to this question will lead you to the type of Bible version that will suit your specific need. Below are some recommendations:

*Know the Basic Nature of the Bible*

1. Get at least one study Bible from the Formal or Functional equivalence category, and another Bible from the Mediating group, as a devotional Bible;

2. If you can afford it, get at least 2 different Bibles from each category, as it will enhance clarity of God's Word;

3. Also, purchase a Bible version that has been translated by a committee, preferably, a committee from different denominations and/or different branches of Christianity, including experts in the original languages, rather than a Bible translated by just one individual. The obvious reason is that a committee will include individuals with expertise from different areas of Bible studies; an individual cannot be an expert in all areas of Bible studies;

4. Always read the preface section of any Bible version before purchasing it, as it will provide relevant information about the scholarship which was involved in its translation process. This information will reveal whether or not a committee was involved during the translation, and the type of committee, etc. Knowing this information will enable you to make a wiser decision.

> *Using multiple Bible translations does not imply that one Bible version is not sufficient; because it is, as God will still speak to you through His Word, if you only use one translation.*

To conclude this section, I want to add that purchasing multiple versions will definitely benefit you; it will enable you to obtain a much in-depth study of God's Word, since you will have the opportunity to study how the different translations render various Scriptures. **Please note that the various Bible translations are saying the same thing, but they present the rendering in different styles. Most importantly, using multiple Bible translations does not imply that one Bible version is not sufficient; because it is, as God will still speak to you through His Word, if you only use one translation.**

**What are the Various Writing Styles of the Bible?**

The Bible is written in a variety of literature styles, including:

1. Poetry, such as the Psalms, Song of Songs, etc;

2. The Law of God (i.e., the details for the Jewish Nation), such as found in the Old Testament books of Exodus (see the 10 Commandments), Leviticus, Numbers, Deuteronomy, etc;

3. Historical Accounts (i.e., almost all of the Old Testament), such as the book of Joshua, 1 and 2 Chronicles, etc;

4. Prophetic Writings (i.e., with accurate prediction of future events), such as the book of Isaiah, Daniel, Jeremiah, etc;

5. Apocalyptic Writing (i.e., a type of prophetic literature writing, warning about a disastrous future event ), such as the book Revelation;

6. Wisdom Literature, such as the book of Proverbs, Ecclesiastes, Job, etc;

7. Gospel Accounts (i.e., recording of the ministry of Christ Jesus), such as the four Gospels of Matthew, Mark, Luke and John. **Please take note that the Gospel recordings are not biographical accounts of the life of our Lord Jesus. Rather, they are brief recordings of His ministry;**

8. Letters or Epistles, such as the book of Romans, 1 and 2 Corinthians, Galatians, etc.

Although they are different in their writing styles, the 66 books of the English Bible have different arrangements as well. I refer to the English Bible because the Hebrew Bible has a slight difference in its arrangement of the same 39 Old Testament books.

## How the English Bible is Arranged

The Old Testament English books are arranged according to the type of writing and subject matter, and not by chronological order. Below is the order of arrangement:

**The 39 Books of the Old Testament English Bible:**

1. 5 Books pertaining to the Law: Genesis through Deuteronomy;

2. 12 Books pertaining to History: Joshua through Esther;

3. 5 Books pertaining to Wisdom and Poetry: Job through Song of Songs;

4. 17 Books of the Prophets: Isaiah through Malachi. These are sometimes referred to as the 5 books of the Major Prophets: Isaiah, Jeremiah, Lamentations, Ezekiel, Daniel, and the 12 books of the Minor Prophets: Hosea, Joel, Amos, Obadiah, Jonah, Micah, Nahum, Habakkuk, Zephaniah, Haggai, Zechariah, and Malachi.

**The expression of minor or major prophet does not pertain to the relevance or importance of the book, for they are all equally important; rather, it refers to the length of the book.**

**The 27 Books of the New Testament Bible:**

1. *5 Books Pertaining to History:* Matthew, Mark, Luke, John and Acts. This category can be subdivided into the four Gospels and the Acts of the Apostles. The book of Acts picks up where the book of Luke ends, thus it is at times referred to as Luke-Acts.

2. *21 Books of Christian Doctrine:* Romans; 1 and 2 Corinthians; Galatians; Ephesians; Philippians; Colossians; 1 and 2 Thessalonians; 1 and 2 Timothy; Titus; Philemon; Hebrews; James; 1 and 2 Peter; 1, 2, and 3rd John; and Jude. Although the entire Bible focuses on Christian doctrine, these 21 books highlight the major doctrines of the faith. These books are mostly letters, or referred to as epistles. Out

of the 21 epistles, 13 are written by the apostle Paul. Three of these epistles are considered pastoral epistles as they offer doctrinal guidelines for pastors and the Church: The book of Titus, 1 and 2 Timothy.

3. *1 Book of Prophecy:* Although most of the Bible can be viewed as prophetic, the book of Revelation is the main apocalyptic book.

## God Has Already Spoken

The Bible teaches that God has already spoken to His creation through the inspired writings in the testaments, in the person of Christ Jesus, and through nature, thus we can fully comprehend the true nature of God (Hebrews 1:1-2; Romans chapter 1). You can rest therefore, with the notion that whatever it is that God wants you to know about Himself, He has already revealed it in the Bible, which has the answers to all of life's problems. As such, you need not look elsewhere for further answers. Because of this complete revelation of God in the person of the Lord Jesus; through nature; and in His written Word, the Bible is considered canonized, and no further writing is authorized or viewed as inspired Scripture.

## The Bible is Already Canonized

The word canon in English comes from the Greek word "Kanon," referring to a measuring rod or rule used to measure something. With regards to the Bible, it is referring to the list of inspired books called "Holy Scriptures," which were selected by church leaders under the inspiration of the Holy Spirit, and are serving as the authoritative voice for the body of Christ (i.e., the Universal Christian Church). By Universal Christian Church, I am referring to all of the churches worldwide, whose congregants have a relationship with God through the Lord Jesus.

## Canonization of the Old Testament Books

Most Bible scholars agree that the Old Testament books were selected and canonized in various stages. For example, by 400 BC (i.e., before Christ), the books of the Law were already selected and canonized, and by 200 BC, the books of the Prophets were canonized, then by 100 BC, the rest of the writings were canonized. And by the time of the New Testament writings, all of the Old Testament books were definitely canonized.

The main criteria for accepting a book into the canon was authorship by a prophet, or a recipient of God's divine revelation (i.e., an individual whom God revealed Himself to). Our Lord Jesus Himself authenticated the Old Testament Scriptures as He frequently referred others to search the Old Testament Scriptures about Himself; and He often quoted from it.

It is beyond the scope of this book to expound on the process of the canonization. But suffice it to say that most of the Old Testament Saints themselves authenticated the selection process of the canonized books, based on their inspired utterances from God, and the Jews believed it. For example, the Prophet Jeremiah stated directly to the people: *"The LORD said to me, "You have seen correctly, for I am watching to see that my word is fulfilled"* ( 1:12); and the Prophet Hosea stated: *"The word of the Lord that came to Hosea son of Beeri ..."* (1:1); and the Prophet Isaiah declared: *"This is what the Lord says to me:"* (18:4), etc, (emphasis author's).

Furthermore, the Jews themselves authenticated the Old Testament as God's inspired Word when they agreed to obey the 10 commandments which God had given to Moses. In addition, in Nehemiah chapter 8, the Jews recognized the authority of the Scriptures as God's inspired Word when they wept and were repentant for their sins, after the Priest Ezra read the Scriptures to them aloud (v. 9).

## Canonization of the New Testament Books

After the ascension of our Lord, the only canonized Scripture was the Old Testament books, and the first Century church mainly read aloud the life and teachings of the Lord Jesus and those of the apostles during their gatherings. Thereafter, under the inspiration of the Holy Spirit, various first Century church leaders began the process of assembling these writings into a single unit. One major reason was because Christianity was rapidly spreading across the Roman Empire and above, and by the end of the first Century, certain inspired church leaders became fully aware of the need to swiftly select the inspired and authenticated books for the canon. Other reasons for canonization of the New Testament books include, but are not limited to the need to:

1. Avoid false writings, false prophets and their teachings under the guise of Christianity;

2. Preserve the inspired written Word for future generations;

3. Have an authoritative voice for the Universal Church; and

4. Prevent the Roman Empire from destroying and confiscating the inspired writings, given the widespread persecution of the church at that time.

The process of compiling the inspired selected books of the New Testament took multiple years. And the explanation of this process requires more space and content than I can discuss in this book. Nonetheless, in a nutshell, Bible scholars generally agree that by the middle of the second Century AD (i.e., Anno Domini, meaning the "year of our Lord," in Latin), the New Testament canon was taking shape, as multiple books were surfacing, such as the letters of the apostle Paul, the Gospels, etc, in a list known as the Muratorian Fragment, discovered by Cardinal L. A. Muratori.

And by 367 AD, a list consisting of all 27 books of the New Testament was published by Athanasius, the Bishop of Alexandria.

After this brave move, under the inspiration of the Holy Spirit, the Church counsel decisively affirmed and officially selected all 27 books of the New Testament as possessing divine qualities, thereby accepting it in the canon.

It is noteworthy to mention that, just like the Old Testament canon, the main criteria for accepting a book as belonging to the New Testament canon was authorship by a firsthand witness of the ministry of our Lord Jesus Christ (i.e., His disciples, who were later called Apostles), or by those who had very close contact with the Apostles. As an example, the Gospel of Mark is written by the apostle Mark, who became a disciple of Jesus Christ after His death, resurrection and ascension into heaven, and had intimate contact with the apostle Peter. In fact, most Bible scholars agree that, under the inspiration of the Holy Spirit, Mark wrote his Gospel under direct supervision and direction from the apostle Peter. Thus, some Bible scholars and teachers actually refer to the Gospel of Mark as the apostle Peter's account of the ministry and teaching of Jesus Christ.

**It is very critical to note that the process of canonization of the Old and New Testament books were equally inspired by the Holy Spirit. Also, the Church council did not select the books to be accepted into the canon.** <u>**Rather, the books that were accepted into the canon already possessed divine qualities as inspired by God, then, under the inspiration and guidance of the Holy Spirit, the church leaders selected the books.**</u>

There are many people who struggle with the notion that God had to speak through mere human beings who wrote down His thoughts, as such, they are uncertain about the trustworthiness of the Bible. If you are one of those people, I want to assure you that you can trust the Bible as God's inspired Word to you (I address this issue in details in <u>chapter 6</u>). But, one easy and subjective way to find out for yourself, whether or not the Bible is inspired, is to invest some time in studying it; and it will supernaturally inspire you, because it is, indeed, inspired.

## PRACTICAL APPLICATION

In spite of how ancient the writings in the Bible might be, it is supernatural how God preserved the content throughout the process of canonization and translation from the original languages into the major languages of the world today. And these writings are still timely, relevant, and applicable for us, today! Under the inspiration of the Holy Spirit, the different authors used various styles of writings, depending on the subject matter at hand, to tell God's story. Amazingly, these different styles of writings supernaturally serve various purposes. For example, the Psalms are written in such poetic styles, thus enabling us to easily embed them into our worship of God. And the wisdom literature, such as the many " to the point" sayings in the Proverbs, foster easy memorization for our daily practical guide.

After the "Fall of Mankind" as noted in Genesis chapter 3, God anticipated the kinds of problems human beings will encounter in this life, thus, He provided His answers and solutions in His Word. There is nothing new under the sun—which means, there is no problem that you, or any other human being will ever encounter, that the Bible has not already addressed, one way or the other. Therefore, as you approach the Bible, keep the following major principles in mind:

- ➢ All 66 books of the Bible contain relevant and timeless instructions from God to you;

- ➢ You can trust your modern English Bible translations, because the primary message from God to you is intact;

- ➢ Trust that God has already spoken through His Word, and rely on the Bible as your primary source of information about God;

With the aforementioned brief overview of the basic nature of the Bible, you may wonder what to expect once you open its pages!

## What to Expect in the Pages of the Bible

- ❖ Revelation of the true nature of the immutable God: the Creator of the heavens and the earth;

- ❖ Hundreds of doctrines about the Christian faith;

- ❖ Answers and solutions to all of life's problems, including guidelines and specific instructions on topics such as marriage, raising children, relationships, conflict resolution, sexual relations, finances, avoiding sin, managing your emotions, growing in your spiritual journey, how to care for your soul and physical health, etc;

- ❖ How to live a holy and godly life, pleasing to God;

- ❖ How to deal with political and social issues (i.e., the government);

- ❖ How this present world will end, plus much more.

In situations when the Bible does not offer specific instructions regarding a specific issue, such as who to get married to, or where to attend college, or which house to buy, practical biblical wisdom can be found in books such as the book of Proverbs, and in the various epistles. As an example, the general principle in the Bible is that God is pleased when His children marry fellow Christians, as it will be much easier to share the most important thing in their lives: their Christian faith, with a like-minded believer. Plus, marrying a fellow Christian increases the probability of raising godly children, which pleases God.

On the other hand, marrying an unbeliever will bring much distress in your life because you will not be able to share your faith, with the person you spend the most time with. This challenge might lead to much strife about various doctrines and practices about the faith. Worst case scenario, this union might cause you to stray from the faith. God loves you, and does not want you to be miserable in your marriage. Hence, even when specific biblical instructions are not offered, adhering to various general biblical principles will honor God and bless you. As another example, in cases such as which house to buy, the Bible may not directly point you to a particular home, but it clearly teaches about practical principles such as those found in the book of Proverbs, warning you not to live above your means, etc.

**A word of caution**: Not everything you read in the Bible is God's prescriptive plan for you. In the Bible, you will find God's prescriptive decrees, instructions, or plan, such as what He specifically wants you to do. Examples of such decrees include, but are not limited to, avoiding sin; loving and respecting others; sharing the Gospel message with others; fellowshipping with other believers; raising godly children; supporting His work on the earth with your finances, prayers and godly service; staying out of debt; marrying a believer, etc.

On the other hand, there are also written descriptive accounts in the Bible that the authors are simply narrating events that took place, such as heinous sinful events, for purposes of warning us, and emphasizing how such events grieve God. For example, incidences of murder, due to individuals' lustful passions and desires, incest, rape, child sacrifice, etc, as recorded in the Old Testament, are not implying that God approved of these events—these are not His prescriptive wish or will for us. Rather, these events are recorded for our learning, so we do not repeat them. So do not get God's prescriptive will and the descriptive narratives in the Bible mixed-up!

In conclusion, the Bible has remained the number one best-selling book throughout the history of the world, because it is applicable globally, as it transcends and speaks to every culture, race, gender, government, etc. You know why? The answer is simple: It is God's instruction for His creation, whom He knows quite well. At the core, beyond the differences in our skin color and physical appearances, all human beings are the same, struggling with the same issues, such as fear; loneliness; anger; wanting acceptance; and the desire to be loved and valued; live meaningful lives; and have a relationship with their Creator, etc. And because the Bible has the answers to all of these issues, it will always be the bestselling book of all times. So, the sooner you trust it as God's inspired Word, and start applying its teachings into your life, the sooner you will start to experience the transformed life that God wants you to enjoy.

In conclusion, I want to acknowledge that, I am aware that some people, even some Christians, are confused about the consistency of God as revealed in the testaments. There are those who erroneously believe that the God of the Old and New Testaments are very different, which is grossly incorrect. Thus, harmonizing the testaments in order to enable you to better understand God's message, to you, is critical. With this in mind, I now turn to the next chapter, where I teach on basic ways to harmonize the testaments.

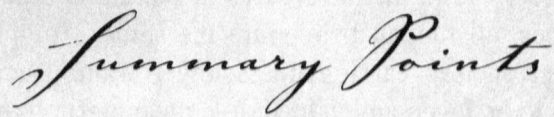

## Summary Points

- The Bible is the primary way in which God has revealed Himself to us;

- The Bible tells God's story about the "Fall of Mankind from Grace," and His plan to reconcile us to Himself, because of His unconditional and unfathomable love;

- Because of the scrupulous work from the discipline of Textual Criticism, you can trust our contemporary English Bible translations;

- At this time, the entire Bible is canonized. God has already spoken through the prophets in the Old Testament and in the person of Christ Jesus, and through the apostles who wrote the New Testament books under the inspiration of the Holy Spirit;

- The books selected into the canon already possessed divine qualities as inspired by God, then they were later selected by Church leaders into the canon, under the wisdom and direction of the Holy Spirit;

- God has supernaturally preserved the Holy Scriptures throughout the process of canonization, including the process of translation from the original languages to the major languages of the world today.

# Chapter 5

# How To Harmonize the Testaments

Some Christians believe that the Old Testament is obsolete, which is not true, and as such, they only focus on the New Testament. Both Testaments are equally important. The Old Testament, which primarily focused on the Nation of Israel and the Mosaic Law, pointed the Jews towards the coming Messiah, Christ Jesus, while the New Testament reveals the Messiah, and is the fulfillment of the Old Testament Laws.

Without a solid understanding of the Old Testament, it will be difficult for anyone to fully comprehend the totality of Scripture, as this might cause you to only understand pieces of the big picture. Since God inspired both the Old and the New Testaments to be used for purposes of correcting and training us in His ways (2 Timothy 3:16); ignoring the Old Testament Scripture could lead to some major problems, errors and confusion in your understanding of God, which might negatively affect your relationship with Him. Besides, the Lord Jesus, God Himself in the flesh, quoted and relied on the Old Testament Scripture throughout His ministry, because it is the Word of God, with its supernatural power.

Many people erroneously believe that the God of the Old Testament is different from the God of the New. This is FALSE, God is immutable in His essence. Part of this confusion is because many Christians who genuinely love God have not taken the time to study and understand the totality of Scripture, thus they cannot harmonize the testaments. Another reason why many people struggle with harmonizing the testaments is because they cannot reconcile the loving and forgiving God as portrayed by the Lord Jesus, compared to the God of the Old Testament, who brought harsh judgments upon many people.

## God's Judgment in the Old Testament

For the most part, those who struggle to harmonize God's judgment of individuals and nations in the Old Testament with His grace in the New, only look at "one side of the coin." They focus on God's love, and ignore His justice. Space limitation in this book prevents me from expounding on this very relevant issue at hand. Nonetheless, let us briefly examine why God commanded much killings as noted in the Old Testament text. As we proceed, keep in mind that there is a major difference between killing and murdering someone. As a brief example, some killings may be justified (i.e., self- defense), while murdering someone is usually premeditated! I begin with the notion of God's love. In order for love to be fully expressed, hatred for evil must be present. If God were to allow the wicked individuals to get away with their wickedness against their fellow human beings and Mankind at large, that would be injustice, which would be inconsistent and incomparable with His nature.

Let us examine an earthly scenario. Imagine that a serial murderer who has confessed to the killings of over 200 people is tried by a jury and released without any accountability or punishment to serve time in prison, because the jury and judge were compassionate towards him for his poor upbringing; and when asked by the media why the serial murderer was not sentenced to death or life in prison; the judge simply responded by saying " someone had to express compassion for this murderer, who had never experienced love from anyone." A scenario like this would definitely lead to much rioting in the streets of the USA, and a judge or jury like the one mentioned above would be punished by the judiciary system for such gross injustice and negligence. You get the point! Hopefully you do! Well, guess what? Such injustice and negligence as discussed in the above scenario would have been said about God, had He not commanded some of the punishments and judgments as documented in the Old Testament text.

God's holy character demands that sin and evil be punished. For example, we are told in the Old Testament how the Canaanites were morally and spiritually corrupt. Their cruelty and abominable acts against God, such as child sacrifice ( i.e., burning their children while alive in the fire, in order to appease their pagan gods); bestiality (i.e., sexual intercourse between a human being and an animal); and a host of other perverse sexual practices were rampant and uncontrollable. In spite of several warnings, they were unrepentant, and essentially took God's long-suffering for granted and in a way, "laughed at Him."

We are told how God, in His love, patience, and mercy, allowed up to about 400 years for them to repent (i.e., the Amorites, one of the Nations who lived in Canaan during that time), but they refused (Genesis 15:16). As such, God had to command His judgment against them, in order to prevent further deaths, protect the innocent children, and preserve future generations — this is actually love, I believe. Had God not enforced judgment, it would have led to an uncontrollable epidemic of massive unjust killings of the innocent, and the spread of wickedness. Much more, had God not intervened, other nations of the world at that time would have "copied" such malignant behaviors. Hence, God had to save His creation, thus, judgment was absolutely warranted and justified.

The book of Genesis documented a similar situation, during Noah's generation, whereby the morality of the human race had hit "rock bottom," and in spite of Noah's preaching to the people for about 120 years, they would not repent, so God imposed His judgment (see Genesis chapters 6, 7 and 8; 2 Peter 2:5-10 ). Sodom and Gomorrah was another classic example of how God could not even find 10 righteous people there. Their unrepentant sexual immorality and moral decay was detestable, thus God had to impose His judgment against them (Genesis 18 and 19; 2 Peter 2:5-10 ).

Some people believe that God was unfair to favor the Israelites, and to command them to savagely destroy their neighboring nations because of their wicked ways. To this end, I pose this question to you: Was God also unfair when He allowed the Assyrians to attack the Israelites? Was God still favoring them then? Of course, the answer is No. God seeks after justice, and there is no partiality in Him. He had to punish even His "elect" (i.e., His chosen ones, such as the Israelites) when they disobeyed Him. Due to the Israelites sins and outright disobedience, they strayed outside of God's will and divine protection. Even after much admonition for them to repent, they did not, thus God allowed judgment against them (see the books of Ezra, Nehemiah, Jeremiah, Lamentations, etc). Also, keep in mind that the Old Testament people were not "born again," so God's punishment during that era was different, compared to His dealings with us in this present Church age (I address this issue later in this chapter).

It is amazing how every reasonable and fair human being would agree that the judiciary systems in the world should punish the wicked, in order to preserve the innocent and upright citizens of their respective countries; but when it comes to God's punishment, it is as if people put blinders in their eyes. **Most people will readily accept God's love, but reject His justice and punishment — We cannot play this game. This attitude is unfair towards God. If we have to accept Him as our Creator, who knows best, then, we must accept Him in His entirety, and not pick and choose which aspects of Him to embrace — it does not work like this.**

Often, people criticize God based on someone else's opinion. The only way to know for sure, is to invest some time and study His Word for yourself, in its entirety, and you will definitely come to the firm conclusion about the consistent revelation of the Triune Godhead across the testaments. For those of you who have never read the entire Bible from Genesis to Revelation, I challenge you to do so, so you can better perceive for yourself God's progressive revelation of Himself to us, until His fullest manifestation of Himself in the person of Jesus Christ; and His immutable nature, as evident in the consistent themes throughout the Bible.

## Harmonizing the Testaments

There are hundreds of consistent themes across the testaments, but due to space limitation, I am only able to discuss a few major ones, in order to enhance your understanding of the unchangable nature of God. There are hundreds of scriptural references pertaining to these themes, but I am only able to cite a few of them here.

**God's Consistent Revelation of Himself Across the Testaments**

➢ *God's Desire for a Relationship with Mankind*

God's deepest desire to have a relationship with His creation, human beings, is consistent across the testaments. In the Old Testament, God sought a relationship with Adam and Eve even after they transgressed His law. And He sought after Abraham and Noah, in addition to His "chosen people," the Nation of Israel, for a covenant relationship ( Genesis 3: 8-9; 6: 8-22; 12: 1-20; 15:1-21; 17: 1-27; Deuteronomy 7:6-10). Then in the New Testament, the same pattern and consistency is noted, as He is willing for none to perish, but for all to come into a relationship with Him, through Christ Jesus (2 Peter 3:9; John 3:16; See the Gospels).

➢ *God's Faithfulness*

God's faithfulness is evident throughout both testaments. He has vowed to never break or violate His covenant with us (Psalm 89:34). As an example, in the Old Testament, God honored His covenant agreement with Noah, Abraham, and the descendants of Abraham (i.e., the Jewish Nation) in addition to providing protective care for them (see Genesis 8:1-2, 21:1-7; 26:24; Exodus 13: 17-31; the book of Esther). And in the New Testament, the same pattern is evident: The promised Messiah, Christ Jesus was born; the Promised Holy Spirit came; the resurrection took place, etc (see the Gospels, Acts 2: 1-13).

> *God's Forgiving Nature*

>> Because of His infinite love for His creation, God did not physically kill Adam and Eve when they sinned against Him, instead He forgave them (see Genesis Chapter 3). As other examples, He also forgave Cain, the first murderer in the history of the world, for the murder of his brother Abel (see Genesis Chapter 4); He repeatedly forgave the Israelites for breaking the covenant relationship He had with them (see Exodus 32; Nehemiah 8 and 9); and He forgave King David for committing the two deadliest sins under the Old Testament Law: adultery and murder (2 Samuel 11-12).

God also forgave the wicked people of Nineveh who repented from their wickedness after Jonah proclaimed God's Kingdom and goodness to them (see the book of Jonah). In the ministry of the Lord Jesus, God's consistent forgiving nature was also obvious— The Lord forgave the woman caught in the act of adultery, even though she deserved to be stoned to death in accordance with the Jewish Law, and He forgave the sins of many individuals who received healing from Him. And God's ultimate forgiving nature was seen on the cross, as He Himself became flesh in the person of Christ Jesus, and died for the sins of the world ( see the Gospels; 2 Corinthians 5:15; 1 John 2:2).

> *God's Grace, Compassion, and Mercy*

>> Because of His mercy (i.e., withholding punishment when it is due), due to His forgiving nature as described above, God did not physically kill Adam and Eve who willfully transgressed His instructions, they lived for hundreds of years thereafter. It was also because of God's grace, compassion and mercy, that caused Him to spare the life of Cain, who murdered his brother, Abel. God's gracious nature was also displayed, as He saved Noah and His family from destruction because of Noah's righteousness. Much more, God spared the life of Lot and his family from

destruction, because of His grace, compassion and mercy (see the book of Genesis).

For centuries, God expressed His compassion and mercy towards the Israelites who chronically rebelled against His Laws, by worshipping false gods and idols, intermarried foreigners (against His specific instructions for them not to do so), and practiced all sorts of evil and divination (e.g., see the books of 1 & 2 Chronicles, Isaiah, Jeremiah, etc). God's grace, compassion and mercy were very much highlighted in the ministry of the Lord Jesus. He was moved with compassion for people and healed them. And the apex of God's grace and mercy was seen on the cross, as God Himself, in the person of Christ Jesus, shed His innocent blood and died for each of us, and paid the penalties for our sins. This act of grace, compassion and mercy, has paved the way for each individual, who so desires, to have direct access to God, even though none of us deserves it (see the Gospels).

➢ *God's Patience and Long-suffering*

This theme is also consistent across the testaments. God was patient with the Israelites in spite of their rejection of Him. He was very patient with the wicked and unrighteous people in Noah's generation, for up to about 120 years, yet they refused to repent. Like mentioned earlier, God patiently waited for hundreds of years for the wicked Amorites who practiced child sacrifices and committed heinous crimes to repent, yet, they would not.

In the New Testament, God's long-suffering is still present in this Church age, as He desires none to perish, but for all to come to Him (2 Peter 3:9). We are told in the book of Revelation that even during the tribulation, some people will still reject God; in spite of numerous opportunities to repent, they will unfortunately refuse (see Revelation chapter 16).

> *God's Unconditional Love*

The death of the Lord Jesus on the cross speaks for itself. God's kind of love is unconditional, because His nature is Love (1 John 4:8). This obvious theme is consistent across the testaments —His love for His creation, human beings. Out of love, He saved Noah and his family and gave Mankind another opportunity to repopulate the earth after the destructive flood (see Genesis 6 through 10). His unconditional love for His chosen people, the Nation of Israel, is easily discernable throughout the writings of the Old Testament, in spite of their rejection of Him. God's unconditional love for Mankind is still in operation, as He is always willing to have a relationship with anyone who will accept the sacrificial work of Christ Jesus (Revelation 3:20).

> *God's Holiness*

Holiness means to be "set apart" and "pure." With regards to God, it means He is 100% pure in everything, and there is no darkness, evil or deceit in Him. God's holiness is a consistent theme across the testaments (Isaiah 6:1-3; Psalms 99:9; 1 Peter 1:16; Revelation 4:8, etc).

> *God's Justice*

God's justice is obvious across the testaments. Since God is holy, sin and evil must be dealt with by God. This is such a consistent theme across the Bible that, in my view, it is the easiest to perceive. The Bible teaches that because of God's holiness, sin cannot abide in His presence. As such, Adam and Eve were dismissed and separated from God's presence after they sinned. This pattern is also evident throughout the Old Testament, such as during the Day of Atonement, when the Jews offered annual scarifies for their sins to be forgiven (see Leviticus chapter 16). Throughout the Old Testament, God's justice is seen as He punished the wicked, in order to preserve the innocent (as already discussed in the case of the Amorites, etc).

Because God is just, the Sinful Nature of Mankind inherited at the Garden of Eden had to be dealt with. Thus, the apex of God's justice was evident on the cross (Hebrews 9:12). Nonetheless, God's final justice will be demonstrated at the final judgment of Satan, his demonic angels, and his wicked followers (Revelation 16).

> *God's Omniscience, Omnipotence, and Omnipresence*

Another major theme across the testaments is God's Omniscience (i.e., His knowledge of all things). There are hundreds of examples to this regard. For example, biblical prophesies across the testaments attest to this truth (to be discussed in the next chapter ). God is always present (i.e., Omnipresence) in the heavens and on the earth (Psalm 139: 7-12). He is eternal and self-existent, and has always been present with His creation.

God's presence, through His Spirit, was well acknowledged during the Old Testament era as noted throughout the creation account, and in the lives of the patriarchs, such as Abraham, Moses, Isaac, etc. In the New Testament, God's presence was obvious throughout the ministry of Christ, and His presence continues in the lives of believers; and in the world today through His Spirit. God's omnipotence (i.e., His power) is obvious. His miraculous works since the beginning of creation of the earth display His absolute power. Furthermore, the miracles displayed during the ministry of Christ Jesus and the apostles, including His continuous miracles in the world today, are all undeniable evidence of His absolute power.

*The fact that God chose to reveal Himself in this progressive fashion does not negate or nullify His Omniscience.*

Remember that I explained earlier how God revealed Himself during the Old Testament dispensation in a progressive manner, with the full revelation evident in the person of Christ Jesus (Hebrews 1:1-3)! Hopefully, you recall! So, **do not get this notion of progressive revelation confused with God's Omniscience (i.e., God's all knowing nature), like some people do. The fact that God chose to reveal Himself in this progressive fashion does not negate or nullify His Omniscience**. It is my belief that God revealed Himself in such a progressive fashion because in His wisdom and timing, Mankind was not yet ready for His full manifestation; thus, at the proper time, He revealed Himself fully to us, in the person of Christ Jesus.

> ➤ *God's Righteousness is Imputed by Faith*

> This theme is noted in the Old Testament even before the Lord Jesus died for our sins (see Genesis 15:6). Abraham believed (i.e., exhibited faith in God), and God considered him as righteous (because of his faith), and thus credited it to him. Then in obedience, Abraham performed the rite of circumcision (see Romans 4; Genesis 17:26). It was a credit to Abraham because the sacrifice (i.e., the death of Christ) had not yet happened. So it is obvious how even in the Old Testament era, faith was God's standard for righteousness, and this pattern is consistent across the testaments.

> In the New Testament, after the sacrifice of Christ Jesus, the Bible teaches that we are saved only by the grace of God through faith (Ephesians 2:8-9; Romans 4). Then once we believe in the Lord Jesus, we are made righteous (i.e., righteousness is imputed to us because of our faith, just like it was with Abraham). Therefore, God's righteousness is a free gift to all those who believe.

> ➤ *God Rewards Faith*

> The Bible is very clear, from the book of Genesis to Revelation that without faith it is impossible to please God (Hebrews 11:6). God is a Spirit (John 4:24), so you must accept Him by faith. All of the patriarchs of the Old Testament, such as

Abraham, Moses, Jacob, Isaac, Elijah, etc, believed in the promises of God without much physical evidence, and God blessed, and used them mightily (see Hebrews chapter 11).

We see the same pattern throughout the New Testament. The apostles, such as Paul, Peter, James, John, etc, believed in the promises of God by faith, and they were used mightily by God to spread Christianity rapidly across the world, after the ascension of Christ Jesus. Today, many faithful Christians are following suit, and by faith, are spreading the Gospel of Christ, believing in the promises of God, and are seeing results: signs and wonders (i.e., miracles).

➢ *The Triune Nature of God*

Like already discussed in chapter 3, the fullness of the Godhead is quite evident across the Old and New Testaments. Other scriptural examples of Christ Jesus in the Old Testament, in His pre-incarnate form (i.e., before He became flesh) include, but are not limited to Genesis chapter 16: 10-13; 32:24-25; Exodus 3:2; Judges 13:18; 13:22; Joshua 5:14; Daniel 3: 24-25, etc).

➢ *God's Sovereignty*

God is the absolute "boss." He is self-existent, and no one tells Him what to do ( Psalm 135:6 ). But, by His choice, He decided to create human beings in His image, and has given us a Free Will. His Sovereignty is evident across the two testaments. He created the heavens and the earth (see Genesis chapter 1 and 2); He destroyed the earth with a flood, and decided to repopulate it (see Genesis chapters 6 through 9); He parted the Red Sea (see Exodus chapter 14), etc.

Other scriptural examples of God's sovereignty are evidenced in the books of Ruth, Esther, Job 1:12; 2: 6; 37: 14-24; 42: 2. God even worked through pagan leaders (those who did not believe in Him), in order to accomplish His will (see Genesis chapters 7 through 12, Genesis 20:3), hence emphasizing His sovereign nature.  In the New Testament, God's sovereignty is obvious throughout the ministry of Christ Jesus. For example, the perfect timing of His birth, death and resurrection, were all examples of God's sovereignty.  During this present Church age, God's sovereignty is still in operation, evidenced by His continuous miraculous work in the lives of His children and on the earth.

Other major consistent themes across the testaments include, but are not limited to God's humility, hatred for sexual immorality, disobedience and sin, etc, which will quench His presence and power in the lives of His children .

## How Are the Testaments Different?

Hopefully, you agree that harmonizing the testaments is essential in developing a deeper understanding of God and His Word, as encased in the Bible. **It is noteworthy to mention that the progressive manner of God's revelation of Himself to us, is the major reason for the major differences between the testaments.** So keep this fact in mind as you read the discussion below, pertaining to the major differences between the testaments.  Because I have already discussed these major reasons in previous chapters, I only present a succinct discussion below.

> *It is noteworthy to mention that the progressive manner of God's revelation of Himself to us, is the major reason for the major differences between the testaments.*

1. *Christ Jesus Fulfilled the Old Testament Laws 100%.* This includes the 10 commandments given to Moses in Exodus chapter 20, in addition to all of the other Mosaic Laws

found in the books of Exodus, Leviticus, Numbers and Deuteronomy. Bible scholars have noted that there were over 600 such Laws given to the Jews to adhere to. But since Jesus fulfilled all of these Laws perfectly, God is dealing with the New Testament believer based on grace, and not based on the Mosaic Laws.

2. *A Personal Relationship with God.* During the Old Testament period, the Jews did not have such close and personal relationship with God, as we are privileged to enjoy today. They could not address God as their " Father," as we can do today, if we choose to. This was because the Lord Jesus had not yet paved the way for such a relationship through His death and resurrection.

3. *God's Spirit did not Permanently Indwell the Old Testament People.* Today, all true believers are permanently indwelt by the Holy Spirit, and are sealed. Like I already discussed in chapter 3, God's Spirit filled the Old Testament Saints for specific purposes only, in order to accomplish His will, thereafter, the Spirit departed from them.

4. *The New Testament Believer can Directly Discern the Voice of God.* I am not referring to an audible voice, but rather, the ability for Scripture to be illuminated in their hearts by the Holy Spirit. And also, the ability for the believer to discern, in their hearts, the convictions or revelations of the Holy Spirit directly to them. Please note that, whatever promptings or convictions you might be discerning as coming from the Holy Spirit, they must be consistent with His written Word. This is because God will never speak to you contrary to His Word; His Word is the primary way He will speak to you.

On the other hand, during the Old Testament era, God primarily spoke to the people through His prophets and through His various Laws. Additionally, God's Law was not written in the people's heart during the Old Testament era, as it is now, in the hearts of all those who have placed their faith in Christ ( Ezekiel 36:26). This was because the Old Testament people did not have a regenerated spirit (i.e., they were not born again since Christ had not come in the flesh), but all New Testament believers have a regenerated spirit.

With the above major differences, some of you may be wondering why God gave the Law in the first place? This is a very valid question, which I am unable to expound on in this book, lest I would stray from the subject matter at hand. Nonetheless, let us briefly examine this issue of the Law.

## Why the Old Testament Law was Given

Keep in mind that since the Old Testament Jews were not yet born again, God had to give them specific instructions on how to live daily. While some people may laugh at the details found in the Law, it was absolutely necessary then, lest the Jews would have ended up as wanderers on the earth without any guide. Details of the Law can be found in the books of Exodus, Leviticus, Numbers and Deuteronomy. Below are some major reasons why God gave the Law:

- *To Emphasize His Holiness*: The Law was perfectly holy, because it reflected the nature of God. And God wanted His chosen people, the Israelites, to reflect His holiness on the earth;
- *To Learn How to Relate to God*: God gave the Law to teach the Israelites how to relate to Him, including how to worship Him, etc. The Law also was intended to teach the Israelites how to relate to one another (i.e., several Laws pertaining to sex, marriage, law suits, social and legal issues, etc, were given), including how to interact with their neighboring nations;
- *The Law Served Like a "School Master"*: The Law was meant to teach the Israelites the ways of God and to remind them of God's perfect righteous standards, until the Messiah came;
- *The Law Revealed the Sinful Nature of Mankind*: Because the

Law revealed the holiness of God, and how sinful Mankind was, it pointed the Jews towards a Savior, Christ Jesus. Once the Law was given, the Bible teaches that it made sin to "come alive," because it made people more conscious of their "Fallen" sinful human nature. As an illustration, without Laws, people might not even be aware that certain behaviors are unlawful, hence, they would have no temptation to transgress the Laws. But with full knowledge of the Laws, the temptation and likelihood of transgressing it would probably increase. Thus, the Mosaic Law led people to become more aware of their sins. Nonetheless, since the Law was only temporary, until the Messiah, Christ came; it could not produce justification, righteousness or salvation (Galatians 2:15-16, 3:21; Romans 3:20);

- *The Law Was an Administration of Death*: The Law enabled the Jews to realize that they could not keep it. As such, it brought emotional death and torture, such as constant guilt, fear, condemnation and shame (see 2 Corinthians chapter 3);

- *The Law Had Some Usefulness*: Although the Law could not redeem the Jews, its major advantage was that, it caused people to detect and avoid evil (Proverbs 16:6). It also "exposed" the erroneous perception of "self-righteousness," and the deceit that an individual can, on their own effort, overcome their own Sinful Nature and sins. Hence, the Law was good in this regard.

<u>Please keep in mind that God had only given the Law to His chosen people, the Nation of Israel, and no one else</u>. Nonetheless, remember that as born again believers, Christ Jesus is our Sabbath, meaning, He perfectly fulfilled all of God's Laws on our behalf; thus, we can rest in Him (see Hebrews chapter 4).

## PRACTICAL APPLICATION

Hopefully, after studying this chapter, you are convinced about the consistent themes across the testaments, and have come to the conclusion that God's revelation of Himself to us is immutable. With this understanding, approach the Bible from the perspective that God is the same yesterday, today and forever (Hebrews 13:8), and consider the following recommendations:

> *The Lord Jesus fulfilled all of the Old Testament Law, but He did not abolish it. Rather, He taught us the proper interpretation of the Law, which focuses on unconditional love.*

1. View all Scripture as God's specific instructions to you, none of it is obsolete.

2. Trust that God can speak to you through any of the Old and New Testament Scriptures, thus approach all of the Scripture with equal authority. Please keep in mind that **The Lord Jesus fulfilled all of the Old Testament Law, but He did not abolish it. Rather, He taught us the proper interpretation of the Law, which focuses on unconditional love.**

3. Although you are not to live by the Mosaic Law, God's Law of love has been written in your heart, as a true Christian. **And as you allow the source of love—the Holy Spirit, to lead you daily, you will effortlessly display unconditional love to others, thus living out God's Law.** By doing this, you will not steal, cheat, worship idols, or murder; instead, you will honor and respect your parents, care for your neighbor, revere the name of God, etc. In fact, God's kind of unconditional love (i.e., agape love) will enable you to live

in accordance with His Laws, written in your heart. This explains why the Lord Jesus said that all of God's Law and the teachings of the Prophets are based on love (Matthew 22:36-40); they surely do! Do you perceive that? I hope you do!

4. Through studying the Scriptures, gain a deeper understanding of God and appreciate His goodness. Always approach His Word in context, in the totality of Scripture, from Genesis to Revelation, rather than from bits and pieces of information from others or from specific verses (I discuss more about this in chapter 7). Approaching the Scriptures in context will prevent erroneous interpretations.

5. As a New Testament believer, take note that you have a much better covenant with God. Thus, keep in mind that since God used the Old Testament Saints mightily like He did, in spite of their imperfections and, an inferior covenant with them, He can work through you as well, in order to accomplish His will, as you abide in Christ and live in obedience; because, He is no respecter of persons (Romans 2:11; Acts 10:34).

   In conclusion, as we comprehend the nature of God through His written Word and appreciate His love, mercy, compassion, justice, and the remainder of His holy character, it will become evident that God is the same: yesterday, today and forevermore. Therefore, having a basic understanding of the true nature of God will enable us to easily trust His Word. With this in mind, let us turn to the next chapter, where I discuss the trustworthiness of the Holy Scripture as God's inspired Word to you.

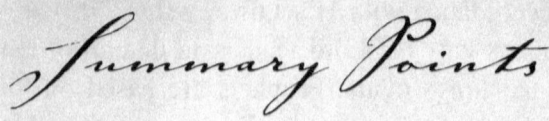

# Summary Points

- God's immutability is readily evident across the testaments;
- Approach both Testaments as inspired by God;
- In order to develop a deeper understanding and appreciation of God's Word, it is necessary to harmonize the Old and New testaments, which are all considered to be Holy Scripture;
- God can speak directly to you either through the Old or New Testaments;
- There are hundreds of consistent themes across the testaments, some major ones include, but are not limited to God's unconditional love, holiness, humility, justice, grace, long-suffering, desire for a relationship with human beings, forgiving nature, etc;
- God dealt with the Old Testament Jews through the Law, but He is dealing with the New Testament believers through grace, because of our relationship with the Lord Jesus;
- Overall, the New Testament is a much better covenant compared to the Old. Although Christ Jesus fulfilled all of the Old Testament Law, He did not abolish it, because all of God's Law and the Prophets are now based on agape love (i.e., God's kind of love).

# Chapter 6

# TRUST THE BIBLE AS GOD'S WORD TO YOU

Did you know that among all of the Sacred books of all of the world religions, only the Bible has proven, verifiable, and consistent evidence as inspired by God? Yes, indeed! Before I discuss how to apply God's Word into your life and expect godly results, it is essential that I establish the trustworthiness of the Bible especially, because, some of you may have never considered the evidence.

There are numerous internal and external evidence that support the trustworthiness of the Bible as God's inspired Word. In the ensuing section, I have decided not to categorize the discussion as internal (within the Bible), and external (extra biblical) evidence. Rather, I will approach the discussion in a narrative style, for purposes of simplicity. Because of space limitation, I will only present an overview of the supporting evidence. Those interested in further reading should consult the endnotes in this book for further resources.

Since the Holy Spirit inspired all of the writings in the Bible, He is the best person to ultimately reveal to you how trustworthy His Word is. Thus, if you are struggling in this area, I strongly recommend you ask the Holy Spirit to assure you; as you do, willingly open your heart to evaluate, ponder, and hopefully come into agreement with the evidence.

## The Trustworthiness of the Bible

### What the Bible Says About Itself

The written Words found in the Bible attest to its trustworthiness as inspired by God. Old Testament believers revered God's written Word as inspired. We have several examples of the Israelites who repented and wept when the Scriptures were read to them, as they recognized, acknowledged and realized they had disobeyed God's Word (see 2 Chronicles chapter 34; Nehemiah chapters 8 and 9).

The Bible teaches that the Word of God is flawless (Proverbs 30:5); incorruptible, meaning perfect (1 Peter 1:23); and it provides the light ( i.e., direction and guidance), to our path in this dark world (Psalm 119:105). A lot of people struggle with the notion that the Word of God is perfect, probably because they have never experienced the results they desired, for various reasons. Some of it could be incorrect doctrine, and subsequent wrong application of the Word; but that has nothing to do with God, or His Word.

> *The Word of God always works, when applied correctly, in faith. It is never the Word of God that is the problem; it is us, who do not have 100% revelation of how to apply it in our lives.*

**The Word of God always works, when applied correctly, in faith. It is never the Word of God that is the problem; it is us, who do not have 100% revelation of how to apply it in our lives.** The Word of God is eternal and has always existed (John 1:1; Psalm 119:89). And God has magnified (i.e., elevated) His Word above His name (Psalm 138: 2), which reveals how critical God regards His written Word.

The Bible further teaches that the Word of God is the best way to evaluate our thoughts, attitudes, or those of others to determine whether or not they are godly. As an illustration, if you know what the Word of God teaches about a particular issue, you will be able to tell if an individuals' attitude or reaction about that issue is godly, from the flesh (i.e., based on selfish carnal desires), or from Satan (Hebrews 4:12). The Word of God is therefore the best standard for the evaluation of everything, because the Bible has the answers to every issue pertaining to life.

Much more, the Bible teaches that the Word of God spoken in faith will yield its desired results (Isaiah 55:11), such as healing of physical and emotional sicknesses and diseases (Matthew 8:5-13; Psalm 119), and salvation for the sinner (Romans 10: 9-10), etc. Because the Word of God is God, and God is His Word, it has the power to accomplish supernatural works in the presence of faith.

## What the Lord Jesus Said About the Holy Scripture

Christ Jesus, God Himself in the flesh, was the Word of God (i.e., the seed), which supernaturally became flesh (i.e., a human being) and dwelt among us (see the Gospel of John chapter 1). During His earthly ministry, the Lord affirmed the reliability and trustworthiness of the Scripture by depending on it to overcome the devil, when He was tempted. If there was another way to deal with the devil's temptation, the Lord Jesus would have used it. But He proved that the Scripture is the only antidote available to overcome the lies from the devil. Thus, Christ has set the precedence for using the Word of God as the best weapon to overcome the Kingdom of darkness, ruled by Satan (see Luke chapter 4).

Christ Jesus taught that the Word of God can never be broken (John 10:35), and throughout His ministry, He rebuked the Religious leaders (the Pharisees and Sadducees) for not knowing the Old Testament Scriptures which testified about Him, as the Messiah (e.g., see John 5:39). Then in the Gospel of John chapter 6, He further attested to the authority of Scripture when He declared that the Word of God is the only source of life. The Lord stated: *"The Spirit gives life; the flesh counts for nothing. The words I have spoken to you—they are full of the Spirit and life" (v. 63)*, (emphasis author's).

The Lord further affirmed Scripture when He declared that the Word of God is the Only Truth that sanctifies us. In John 17:17, He said, *"Sanctify them by the truth; your word is truth"* (emphasis author's). Then in Matthew 24:35, Christ Jesus noted on the permanency of Scripture: He stated "Heaven and earth will pass away, but my words will never pass away," (emphasis author's).

## What the Apostles Said About the Holy Scripture

In his writings, under the inspiration of the Holy Spirit, the apostle Peter referred to the apostle Paul's writings as Scripture, inspired by God (2 Peter 3:14-16). Also, in the apostle Paul's teaching to Timothy as noted in First Timothy 5:18, it is noticeable how he cited or quoted from the inspired writings of another apostle (see Matthew 10:10; Luke 10:7), thus corroborating the Holy Scripture, and supporting its validity, consistency and trustworthiness as God's Word.

In addition, the apostle Peter was with the Lord Jesus, as a firsthand witness of His miracles, love, forgiveness, compassion, etc. And after His resurrection, the apostle Peter saw the "Risen Christ", and he was fully convinced that the Lord Jesus was God in the flesh. In spite of this firsthand eye witness account, the apostle Peter wrote that the prophetic message (i.e., the written Word of God), is a sure way to know that the Holy Scripture is God's inspired Word, spoken through godly men who wrote everything down (2 Peter 1:19-21). Furthermore, the apostles quoted heavily from the Old Testament Scripture throughout their various epistles, thus authenticating the trustworthiness of the Holy Scripture (see Romans 4; Acts 2; Hebrews 11; the book of Jude, etc).

## Other Verifiable Significant Body of Evidence

Besides the aforementioned evidence, below are 10 significant reasons, presented in brief, for the trustworthiness of the Bible as God's inspired Word which is inerrant, infallible, and authoritative for His Universal Church.

1. **Archeological Evidence**: A plethora of archeological evidence supporting events, places and stories told in both the Old and New Testaments have been discovered. Archeological evidence cannot prove that the Bible is indeed God's inspired Word. However, they add validity to the claims of the Bible, as their findings are consistent with biblical accounts of events, places, and characters, etc. There are hundreds of such findings, but as an example, evidence of the collapsed walls of the City of Jericho as described in the Bible has been found; evidence of the Philistines as discussed in the Bible has been found; the City of Nineveh as discussed in the book of Jonah has been found, etc. And in the New Testament, Jacob's Well, as described in John 4:1-10 has been found; the Pool of Bethesda, as described in John chapter 5; and the Pool of Siloam, as described in John chapter 9, have all been discovered by Christian and non-Christian archeologists alike.

2. **Biblical Miracles**: Only the Bible has verifiable miracles compared to other self-proclaimed Sacred writings of various world religions. For example, in the Old Testament, Elijah raised the dead as recorded in First Kings chapter 17; Moses parted the Red Sea, as noted in Exodus chapter 14; Elijah called down fire from heaven as recorded in First Kings chapter 18. The New Testament is replete with miracles: Christ Jesus performed hundreds of miracles such as raising the dead; feeding the multitudes; walking on water; etc (see the Gospels). Likewise, His disciples, who were later called apostles (i.e., the sent ones), performed countless miracles in the name of Jesus, such as raising the dead; healing the sick; and were emboldened to proclaim the Gospel Message of Jesus Christ against fierce persecution, etc, as noted in the book of Acts, and in the various epistles.

3. **Bible Prophecy:** Biblical prophesies have precisely and accurately come to pass. For example, over 50% of the prophesies in the Old Testament have been fulfilled exactly

as prophesied, such as the birth of Christ Jesus, which was prophesied hundreds of years in the Old Testament (Isaiah 7:14); the destruction of various nations, as prophesied by the Prophet Isaiah (see the book of Isaiah), etc. The Old Testament prophet, Isaiah, also prophesied that the Lord Jesus would have a forerunner in His ministry (Isaiah 40:3), and it happened, exactly as prophesied. John the Baptist was that forerunner of the Lord Jesus' ministry (see Matthew 3:1). The betrayal of the Lord was also prophesied in the Old Testament (Zechariah 11:12-13), it happened just as prophesied (see Matthew 27:5-10), etc.

In the New Testament, the Lord prophesied how He would be betrayed by one of His disciples, it came to pass; He prophesied that Peter would deny Him three times, it happened exactly that way; He prophesied about the destruction of Jerusalem, it happened in 70 AD; He prophesied His death and resurrection after three days, it accurately happened as predicted, etc (see the Gospels). The list is endless, but suffice it to say that, biblical prophecies speak for themselves as verifiable, proven evidence for the trustworthiness of the Bible.

4. **Biblical Testimonies**: Compared to other self-proclaimed religious books of the world today, only the Bible has testimonies of transformed lives of individuals, who had supernatural encounters with the living God. For example, the apostle Paul was once a persecutor of Christians, but when he saw the "Risen Christ," he experienced a supernatural transformation. He became the individual that God initially used to spread the Gospel of Christ in the first Century, and he later wrote over 50% of the New Testament under the inspiration of the Holy Spirit. Even the lives of Jesus' disciples were supernaturally transformed from weak men to bold, fearless men, after their encounter with the "Risen Christ," and their experience of being filled with the Holy Spirit (see the book of Acts). Only the supernatural power

from God can enable such a transformation as was evident in the lives of the apostles, as recorded in the Bible.

In spite of the thousands of self-proclaimed religious leaders of the world representing the various religions, none has ever manifested such supernatural transformation, accompanied by documented, verifiable, and corroborated eye witness accounts of miracles, except the individuals recorded in the Bible. You know why? Because the One and Only True living God is the God of the Bible, who manifested His miracles through these individuals, as recorded in the Bible.

There is only One God: The living God of the Bible. And This God of the Bible will not perform His miracles through counterfeit self-proclaimed religious leaders of the world, because they (i.e., counterfeit religious leaders ) have rejected the Holy Spirit; this explains the absence of the verifiable and corroborated miracles in their lives! These counterfeit religious leaders must come to the Only True God of the Bible through a relationship with His Son, Christ Jesus. To the extent that they reject Christ, the True living God will never be present in their lives.

5. **Number of Biblical Manuscripts**: There are over 5,000 different Greek manuscripts (i.e., hand written document or text) of just the New Testament alone, such as the Vatican; Alexandrian; Sinaitic Codex, etc. Then there are over 19,000 other available manuscripts in other languages such as Latin, Syriac, Aramaic, Coptic, etc. All in all, making a total of about 24,000 New Testament manuscripts, way above and beyond other popular ancient manuscripts, such as Aristotle's Poetry, Plato, Caesar's etc.

With regards to the Old Testament, there are over 10,000 available manuscripts, such as the Samaritan Pentateuch; the Dead Sea Scrolls; the Septuagint, etc. The thousands of Old and

New Testament manuscripts make it possible for a thorough and accurate investigation of their (1) consistency; (2) accuracy; and (3) discrepancies or variances, thus lending itself to open public scrutiny. Well, the good news is that, all of the scrupulous studies of all of the manuscripts have yielded the same results— accuracy and consistency across all of them with regards to the content: Whao! This is God preserving His Word, you can trust the Bible!

6. **Honesty of the Holy Scripture:** We serve a God who cannot lie, and because of this the Bible does not present the Saints of God as flawless and perfect individuals. The Saints of the Bible are presented just as they were: imperfect individuals. Yet they trusted God, and He used them mightily. As an example, Moses was a murderer, yet God transformed his life and performed mighty miracles through him. Abraham lied about his wife multiple times, disobeyed God and had sexual relations outside his marriage, yet God forgave him after a genuine repentance, and thus used him mightily to accomplish His will.

   King David was called "a man after God's heart" yet he committed two of the deadliest sins of the Old Testament Law: sexual sin and murder, but because of his true repentance, God accepted his repentance and worked through him (see 2 Samuel 11). No other self-proclaimed religious book in existence today, has such transparency and honesty about their heroes, except the Bible. This is because the living God of the Bible is the Only God of Truth, and there is no deceit in Him. You can trust the Bible!

7. **Consistency of Scripture** : The Bible is written by about 40 different authors, throughout different generations, and in different languages; yet, there is supernatural consistency in the writings. **All of the writings of the different authors of the Bible are 100% consistent in their vision of God the Father, God the Son, and God the Holy Spirit**. Plus, they all pointed the Old Testament Jews towards Christ Jesus,

the Messiah. All other self-proclaimed religious books are based on just one man's vision, the founder of the religion, which is usually inconsistent, not corroborated or verifiable; in fact, some of them are even embellished.

8. **Extra Biblical Writings**: These are mostly historical writings from many non-Christian and Christian writers about biblical events and characters. Please note that these writings are called "extra biblical," because they are mostly historical accounts and are not considered by the Universal Church as inspired by God, as such, were not canonized. Nonetheless, these writings add much historical validity to the Holy Scripture, as they are consistent with the inspired written accounts found in the Bible.

Since the Bible is considered to be a historical account of God's story, it is necessary that we compare its content with what historians have written, in order to evaluate its accuracy, reliability, and validity as a trusted text. For example, there are various writings from the Romans; Jews (i.e., Jewish Tallmud); Babylonians; and Assyrians, which supported biblical events as recorded in the Bible. Also, there are writings of historians, such as the famous first Century historian, Flavius Josephus, who wrote extensively about the Jews. His writings are also consistent with biblical accounts of events. All in all, these historical accounts validate what the Bible says, thus we can trust the Bible as God's story to us.

9. **Scientific Accuracy:** Science supports the Bible. God told us various things about the earth He created, even before scientists were born; scientists discovered these things much later. For example, the Bible teaches that the shape of the earth is round (Isaiah 40:22); it talks about the innumerable stars ( Genesis 15:5); the collections of waters (Genesis 1:10), etc, and science supports this body of evidence. Also, medical science confirms and supports biblical principles

and teachings, such as the fact that life is in the blood (Leviticus 17:11 ); humans are made up of a mind, body, and a spirit bound together as one; spiritual distress contributes to various life threatening physical illnesses and diseases; selfish emotions such as unforgiveness, anger, jealousy, bitterness, etc, lead to a host of chronic diseases. You can trust the Bible as God's inspired Word.

10. **The Resurrection of Christ Jesus**:  Only the Bible has verifiable accounts of people being raised from the dead. No other religious book in the history of the world has this, only the Bible.  For example, Christ Jesus Himself, prophesied about His own resurrection, and it occurred exactly as prophesied. Other Saints used by God such as Elijah, the apostles Paul, Peter, etc, raised people from the dead. Only the True living God of the Bible who gives life can raise anyone from the dead, and He did it several times as recorded in the Bible. And during this present Church age, God is still working through godly men and women as He continues to raise people from the dead. You can trust the Bible as God's Word!

## PRACTICAL APPLICATION

What the above body of evidence is telling us is that you can trust the Bible as God's inspired Word. All of the various religions of the world are also claiming that their Scripture is inspired by some god, but it is not from the One True living God of the Bible. You know why? Primarily because God has Only revealed Himself through His Son, Christ Jesus, and through His written Word which Christ relied on throughout His earthly ministry.

*If you believe in Christ Jesus, how can you not believe in His teachings, or in the preeminence, authority, and authenticity which He placed on the Holy Scriptures?*

The Lord Jesus revered the Holy Scriptures as inspired by God, the Father. **If you believe in Christ Jesus, how can you not believe in His teachings, or in the preeminence, authority, and authenticity which He placed on the Holy Scriptures?** Additionally, here is another interesting common sense logic which adds a different dimension in the way you should view the Bible.

Being a reasonable and intelligent human being that I believe you are, think with me for just a second! **It is logically impossible for the Bible and all other religious books, such as the Koran, Book of Mormons, Jehovah's Witness Bible, etc, to be inspired and accurate at the same time. Only one of these can be right, especially because they contradict each other, and espouse different teachings. You know why? The answer is simple: The simple Law of Contradiction from Philosophy states that two mutually exclusive positions cannot be true at the same time; one is wrong.** What this means is that the Bible, the Koran, the Book of Mormons, the Jehovah's Witness Bible, etc, cannot all be correct! Only one of this is absolutely God breathed! You have to decide!

The greatest news is that, no other religious book on the planet earth has such proven, verifiable, consistent, corroborated, and reliable evidence as the Bible. You may wonder why? Because the Bible is the Only inspired book from the Only living God. <u>There is only One True God, who inspired One Holy Scripture, and not several: You must make a decision.</u> As an example, the Koran, which is the main scripture for the Muslims, was written approximately 500 to 600 years after the Christian Bible was already written, canonized and well established and validated as God's inspired Word. So, let me ask you a question: Which is trustworthy, the Koran, which is a secondary source, an individual's vision, with no verifiable corroborated eyewitness account, or the Bible? Let God be true; and every other person be a liar (Romans 3:4); I choose to believe God! What about you? Only the Bible is the True Word of God, as the above body of evidence has proven. I hope you are in agreement. Hallelujah! Let us praise the Lord!

The mighty signs and wonders (i.e., miracles) of the apostles, are well acknowledged in the Bible. And we have the evidence, and we do believe, that these apostles actually existed in time and space, and that God, indeed, worked through them. If these apostles trusted the Scripture as I have already established, and God worked through their ministries, I wonder why anyone would doubt the trustworthiness of the Holy Scripture? Hopefully, you are no longer in the doubting category!

Some of you may be wondering why I am so confident about the trustworthiness of the Bible as God's Word? It is a fair question, which I have been asked many times. For me, the answer is simple and straight forward. <u>Firstly</u>, because God says so in His Word, and I have spent many years studying and meditating on the Scripture, hence I need no further external evidence to accept this Truth; I trust God 100%, period! And <u>secondly</u>, because the Word has yielded countless results in my life; I have the experiential evidence to back it up. I am a living testimony that the Word of God is inspired; it works.

Some of you may not be aware of my testimony. I was diagnosed with metastasis Colon Cancer and given a very, very dire prognosis (I discuss my testimony in another book). But suffice it to say that, I stood on the Word of God and His promises, and put them to practice in my life during my deadly battle with Cancer. Because I believe the Word of God is God, and God is His Word, I trusted what God has already told us in His Word about healing. Without anyone laying hands on me, I received the revelation of healing from God's Word, and it became a reality to me. Shortly thereafter, I received my healing. Today, it has been about 8 years, and I am 100% cancer FREE. Plus, all of the other diagnoses labeled against me as a result of the Cancer disappeared without any medical intervention, because I stood on the Word of God with unwavering faith and expectation. Friend, the Word of God is indeed inspired! It works!

So please, do not tell me that the Word of God is not real; you are too late for that. I am here as a testimony to say that the Word of God is as real, consistent, reliable and dependable as God Himself: it works! The sooner you come into agreement with the teachings in the Word, the faster you will start seeing its results in your life. For God has asked the question—How can two walk together, if they do not agree? (Amos 3:3). If you disagree with God's Word, then you will not experience its desired results, because you will not be "walking" with Him, as the Scripture cited above, out of the book of Amos, tells us. It is up to you, but remember, God is always willing to reveal Himself and His goodness to you!

In conclusion, as I mentioned earlier, one easy and subjective way for you to find out if the Word of God is indeed inspired, is for you to study it for yourself, and faithfully put it to practice as you live in obedience and abide in Christ. As you do that, I guarantee you, if you are genuinely seeking God, He is faithful; and He will speak to you through His Word, and you will be inspired, because the Word is supernaturally inspired! Now that I have established the trustworthiness of God's Word, and hopefully, you have come into agreement, let us proceed to the next chapter to study how to meditate on the Holy Scripture.

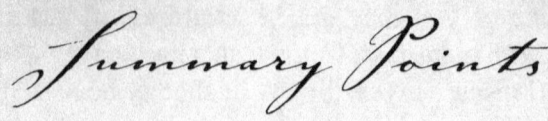

## Summary Points

- The writings of the Bible speak about its trustworthiness;
- Christ Jesus authenticated and verified the Holy Scripture as inspired by God throughout His earthly ministry;
- The apostles authenticated the writings of the Bible as inspired by God;
- The Bible has more manuscripts than any other ancient book in the history of the world, and the various manuscripts have been proven to be consistent and accurate in their writings;
- The Bible is the Only Religious book in the history of the world with much proven, verifiable, authenticated, and consistent evidence to support its claims;
- The best way to trust the claims of the Bible is to study it for yourself firsthand, put it to practice, and then evaluate the results, as you abide in Christ and walk in obedience;
- The Bible is eternal, whether you accept the Truths in its pages or not, it will not change the absolute Truth that it is inspired by the Only True living God of the heavens and the earth: the God of the Bible;
- The teachings of the Bible have transformed millions of lives across the world, including the life of the author of this book;
- The Bible has remained the number one bestselling book of all times, and it will continue to be so, because of its divine ability to transform lives.

# Chapter 7

# How to Study and Meditate on the Scriptures

Having an unshakeable confidence about the trustworthiness of the Bible is the beginning of knowing the true nature of God. But, knowing what the Bible teaches, learning how to study and meditate on the Scriptures, and then, applying it into your life and seeing the expected results, is a completely different matter. It is not sufficient to be casually acquainted with God's Word; it is best to have a deeper revelation of what the Bible teaches, and the best way to accomplish this task is to master the "art" of meditation. It is through meditating on the Scriptures that you will receive the life-changing revelation from God's Word to you. Before I teach you how to meditate, it is necessary that I discuss some basic recommendations for studying God's Word, because you cannot meditate on something, if you do not first know it, right?

## Some Recommendations For Studying the Bible

The initial ingredient for an effective Bible study is to have a sincere desire, hunger and thirst to know God better. The Lord Jesus said all those who are hungry and thirsty for righteousness (i.e., the Truths found in God's Word) are blessed, and will be filled (Matthew 5:6). If you desire to know God more through His Word, below are some recommendations which I believe will help you to get started. Always remember to pray and ask the Holy Spirit for revelation each time you begin your study of God's Word.

1. *Invest in an In-depth Study Bible, and at Least One Other Bible For Devotional* Purposes.

   Get a study Bible such as the New International Version (NIV); New King James Version (NKJV); New Revised Standard Version (NRSV) or any other. Be certain it is a study Bible because it will provide a good introductory summary, including cultural and historical insights pertaining to each book of the Bible. An in-depth study Bible will also include a timeline when each of the books of the Bible was written, in addition to the main themes and purpose(s) for each book. Most study Bibles also have a concordance that can help you with your studies.

   Before you start studying any book in the Bible, it is necessary to have a general idea about why the book was written, and who was the target audience. Also find out what the major themes of the book are, and what was happening during that time when the book was written. Knowing this information before you begin studying any book in the Bible will enhance your understanding significantly. Additionally, invest in an easy to read Bible with a contemporary English translation such as the New Living Translation, The Message Bible, etc, as such translations incorporate our modern vernacular, and thus, may be easier to use as a devotional Bible.

   Like I already discussed, you can trust the majority of our modern English Bible translations, because for the most part, they are all saying the same thing, but presented in different styles, in order to suit different audiences. It will be wise to invest in multiple translations, like explained already. Also, consider purchasing a Bible dictionary, and a Bible language book such as the Vine's Complete Expository Dictionary of the Old and New Testament Words, which can help you with studying various words in the Bible.

Investing in these extra biblical resources will pay great dividends, as you will be well-equipped with the necessary tools to better understand God's Word for yourself. You want to make it your ultimate goal to study through the entire Bible, from Genesis to Revelation, in order to have a complete picture of who God is. After investing in some of the resources mentioned above, I recommend you begin your study by knowing more about the Lord Jesus.

2. *Begin Your Study of the Bible with the Gospel of John.*

This Gospel is written by the apostle John to explain to you that Christ Jesus is the Messiah, the Only way to the One living God of the Bible. This Gospel teaches the readers how to find eternal life in Christ, and it will help you to better know the Lord as your personal Lord and Savior, and, as your friend, who will never leave or forsake you. When you read through the Gospel of John, you will find that almost every chapter is packed with evidence of Christ Jesus as the Messiah. This will enable you to better understand the Deity (i.e., that Jesus Christ was God), and His humanity (i.e., that Jesus Christ was a Man also, a human being, like one of us).

Investing the time in this Gospel is crucial, because you want to have an unshakable personal revelation of who Jesus is! And, as you ask the Holy Spirit to impart this revelation to you, you will come to know Jesus personally as your friend; without this basic knowledge (i.e., baby Christianity "stuff"), you will struggle in your relationship with God. After developing a deeper understanding of the Lord Jesus' ministry and His mission, I recommend you proceed to the beginning of the Bible, to know how things started, and why they "fell apart": go straight to the book of Genesis.

3. *After the Gospel of John, Read the Book of Genesis.*

Every book of the Bible is absolutely important. However, the book of Genesis is the key to believing God as your Creator, and in gaining a firmer understanding of His story. The book of Genesis is where many godly Christians can "fall" into error, because they struggle to accept that God created the heavens and the earth in six literal days. Refusing to accept a six-literal day creation has led many godly Christians to come up with all sorts of erroneous conclusions, that the earth is billions of years old versus, just six to seven thousand years old. This erroneous conclusion has also led some godly Christians to conclude that God used evolution to create the heavens and the earth, which is unscriptural and wrong.

If you were to invest some time studying the book of Genesis and the totality of Scripture pertaining to creation, you will come to the firm conclusion that the six-literal day creation is the only biblical and correct view. Thus, the book of Genesis is critical, lest you will miss God's view of how things started. Additionally, getting into error in the book of Genesis has the potential to lead to other different errors in your view of God; and this wrong knowledge will subsequently affect your relationship with God.

Much more, knowing God's account of events as recorded in the book of Genesis will help you to better understand and appreciate the Ministry of Christ Jesus; why God had to die for your sins; how evil and death entered into God's perfect creation; how the various languages and nations on the earth started, etc. All these information will give you a richer perspective as you approach the rest of the books of the Bible (essentially, things will make sense). **The book of Genesis is the book of beginnings, the beginning of all things on the earth —Read it; know it!**

4. *After Completing the Book of Genesis, Read the Epistles of 1st, 2nd, and 3rd John.*

These short but powerful books will teach you how to recognize the many antichrists out there, and it will help you to be grounded in your relationship with Christ, and assure you about your citizenship in God's Kingdom, and of God's infinite love for you. These books will definitely equip you with tools to discern counterfeit Christians and leaders.

5. *After Completing the Epistles of 1st, 2nd, and 3rd John, Start Reading the Bible in Chronological Order.*

    I recommend that you primarily study the Bible as you are led by the Holy Spirit. Notwithstanding, most people find it easier to read chronologically as the Bible is arranged; meaning, from the book of Genesis to the book of Revelation, book after book, etc, this is very acceptable, in fact, I prefer this methodology. However, others study the different books of the Bible out of order; it is okay too, the key is to just start studying. The most important thing is to study through the entire Bible, book by book, chapter by chapter, and verse by verse, in order to get God's story in context and allow Him to speak directly to you. <u>For those of you who need help with this, our Ministry offers an in-depth discipleship program to help you with studying through the entire Bible</u>. Please refer to the end of this book for details on how to sign up for this program, which is accessible across the world in the English language.

6. *Never Study the Bible Out of Context.*

    There are three major principles I want to briefly emphasis here about studying the Bible correctly: (1) always study the Bible **contextually**, by examining each verse in its context. You will do this by studying the chapters before and after the verse; (2) **comparatively**, by studying each book, chapter or verse of the Bible within the context of other books in the Bible (i.e., within the totality of all Scriptures); and (3) **practically**, by examining how each book, chapter or verse will apply to your personal life directly, today.

    Earlier, I mentioned how knowing the summary

information such as why the book of the Bible you are reading was written, the audience, etc, is important in enhancing your understanding of the book. With this information in the forefront, as you examine the practicality of each book, chapter, or verse, ask the Holy Spirit to reveal to you how you can apply the teachings into your life today, in the " here and now." Remember that, while the Bible was written thousands of years ago, human beings are still dealing with the same issues, and the solutions are the same: God's Word, which transcends generations, cultures, language barriers, etc.

> *When you take chapters or verses, or even entire books of the Bible out of context, it will definitely lead to misunderstanding, incomplete understanding of the nature of God, and definitely result in major errors in interpretation.*

As you study the Bible in context, desire to know God personally and how He dealt with the different individuals and themes discussed in each book, because it is still applicable today. As an example, if someone sends you a letter, you would not get the fuller understanding of the content of that letter if you were to read just the first two sentences, then a few paragraphs in the middle, and lastly, the concluding remarks, right? Likewise, **when you take chapters or verses, or even entire books of the Bible out of context, it will definitely lead to misunderstanding, incomplete understanding of the nature of God, and definitely result in major errors in interpretation.** This explains why we have pseudo-Christian cults (referring to those who deviate from God's Truths as found in the Bible), such as the Jehovah's Witnesses and the Mormons (I discuss briefly about these cults in chapter 10).

Let us go over a simple illustration of how to study God's Word in context and avoid errors. For example, If you are interested in understanding what Romans chapter 8 is teaching, which focuses on life in the Spirit, it will be best to read the entire book of Romans first. Thereafter, reread Romans chapters seven and nine, in order to get a fuller understanding of what the apostle Paul is highlighting in chapter eight. I will also recommend that you read other books of the Bible, such as the book of Galatians, Colossians, Ephesians, etc, which have entire chapters pertaining to life in the Spirit. Please keep in mind that the entire Bible teaches about life in the Spirit, but the epistles mentioned above will provide you with a balanced, accurate, contextual, and comparative analysis and understanding of Romans chapter 8.

Investing some time doing such a study as described above will minimize much error and misunderstanding. Besides, once you do such in-depth study, it gets easier the next time around, and you will be planting deep Truths about God in your soul; it is worth the time. Additionally, most study Bibles offer cross references for other books or Scriptures with similar themes, so finding this information is relatively easy, if you own a study Bible like one of those mentioned earlier.

**There is a popular saying that a Bible text without a pretext and post text, is just a text, with no real meaning; this is so true.** And in fact, such a text is dangerous, and is the primary reason for heresy (false teaching), which continues to lead thousands of people astray, and into the multiple cults we have today in the world in the name of Christianity, which is not true Christianity at all.

Furthermore, many godly Christians are still living in bondage today and not enjoying their relationship with God, primarily due to legalism, because they do not know the totality of Scripture (I discuss more about legalism in chapter 13). So knowing God's Word in totality is not an option, it is mandatory, in order for you to live the blessed life that Christ died for you to enjoy, while in this life!

With this basic understanding of how to approach your study of the Bible, let us begin with the discussion on how to meditate on the Scriptures.

## What is Meditation?

Understanding the Word of God is great. But the life in the Word only becomes a revelation and a reality during the process of meditation (Joshua 1:8). According to the Strong's Concordance, the word meditate refers to a quiet contemplation of spiritual truths for purposes of gaining spiritual insight or understanding. The Vine's Dictionary of the Old and New Testament Words explains that to meditate means to ponder, to attend to, and/or to engage in imagination (referring to visualizing in your heart God's promises coming to pass in your life).

The Oxford Dictionary provides added clarity to the meaning of meditation. It defines meditation as involving a careful, focused or deeper thinking for a period of time. All these descriptions are teaching us that meditation involves a process of quietness, deeper thinking, pondering, and focusing on the spiritual Truths found in God's Word, over a period of time.

To the Christian, meditation is not the same as the Eastern Religions' teachings of Transcendental Mediation, which is a process of emptying the mind. As a Christian, you do not want to dismiss all thoughts when you meditate. Rather, you want to disregard all ungodly thoughts, while giving special attention to godly thoughts as written in the Bible, and allowing the Holy Spirit to directly speak to you through the Scriptures.

## What the Bible Says About Meditation

The Bible highly encourages meditation. For example, in First Timothy, the apostle Paul had been instructing his protégé

Timothy about living a godly life, and encouraging him to be steadfast in the doctrines (teachings) of the faith. Then in chapter 4, he advised him by saying: *"Be diligent in these matters; give yourself wholly to them, so that everyone may see your progress* (v. 15), (emphasis author's). The admonition, be diligent, used in this verse was translated from the Greek to the English language as meditate. So Paul was advising Timothy to ponder, pay attention to, contemplate (meditate) on the things he had been counseling him about.

Then, in the Old Testament, Joshua was called by God to take over from Moses as the leader to lead the Israelites into the Promised Land. For just a minute, pause and contemplate on the magnitude of this task, and the pressure that Joshua was facing, especially as he had witnessed firsthand the miracles God had performed through Moses, in addition to the challenges Moses had experienced with the Israelites' disobedience. I believe all of these must have been a very scary position for Joshua. But the amazing thing is that, when God was encouraging Joshua about his leadership, as recorded in Joshua chapter 1, He did not promise to perform miracles like He did through Moses; rather, He instructed Him to meditate on His Word, in order for him to succeed in his new role. Here is what the Lord said: *"Keep this Book of the Law always on your lips; meditate on it day and night, so that you may be careful to do everything written in it. Then you will be prosperous and successful"* (v. 8), (emphasis authors).

Let me ask you a question: Don't you think that God would have reassured Joshua by promising to perform miracles through him? Don't you think that would have encouraged him and affirmed his new position? I am sure most of you would say yes! But God did not! Instead, He promised Joshua that his success would be primarily dependent on him meditating on His Word, which back then, was only some of the Old Testament Scriptures. Likewise, to succeed and prosper as a Christian, you will have to learn how to meditate on God's Word, in order for the life in His Word to become a reality to you.

The Psalmists and other Biblical Saints meditated on God's Word continuously for wisdom (e.g., see Psalm 63:6; Psalm 119:148; Genesis 24:63). We too can likewise, meditate on God's Word all day long, and continuously (Psalm 119:97), for our spiritual benefits. So why do you suppose God wants us to meditate on His Word? Below are some obvious reasons.

**Meditation Is Essential Because: You Develop**

> A fuller understanding of the nature of God as revealed in His Word;

> A deeper spiritual insight and revelation of God's Truths in His Word;

> A godly wisdom and superior knowledge;

> An unshakable foundation and stability in your life.

## PRACTICAL APPLICATION

For purposes of clarification, I will present the process of meditation below in 5 simple stages, although the process is not always this linear, because it is primarily guided by the Holy Spirit, as you seek Him. Remember to always begin by asking the Holy Spirit to give you the revelation in the Scripture.

An analogy that may help you to approach this process is that of eating. You eat a piece of bread because you want the nutrients in that bread to nourish your body, right? But placing the bread in your mouth does not automatically release the nutrients, you know that, right? You must start chewing the bread for the digestive process to begin, so that the nutrients would slowly be released into your stomach, and then into the rest of your bodily organs, thus giving you the necessary energy to sustain you for the day. Likewise, when you study the Word of God, you have to meditate on it for the "nutrients" (i.e., the life, reality or revelation in the Word), to be "rooted or grounded" in your soul, in order for it [God's Truths] to speak directly to your circumstance, which will in turn make it much easier for you to put into practice.

With that analogy in mind, let us examine this process closely.

### Some Recommendations on How to Meditate on Scripture

1. **Step 1**: Spend quantity and quality time reading and studying the Scripture in context, whatever passage of Scripture you desire. You cannot meditate on something without first becoming familiar with the passage and content of it. This is a very critical step. And remember, never take a passage or verse of Scripture out of context.

As an example, If you are interested in understanding the teaching about your new life in the Spirit, such as discussed in Romans chapter 8, you would want to spend some time studying Romans chapter 7 and 9, at the very least, in order to get a fuller understanding of what the apostle Paul is emphasizing in chapter 8. Like I mentioned earlier, ideally, it would be best to study the entire book of Romans and other books of the Bible regarding this topic. But if you do not have the time, that is okay to "stay put" with the book of Romans, at least for now. Consider reading Romans chapters 7, 8 and 9 several times to become familiar with the content and the various themes discussed. Then, as an example, if you want to meditate on Romans 8:1-4, referring to how there is no condemnation in those who have a relationship with Christ Jesus, consider doing the next step.

2. **Step 2**: Study Romans 8:1-4 in a couple of different Bible translations such as the New Living Translation (NLT); The Message Bible; New king James Version (NKJV); etc, if possible. Doing this comparison would enable you to get a deeper understanding of how the different versions render the Scripture. You will be amazed how looking up Scripture from different translations will add much clarity and enhance your understanding. **But I insist, again, do not get, and never use the Jehovah's Witnesses bible called: New World Translation (NWT), because it is false, distorted, and not inspired by God.** If you come across this so called bible, please, put it in the "trash," that is exactly where it belongs (I offer some reasons why in chapter 10). After studying Scripture from the various translations, proceed to step 3.

3. **Step 3**: Look up and study unfamiliar words you encounter in the text. This is the stage where a Bible dictionary would be quite handy. If possible, do a brief word study from the Greek or Hebrew languages, in order to better understand the fuller meaning(s) of the translated word(s) in the English

language. The majority of study Bibles have a glossary and a concordance that can help you with this process. This process does not take as much time as you might think; it will be worth it. At this stage, you will be getting very familiar with the text, now proceed to step 4.

4. **Step 4**: Now that you are familiar with the text and its content, go back and repeat the first three steps as often as possible, until you begin to get a deeper understanding and revelation of the Scripture from the Holy Spirit. At this stage, the gist of the Scripture, per our example (i.e., Romans 8:1-4) would be much clearer to most people; I am sure it will be the same for you. While this process may appear tedious as you are reading it, it is not in reality, when you put it into practice; and the time spent will pay great dividends, so be patient, it works.

   Besides, it should take less than an hour of your time to do this; this would be time spent with God, your Creator, who loves you, and it would not be wasted time watching lies, gossip, and other ungodly shows on TV that will not edify you. This special time with God is priceless. You will be planting godly seeds into your soul, life, and fostering stability in His Word. Like everything else in life, as you become acquainted with the process, you will gain the skill to accomplish it much faster, which is why I call this process an "art" to be mastered. But much more, you will be planting indelible godly seeds into your soul; it will be worth it! And remember, God is not mocked, whatever you sow into your life, you will reap bountiful results (Galatians 6:7). At this stage, I believe the Scripture would be speaking directly to you, thus proceed to step 5.

5. **Step 5**: In stage 5 of this process, you would be very familiar with the content of the Scripture you have been reading, studying and looking up from various Bible translations; thus, it is time to stop studying for just a little while and

close the book (Bible). Once you close the book, you will engage in intentional quiet contemplation on what you had been studying. Engage your senses, by visualizing the scene(s) described in the Scripture; imagine yourself as one of the characters in the Scripture; visualize yourself in their situation; imagine yourself being touched by God as He touched the characters in the text, etc.

Using Romans 8:1-4 again as our example, visualize all of your sins being placed on the body of Christ Jesus on the cross. Mentally visualize how each whip He took on His body represented every sinful thought or act of sin(s) you had ever committed knowingly or unknowingly. Then visualize how each open wound in His body has completely and permanently deleted all of your sins, hurts, failures, and all other issues you are currently struggling with, right now! Visualize His precious blood that was spewed, and how that blood is continuously cleansing your entire body, setting you FREE. Then pause, thank Him, and visualize yourself completely cleansed, pure as God sees you through Christ. Accept that you have been 100% absolved from your past, guilt, and condemnation, because of the precious blood of the Lord Jesus, receive it by faith, it is done; Jesus said it is finished! He has set you FREE!

Are you struggling to overcome the lies from Satan and feelings of guilt about your past sins? Firstly, quickly acknowledge that this thought is not from God. Nonetheless, it will benefit you to still meditate on Romans 8:1-4, in order for that Scripture to change your perspective and specifically speak to your heart. Doing this will better equip you to accept and believe the "reality" of your salvation in Christ. This is such a powerful exercise that, if you faithfully do this, it will change the way you view the "Cross" of Christ Jesus and your new identity in Him. Many Christians casually believe on the significance of the "Cross," but if they were to meditate on this, it will transform their lives. I believe that doing this simple exercise will cause you to fall in love with God all over, and you will want to do your best not to disobey Him, or go back and taste your vomit (i.e., living again like you did before Christ).

This last step can be done while sitting and meditating on the Scripture, or you can write the Scripture on a 4 by 4 card and carry it with you as you go about the rest of your day. The key here is that while going about your day, you would have the Scripture in the forefront of your mind, focusing on its Truths. As you pay attention to the Scripture over a period of time, the Holy Spirit will begin to slowly speak to you directly through that Scripture, and it will become a deep rooted reality to you in such a way that, neither Satan, nor anyone else, will be able to steal it [the Truths] from you (see Mark 4; Matthew 13; Luke 8).

Once you experience this kind of illumination or revelation knowledge from any Scripture, applying it into your daily life will be effortless. By undergoing this process, you will also be renewing your mind to be consistent with the Word of God, and positioning yourself for God's perfect will to come to pass in your life (Romans 12:2). For some people, this process may take just days, for others, it may take weeks, or months, depending on how much time you invest in it, and on your baseline understanding of the Scriptures when you started the process.

Personally, during the acute stages of fighting metastasis Colon cancer, it took me about 11 to 12 months to meditate on all of the healing Scriptures before I reached a place where my thoughts were transformed (or be in agreement) with the Word of God about healing, before the "life" or reality in those Scriptures became "MINE" (meaning, the Holy Spirit started to speak directly to me through those Scriptures). This was because my thinking pattern was very "messed up" as a doctor, as I primarily viewed medicine as the main source for my healing; hence, it took that long for me. But once I received the revelation or illumination through meditating on the Scriptures that Christ Jesus was my primary healer and not medicine, I received my healing, and I was set free from cancer and other diseases. This can happen to you too, today! Because God has promised us that we will become successful and prosperous, as we meditate on His Word (Joshua 1:8).

## Other Expectations As You Meditate on God's Word

Do not be discouraged, this process is not daunting, and you already know how to meditate, except in the wrong things. Here is what I mean: Think of those days that you are troubled with a particular problem at home, work or elsewhere, and you spend time and energy focusing on the problem and the possible various options to resolve the issue. For some of you, it might have taken hours, days or even weeks before you could come up with any kind of solution, if any, right? Well, guess what? The time you spent dwelling on those problems and the various solutions is just like meditation, but meditating on the wrong things; this time however, you will be meditating on God's promises and solutions, and not on your problems, you get the picture? Hopefully you do! So again, be certain to spend quantity and quality time meditating on the solutions—the Word of God, and not on your problems, then you will overcome, just like Joshua and many others have!

Because the Word of God is alive, potent, and can penetrate into the hearts and souls of individuals, one of three things will happen when a person meditates on God's Words, even for just a short period of time:

- **It Will Bring Conviction to the Christian:** By conviction, I mean that the Holy Spirit will use His Word to alarm you that you are in disobedience, or in the wrong, pertaining to a matter in your life. God will never force or coerce you to repent, you would have to willingly obey Him and do it. The Holy Spirit will convict the believer in a loving and gentle way, especially if he or she is practicing sin, so that repentance can take place. Keep in mind that God is always speaking when we meditate on His Word, but it is up to us to listen. So if you do not agree, then you are in the wrong, because God always speaks.

If you are struggling with discerning God's voice in the Word, it means that you need to grow on how to be more attuned to Him as you study. Or, it could mean that you are expecting an emotional response before acting on God's Word, which is wrong. God has already spoken to us through His Word; we have to, by faith, act on it (2 Corinthians 5:7). Also, remember that the issue is never God, it is us, who are still in the process of learning. And this has nothing to do with God withholding Himself from us: NO! So by faith, accept that God has already spoken to you, and put His Word to practice!

- **It Will Give Assurance:** By assurance, I mean that the Holy Spirit will assure you that you are walking in the "light," meaning, in accordance with the Truths in God's Word. This assurance will produce peace, joy, etc, and affirmation of your relationship with God.

- **It Will Bring Condemnation to Unbelievers:** By condemnation, I mean that the Holy Spirit will condemn and/or convict the unbeliever about their Sinful Nature, sins, and their need for a Savior, Christ Jesus. If they accept the conviction, they will accept the Lord Jesus as their Lord and Savior. **Please keep in mind that the Holy Spirit will not condemn a believer, because the Lord Jesus took upon Himself on the cross our shame, guilt and condemnation** (Galatians 3:13; Romans 8:1-4).

*Please keep in mind that the Holy Spirit will not condemn a believer, because the Lord Jesus took upon Himself on the cross our shame, guilt and condemnation (Galatians 3:13; Romans 8:1-4).*

In conclusion, any person who meditates on God's Word and

claims that the Word does not do any of the above three things to them, is in denial, and is outright refusing the Truth, or is blatantly rejecting it. God says that His Word will never return void, it will always accomplish results (Isaiah 55:11), somehow or the other (i.e., piecing the hearts of people with the Truth), when proclaimed in faith. So doing an honest evaluation of your heart after meditating on the Word would be beneficial to you. Now that you have learned how to meditate on God's Word, turn to chapter 8, to learn some simple ways to apply it into your life, in order to experience the joy and peace Christ Jesus promised to you.

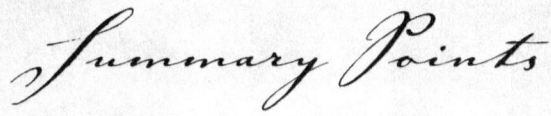

# Summary Points

- Meditation to the Christian means pondering and giving special attention to the Truths found in God's Word;
- The Bible encourages us to meditate on God's Word daily, during anytime of the day, and anywhere;
- You cannot meditate on something that you do not first know. So, the first step of meditating on God's Word is the study of His Word, in order to become familiar with its content;
- Meditation becomes much easier with steadfast practice, although it is a process requiring quantity and quality time, plus much patience;
- It is through the process of meditating that the Scripture is illuminated or becomes a reality to us, because God's Word becomes deeply rooted in our souls.

# Chapter 8

# HOW TO PRACTICE WHAT THE SCRIPTURE TEACHES

While meditating on the Word of God is essential, the Bible teaches that we should take it one step further, by putting it to practice, because only those who practice what the Word teaches receive the blessings (James 1: 22-25). God loves us so much that if we put His Word into practice in our lives by faith in accordance with His prescribed will as stated in the Bible, His promises will definitely come to pass in our lives, in His perfect timing.

Practicing the Word is absolutely critical as it is the only sure foundation that will never crumble in times of trouble. Things, people, fashion, philosophies, academic degrees, friends, children, relationships, honor from others, etc, come and go, but the only stable thing in this life is God and His Word. The Lord Jesus said there is no use to call Him Lord, if we do not practice His teachings. In the Gospel of Luke chapter 6, He explained how putting His Word into practice will result in a solid foundation in every area of our lives. Below are the Words of Christ Jesus:

*"So why do you keep calling me 'Lord, Lord!' when you don't do what I say? I will show you what it's like when someone comes to me, listens to my teaching, and then follows it. It is like a person building a house who digs deep and lays the foundation on solid rock. When the floodwaters rise and break against that house, it stands firm because it is well built"* (vv. 46-48), (New Living Translation), (emphasis authors).

As you can see from the Lord's teaching above, only those whose lives are grounded in His Word receive the blessings and security to buffer the hardships they may encounter in this life. In ministering to others, I find that people are quick to profess Christ Jesus as their Lord and Savior, but they struggle to surrender every area of their lives under His Lordship. Accepting to follow Christ Jesus as your Lord and Savior does not only mean that (1) you will go to heaven when you die, it also means (2) He wants you to allow Him to direct every area of your life, because He knows what is best for you. For most people, the Savior part is much easier to do; but the Lordship part of this equation is a major struggle for them. But I guarantee you, if you allow God to direct every area of your life as you obey His Word and put it to practice, you will not regret it, He has the best plans for you.

In my own relationship and journey with God, I have realized that the areas where I had struggled the most were areas where I had resisted surrendering to Him. But now that I have learned how to surrender every area of my life to God daily, I am experiencing His peace, contentment, assurance, safety, plus much more. I know with absolute certainty that God loves me, and He wants the best for me; so each day, I surrender my plans and decisions under His Lordship and trust His guidance, and it is working very well for me. I recommend you do likewise, and give God a chance, especially if you desire to enjoy His perfect will for your life. You may wonder how to put the Word of God into practice — it is as easy and as simple as just doing what the Word teaches, by faith.

## Live By Faith and Not According to Your Emotions

The Bible teaches that as Christians, we live our lives by faith (based on the teachings of the Bible) and not by sight (i.e., referring to our five senses: sight, feelings, taste, smell or hearing) ( 2 Corinthians 5:7). The Bible describes a Christian who is predominately led by their five senses or fleshy desires as "Carnal."

Such a person, according to the Bible, will definitely quench the Holy Spirit, and it will lead to "spiritual suicide" such as anxiety, depression, fear, worry, etc. Because it is impossible to please God from your selfish or carnal desires, you must obey His Word by faith if you desire His favor and blessings (Hebrews 11:6).

Our five senses in and of themselves are not bad, God created them to serve as protective mechanisms to guide and protect us. But when you allow your five senses to guide, rule or dominate your life and decisions instead of the instructions from the Bible, it will become a major problem which will lead to "spiritual death", because your senses are inconsistent, subjective, and unreliable as a guide to navigate through life and its multiple challenges. But a Christian who allows the teachings of the Bible to serve as their guide will experience God's peace, joy, stability, etc (Romans 8: 5-11).

The type of faith Second Corinthians 5:7 is teaching is biblical faith, and not faith like the unbelievers perceive. Hebrews 11:1 teaches that Bible faith is having a confident hope and expectation that God's promises will come to pass in your life. I like the way the New Living Translation Bible renders this verse: *"Faith shows the reality of what we hope for; it is the evidence of things we cannot see"* (Hebrews 11:1), (emphasis author's). This implies that you accept what the Bible teaches, and you put it to practice in your life by trusting God's Word and promises without any immediate accompanying physical or emotional evidence.

*Our emotions are relevant, but for the Christian who is believing in God's promises and "walking" by faith, emotions are secondary, and they will manifest later, as we walk by faith.*

Anyone can be joyful, then celebrate and give thanks to God after crossing the "Red Sea" (Red Sea is used here to refer to major hurdles or circumstances in life). However, it takes a person who is walking in biblical faith to celebrate, be joyful and give thanks to God for

His promises before experiencing a successful resolution to their "Red Sea". It is this kind of a heart attitude and faith that God honors. **Our emotions are relevant, but for the Christian who is believing in God's promises and "walking" by faith, emotions are secondary, and they will manifest later, as we walk by faith. Much more, Bible faith is based on known realities, the Truths found in God's Word, rather than just ideologies.**

Let us examine an illustration of what Bible faith looks like. For example, the Bible teaches that God is your provider. So if you need a new job, you would first believe, by faith, that God, your provider, is already aware of your specific need and has provided the answer before you even asked. Then, you would pray and ask Him, in faith, to release the promise as stated in His Word. You would then proceed to thank Him, and rejoice in the Truth that He has already provided the answer to your prayer (i.e., new job), and it is already available in the spiritual realm, and in His perfect timing, it will manifest into the physical realm. The Bible teaches that faith without corresponding action(s) is incomplete and essentially useless (James 2:14-26). Therefore, with steadfast confidence and realistic hope and joyful expectation, you would step out in faith and do your part in searching for that new job, while trusting that God will lead and direct your steps, and align you with the right employer and/or open divine doors for you.

It is important, again, to take note that with biblical faith, you would first believe and rejoice to have received the promise by faith (doing this would enable you to release your faith), then expect the physical manifestation [of the promise] later, in God's timing; this is the type of faith which pleases God. On the other hand, faith in the world (i.e., among the unbelievers) means that, a person has to first see the actual physical manifestation of what he or she desires, then believes and rejoices afterwards. This type of worldly faith or carnality will not please God; in fact, it would be unbelief according to Jesus, who taught that we should believe we have already received the promise at the time we pray ( Mark 11:24).

As Christians, we believe and rejoice before physically seeing or receiving the blessings because all of God's promises in Christ Jesus are Yes and Amen, as we practice His Word and live in obedience (2 Corinthians 1:20). But unfortunately, many Christians pray without even believing first; in fact, they pray, then believe later, which is a recipe for unanswered prayer ( I discuss more on prayer in chapter 9).

Appropriating the abundance which Christ died for us to enjoy will not happen automatically; we have a role to play, such as learning how to overcome the lies and doubts from our enemy, Satan, when we step out in faith to practice what the Word teaches. The biggest hurdle you will have to deal with as you practice what the Word of God teaches is to deal with the constant lies and doubts Satan will plague you with about the integrity of God's Word and His promises to you.

Without learning how to overcome doubt, you will struggle with practicing God's Word. If you can learn how to recognize the lies from Satan and quickly demolish them as FALSE, it will be much easier for you to trust God's promises and put them to practice. So, the initial step in practicing God's Word and seeing results is to master the "art" of overcoming doubt. And, as you learn to overcome doubt and be steadfast in appropriating God's promises to you, you will indeed be practicing God's Word.

## Dealing with Doubts From Satan

Practicing the Word of God will bring its own challenges, and the biggest challenge would be the lies from Satan, pertaining to God's promises to you. If you can grow in this area, you will position yourself to easily practice God's Word. As finite beings, we cannot eliminate doubt 100%, but we can learn to recognize and quickly deal with it "head on." Doubting the promises of God is something that I believe every Christian has to deal with at some point in their journey with God. In my case, my biggest battle was when I had to fight the lies and doubts from Satan about receiving my healing from metastasis colon cancer.

We have an enemy called Satan, and his will is to prevent us from appropriating God's blessings in our lives. And He does it by planting doubtful thoughts about the Word of God in our minds, thereby causing us to question God's promises, thus fostering unbelief. Satan has not changed in his method of operation. He is using the same tricks he used to deceive Adam and Eve: planting doubts into people's minds and causing them to question the integrity of God's Word. If you believe his lies, then he will deceive you; the determining factor is you! You know why? Because Satan can only deceive a Christian who consents to him, by believing and accepting his lies. Satan has been completely defeated by Christ Jesus in every area; as such, he has no power or control over the life of a Christian who is obedient to God and walking in the light; thus, his only weapons are lies and deception.

As a Christian, you have God Himself living on the inside of you, and the power and authority in the name of the Lord Jesus is sufficient to overcome the lies from Satan. Although Satan is powerful, he has been "crushed," and you, as a Christian, has God Almighty on your side, protecting you, so you do not have to be afraid of Satan. The Bible also teaches that greater is [He] who is in you, referring to the Godhead, than he (referring to Satan), who is in the world (1 John 4:4); so do not be afraid of Satan. He is just a defeated foe (i.e., Satan), roaring around like a lion without teeth, and seeking for a victim to attack; he is just a bully, and a coward (1 Peter 5:8). In fact, Satan is afraid of you, if you are walking in the "light" with God.

I am originally from Cameroon, West Africa, and in Cameroon, like most African Countries and villages, the fear of witchcraft and other demonic activities are still very rampant. I often tell my relatives that I am not afraid of demonic forces. I tell relatives that when the devil and his angels see me approaching the villages, they must run away, far from me, because they know God is in me, and I bring the light of God into their darkness. While that statement may shock some of you, it is actually biblical. During His earthly ministry, demons recognized Christ Jesus and even pleaded with Him to depart from their Region (Matthew 8:28-34). Likewise, abide in Christ and live in obedience, and as you resist Satan by standing firm on the Truths found in God's Word, he will flee from you (James 4:7).

Many Christians undergo hours of rebuking the devil and spending hours of their time asking the devil to leave them alone. But the easiest way to rebuke the devil is to simply live in the "light" by obeying and practicing God's Word, and the blood of Christ Jesus will continuously cleanse and protect you ( 1 John 1:7). Then, when Satan attempts to attack your mind, simply remind him of the Truths in God's Word by speaking aloud Scriptures, and he will flee. Once you have God's Word ingrained in your soul, rebuking the devil is really easy, as you will be able to readily recognize his lies and come against them with the best antidote: the Word of God.

As part of his schemes, Satan may even use your closest friends to attack you, so that you would doubt God's promises. For example, you may notice that some friends, relatives or other close associates may start criticizing you for putting God's Word to practice. Do not be alarmed, rather, focus on God, and do not allow anyone to steal God's Word from your soul. Keep doing whatever is necessary as you put God's Word to practice, while asking the Holy Spirit to strengthen you to stand firm. In due time, God has promised that you will reap a bountiful harvest if you do not give up (Galatians 6:9).

Remember that Satan's biggest goal is to prevent you from practicing God's Word, in order to prevent you from receiving His blessings (Mark 4; Matthew 13; Luke 8). So, if you are persecuted because of your godly lifestyle, then rejoice, because that is a good sign that God is doing a mighty work on the inside of you and Satan is threatened, and he wants to steal from you—do not allow him! As you grow in the knowledge and practice of overcoming doubts,

Satan will flee from you for a while; but do not relax, he will come back at a later opportuned time to attack you. Thus, always be alert and well prepared to fight him [Satan].

## Some Recommendations For Overcoming Doubt

A. *Never Waver about God's Promises in His Word*

Do not compromise or rationalize your position; doing this will enable Satan to deceive you. For example, since the Bible teaches that stealing or lying is sin, do not attempt to justify why you should steal or lie, period! If you do this: STOP, and simply be honest and repent! Then ask God to strengthen you to overcome this problem. If you do not, you will limit God's influence, protection and power in your life, thereby opening the door for Satan to use this problem (i.e., your issue with lying or stealing) to hurt and disgrace you, sooner or later. The Bible teaches that if you waver about the Truths in God's Word, it means you are double minded (i.e., indecisive, unable to make up your mind), and such a person will not receive anything from God (James 1: 7-8).

Pause and think about this for a moment. Imagine how difficult it would be to put to practice something you are unsure about? The effort required from being indecisive would probably cause many people to quit and become passive. Unfortunately, this is what happens when Christians become double minded about God's promises. Just the emotional and mental stress from wavering would cause many of them to quit believing God, which will be a victory for Satan. You get the picture?

B. *Obey God's Word Completely, and not Partially*

Do not choose and pick how and when you will obey God, do it 100% as you yield your desires to the Holy Spirit. Complete obedience to God will definitely stop Satan in his "tracks." Satan knows if you are not completely obedient in an area of your life, based on your actions and words (i.e., words of doubts, fear, uncertainties, etc). And sadly, he will tempt you to doubt God in those areas of partial obedience, thus making it difficult for you to overcome and put God's Word to practice. God is fair and just, and He will only honor complete obedience and practice of His Word, period!

C. *Do Not Alter, Add or Delete Parts of God's Word to Suit Your Lifestyle*

Doing this will prevent you from overcoming the lies and doubts from your enemy, Satan, and it will make it difficult for you to correctly practice the Word. Learn to accept God's Word as it is written. If unsure, ask the Holy Spirit for clarity, and seek counsel from a mature Christian who has some evidence of God's Word working in their life. Or, seek help from your local church (I discuss more about the church in chapter 10). God will expose you as a liar, if you attempt to add to His Word or alter it (Proverbs 30:6).

D. *Do Not Spend a Second of Your Time Considering Unbiblical Thoughts*

Such thoughts are probably from your flesh, the world (i.e., from unbelievers) or Satan, and they will pose a challenge for you when you attempt to readily put God's Word to practice. The moment you start considering ungodly thoughts, you will open the door for Satan to plant more doubts in your mind, which will cause you to start rationalizing, thereby leading to the compromising of God's Truths. So, immediately ungodly thoughts attack your mind, instantly reject to entertain such thoughts in the name of Jesus (2 Corinthians 10:5).

By quickly demolishing the wrong or ungodly thoughts, you will prevent such thoughts from taking "root" in your soul; this is what the Bible calls spiritual warfare, which is mostly in your mind. And since you cannot act on something without first considering it in your mind, the faster you get rid of ungodly thoughts, the easier it will be for you to overcome doubt and practice God's Word.

E. *For Every Doubtful Thought, Use the Word of God as the Antidote*

Scripture is the best and the only antidote we have to overcome the lies from the enemy, Satan. If Jesus, who was God Himself in the flesh, had to rely on Scripture to overcome the lies from Satan, know that we ought to do the same (Luke 4: 1-13). As an example, if Satan is lying to you that no one loves you or cares about you, simply quote Scripture aloud thereby reminding him about the absolute Truth that God will never leave or forsake you ( Deuteronomy 31:6); and that He loves you indefinitely, and nothing shall separate you from His love in Christ Jesus (Romans 8:38-39). Doing this will cause Satan to flee from you! Because he cannot stand to listen to the Truths in God's Word, he will run away!

Or, if he is lying to you that you will die of poverty, remind him [Satan] that God, your provider, says you will never go without bread or food (Psalm 37:25). If, it is a disease in your body that he is lying to you about, remind Him that the Lord Jesus, your healer, died for your physical health as well, and by His "stripes", you have been healed (Isaiah 53:4-5). Speaking God's Word aloud will strengthen your faith and edify you, thereby fostering your ability to put it to practice, because faith comes by hearing the Word of God (Romans 10:17).

F. *Do not Evaluate God's Word Based on Your Circumstance*

No matter how dire your circumstance may appear, if God says you have been set free, you really are set free, so accept and receive it by faith, because we live by faith and not by sight, remember? Instead, learn to view your circumstance(s) in accordance with God's perspective (i.e., His Word). Therefore, **no matter how bad your circumstance(s) appear, remind yourself that you have already overcome or won the battle according to God's promises, and in just a little while, the manifestation will be evident.** It is very crucial for you to gain this godly perspective, as it will enable you to easily practice God's Word.

G. *Be Patient, it Will Come to Pass if You Do Not Give Up*

God will not allow you to be tempted above your ability to handle it, so be patient. God is faithful, and with every temptation, He will give you a way to escape, endure and overcome it (1 Corinthians 10:13). Take heart and walk by faith; it will come to pass. You are already a winner in Christ! All of us, as Christians, struggle at times, in different areas of life; but we must learn to be steadfast, because God is with us, and He is for us!

## PRACTICAL APPLICATION

Now that you can overcome the doubts from Satan, below are some basic recommendations for applying God's Word in your life daily. These recommendations are not intended to be dogmatic, for God guides each of us differently. Most importantly, be open to the promptings of the Holy Spirit and obey them as you practice His Word.

### Some Recommendations as You Practice God's Word

1. You have to come into agreement with God that His Word is the only Truth, inspired by the Holy Spirit, inerrant and infallible. If you struggle with this, you will experience major challenges from Satan, the world, and from your selfish "fleshy" thoughts and desires, as you attempt to practice what the Word of God teaches. In the book of Amos chapter 3, God asked a very interesting question, He said: *"Do two walk together unless they have agreed to do so?"* (v.3). If you do not agree with God about His Word, you will definitely struggle, and probably be overcome by doubt and Satan.

   Satan will attack every Christian at some point or another. However, He specializes in planting doubtful thoughts in the minds of those who are new to the Word and are excited about knowing God, or even in the thoughts of seasoned Christians who are not "grounded" in the Word of God. He could not prevent you, a new Christian, from accepting to follow the Lord Jesus, but now that you are a Christian, he [Satan] will do everything he can to prevent you from walking in the Truths found in God's Word. So ask the Holy Spirit to help you in this area, and practice those recommendations listed above for overcoming doubt. Also, review the listed resources at the end of this book for further studies in this area. <u>Our Ministry has an audio CD teaching on overcoming doubt; it has helped many, and I am certain it will help you as well</u>.

2. Never take a Scripture out of context and act on it; that will be a recipe for disaster. I have already discussed this in previous chapters. Remember to always, I mean always, read the Bible in context, and take into consideration the totality of all Scriptures. Like I discussed already, briefly study and consider the purpose why a particular book of the Bible was written? Find out who the targeted audience at that time was? And find out what the major issues or themes surrounding a particular book of the Bible are? If you recall, I previously discussed how most study Bibles provide such answers at the beginning of each book of the Bible. Thus, attempt to ask questions as you study.

Answers to such questions as mentioned above will enhance your understanding of the Scriptures. Then, ask the Holy Spirit to reveal to you practical ways to apply the Scriptures into your life. Many Scriptures are already very practical, such as those found in the book of Proverbs and many other books in the Bible; all you have to do is to put them to practice, in faith. Keep in mind that all of the principles and teachings of the Bible are timeless, and are still applicable to this and every previous Century.

Notwithstanding, there are things in Scripture that you will not immediately understand as you study them, but as you remain faithful in studying, meditating, and asking the Holy Spirit for revelation, your understanding will be enhanced. Most importantly, the Bible itself is an excellent commentary (i.e., offering explanations and providing clarity about various topics, issues, etc). Hence, as you invest time in studying the totality of Scripture, eventually, another writer or book of the Bible will offer clarity to some issue you had difficulty with elsewhere in the Bible. For example, the book of Hebrews and the book of Romans offer an excellent commentary (i.e., clarification) about the Old Testament Law, and how Christ, the Messiah, has fulfilled the Law. Thus, it is relevant to read the entire Bible in context for a deeper understanding of God's Truths.

**God is unchangeable in His nature; and has not, and will not, or cannot change His principles to suit our contemporary ways of living— that will never happen. Rather, our contemporary lifestyles ought to conform to His teachings, which is the Only Truth.** Cultures, people, and circumstances may change, but the Truths in God's Word are immutable and applicable to all Mankind, regardless of their race, gender, culture, century, etc; because, at the core, like I have mentioned before, human beings are the same, although our skin color, nationality, and language may vary. For example, homosexuality, sex outside of marriage, etc, were wrong and were considered sins against God during the Old Testament era, and they are still sinful practices today, regardless of the fact that we now live in the 21st Century. Likewise, thievery, stealing, murder, gossip, were all wrong during the Old Testament era, and they are still wrong behaviors now, you get it?

3. Do not read too much into the Scripture, add or take away things that the Scripture is not teaching. I introduced this notion in the previous section, but I want to briefly advance it here. Many times, the intended meaning or teaching in the Scripture is very obvious, but people make it harder than it is, and at times, struggle with accepting the simplicity in the message. God has a covenant with us Christians through Christ Jesus; I have already established this concept throughout this book. Thus, God has only promised to honor and bless His will as written in His Word, which is

His covenant with us. So, if you add to it, or delete from it in order to suit your preference, God will not be obligated to honor you; in fact, this is one of the primary reasons for unanswered prayers (I discuss more about prayer in the next chapter).

Although we are all aware that God is Sovereign, He has chosen to limit Himself within the confines of His written Word, which is His will for us. And, in His infinite love, He has given each of us a Free Will, to willingly adhere to His will and receive His blessings and favor, or disobey and go without, it is as simple as this.

Here is an illustration of what it looks like when people add or delete from God's Word and erroneously expect His blessings. The general biblical principle is that, it is God's will for believers to be married to a fellow believer, and not to an unbeliever. This principle is taught across the testaments, such as God's instructions to the Jews in the Old Covenant to not marry foreigners, and in the New Testament warning for believers to not be "unequally yoked" with unbelievers. Although 2 Corinthians 6:14 is not teaching about marriage, this principle of not being " unequally yoked together with unbelievers" is very applicable here as well. The obvious reason is that you will not be able to share your faith, which is the most important thing in your life, with someone who does not believe in Christ Jesus, thus you will encounter much strife in every area of your life.

If you follow your own desires and lustful passions and decide to violate this principle and marry an unbeliever, expecting and believing that God will change him or her because of your sincere love for God and for the other person: (a) it will not work, because you cannot change anyone in the first place; and (b) God is not obligated to bless that marriage in accordance with His will, because you disobeyed Him and pursued your own desires in the first place.

In spite of how hard you fast, pray and engage in all sorts of godly activities, due to your willful disobedience, you may experience much pain and suffering in the relationship which will not be God's will for you. You may end up very disappointed and angry at God, but you are the one who first disobeyed Him. Also, God is not impressed by your godly activities when you are in disobedience, but, by your obedience in faith; please take note of this basic difference. **Many godly Christians erroneously think that if they fast, pray or worship God "hard" enough, then He will move or act on their behalf — Wrong, Wrong, and Wrong; and this wrong thinking is pitiful and unbiblical. Your actions do not move God, He has already moved over 2000 years ago in Calvary (at the cross when Jesus died), and He is now expecting you to obey His Word in faith, while praying and engaging in these godly activities, there is a difference! Do you get that**?

Nonetheless, if you are in such an "unequally yoked" marriage due to your own disobedience, in His love and grace, God will give you the ability to endure the suffering, which you would have brought upon yourself. So, whatever a Scripture teaches you to do, do just that. *__A point of caution:__ If you are unsure what a particular Scripture is teaching, do not apply it into your life yet. First seek clarification from the Holy Spirit, and as you are led, seek counsel from a mature Christian who has some evidence of godly results in their lives. You may also seek counsel from your local church, if the Bible is their authority. But most importantly, get clarity before acting, lest you cause more problems for yourself and others.* There are many resources available today that can help you to better apply God's Word in your life, such as various Life Application Study Bibles, Concordances, Lexicons, Bible Dictionaries, etc.

4. Be patient as you practice God's Word: it works. You have to give God enough time to help you. God is not an ATM machine whereby you can "plug in" your request and expect an immediate answer to "pop up." It does not work like that in God's Kingdom. It took you a long time to get into the "mess" you are in right now, right? Likewise, the "mess" will not be cleaned up in an instant, it requires time and patience in order for you to grow.

**God has instantly forgiven all of your sins when you accepted the Lord Jesus, and if you sin as a Christian, and genuinely confess, He instantly will forgive you. But, the consequence(s) of the negative effect of your sin will not disappear instantly. You have to deal with the consequences of your mistake, but God will be on your side, helping you through the process.** Besides, if God instantly delivers you from the consequences of your self-inflicted "mess," you will never learn, grow and build character to prevent the same "mess" from happening again.

Much more, the Word of God has to be grounded in your soul over a period of time; and as you walk in obedience, not quitting when attacked by Satan or others, God will honor your efforts and you will eventually see results (Galatians 6:7-9). While waiting for results, continue to study the Word, love God and others, pray, attend church (I discuss prayer and church attendance in subsequent chapters), and engage in other Christ centered activities.

5. Avoid ungodly events, circumstances and friends as much as possible as you practice God's Word. We are warned that bad company corrupts good manners (1 Corinthians 15:33). If you are unable to influence people with your godly lifestyle, then it would be wise to remove yourself from that relationship or circumstance (i.e., ungodly relationships), lest you would start behaving like them (i.e., in disobedience), which will prevent God from doing His work in your life.

Some of you may think that you are too strong for someone to influence you; boy, if I were you, I would not have that much confidence in the "flesh," and underestimate Satan's power and influence through people around you. As an example, an ungodly person may not overtly influence you to walk away from the Lord and denounce your faith, but, their unbelief, and often minor ungodly language and actions may start planting doubts about the influence and power of God in your life, which may cause you to lose your "fire" for God. This can be very unnoticeable until you one day realize you are totally disinterested in the things of God. So do not be deceived, bad company can indeed affect your godly living. Christ Jesus commanded us to be the salt and the light of the world, thus we should influence ungodly people, and not allow them to influence us (Matthew 5:13-16).

6. Engage in things that enable you to easily stay focused on God, thus making it easier to put His Word into practice. Such things include but are not limited to: fellowshipping with other like-minded believers, prayer, fasting, Holy Spirit led good works or services to foster God's Kingdom, praise and worship, etc. As you surround yourself with people who love God and want to obey and live according to His Word, it will become much easier for you to practice what the Bible teaches, and receive the desired results.

7. No matter how bad things, such as financial problems, failing health, impending divorce, feelings of loneliness, etc, may appear on the surface, do not primarily look at your circumstances to evaluate whether or not God is moving on your behalf. Remember, we live and walk (meaning our lifestyles) by faith and not based on what we perceive from our five senses or environment. Rather, completely give your attention to the solution: God! Trust that He is there with you; He really is, that is a promise, so accept it by faith!

And as you interpret your circumstances in light of God's Word, you will get up in the morning one day, and the answer or solution will be visible. There is nothing impossible with God! He already knows your problem, so stand firm. Each of us is just one Word away from God solving that insurmountable problem we might perceive. And as you focus on God, rather than the problem, He has promised to keep you in His perfect peace, which will enable you to endure (Isaiah 26:3).

## Other Benefits of Practicing God's Word

Practicing the Word of God honors God, and it will keep you holy, and enable you to appropriate God's promises in your life. But most importantly, **practicing the Word will allow the Holy Spirit to do His supernatural work of sanctification in your life: molding and shaping you into the image of Christ Jesus** (Romans 8: 28-30). Other benefits of practicing the Word include but are not limited to:

- Stability in every area of your life, because you will be led by the Spirit of God, who is stable in spite of the circumstances round and about you;
- Evidence of the Fruit of the Spirit (Galatians 5: 22-23) will begin to manifest in your life, as you will become God-dependent, abiding in Christ, moment by moment;
- Enjoying the continuous presence and fellowship of the Godhead and cleansing from sin, because you will be walking in the light ( 1 John 1:5-7).

In spite of the above benefits of practicing the Word of God, it is amazing that there are many Christians who are struggling with allowing God's Word to work in their lives. You may be wondering why that is the case? Let us examine this issue closely!

## Why The Word of God Does Not Work For Some People

Some of you may be convinced that the Word of God does not work for everyone. Well, I am here to say that, that is absolutely not true. God's Word always works if applied correctly. In fact, the problem is never with God's Word; but rather, the condition of our hearts and how we apply the Word in our lives. At times, it is wrong doctrine or teaching about the Word which leads to wrong application and subsequently wrong results. That has nothing to do with God, but us, because God has revealed Himself to us through His Word, and He has given each of us the Free Will and responsibility to know Him for ourselves. While these are some reasons, in His teaching called the Parable of the Sower as recorded in the Gospels of Mark chapter 4, Matthew chapter 13 and Luke chapter 8, the Lord Jesus explained why the Word does not work for certain individuals.

By definition, a parable is an allegory or an illustration used to tell a story containing a life lesson. In the case of the Bible, parables are used to illustrate a spiritual lesson. So in the Parable of the Sower, the Lord is not teaching about farming here; rather, He used farming to illustrate a spiritual lesson for our learning. As you read the parable, keep in mind that (1) the Seed in the parable represents the Word of God; (2) the Soil represents the four different types of hearts of individuals, who would hear the Word of God proclaimed, and their different reactions to the message; and (3) the One stealing the Word from people's heart is Satan, because they [the individuals] allow him to do so. Below is the Parable:

Then he told them many things in parables, saying: *"A farmer went out to sow his seed. As he was scattering the seed, some fell along the path, and the birds came and ate it up. Some fell on rocky places, where it did not have much soil. It sprang up quickly, because the soil was shallow. But when the sun came up, the plants were scorched, and they withered because they had no root. Other seed fell among thorns, which grew up and choked the plants. Still other seed fell on good soil, where it produced a crop—a hundred, sixty or thirty times what was* sown. Whoever *has ears, let them hear"* (Matthew 13:3-9), (emphasis author's).

This is one of the parables whereby the Lord Jesus Himself offers the interpretation, let us look at it:

*"Listen then to what the parable of the sower means: When anyone hears the message about the kingdom and does not understand it, the evil one comes and snatches away what was sown in their heart. This is the seed sown along the path. The seed falling on rocky ground refers to someone who hears the word and at once receives it with joy. But since they have no root, they last only a short time. When trouble or persecution comes because of the word,*

*they quickly fall away. The seed falling among the thorns refers to someone who hears the word, but the worries of this life and the deceitfulness of wealth choke the word, making it unfruitful. But the seed falling on good soil refers to someone who hears the word and understands it. This is the one who produces a crop, yielding a hundred, sixty or thirty times what was sown"* (Matthew 13:18-23), (emphasis author's).

This parable is so clear that in my view, no further explanation is necessary, but for those of you who are visual, I have illustrated this on the table below for added clarity, let us try this:

## An Illustration of The Parable of the Sower

| THE SOIL = YOUR HEART | THE SEED = WORD OF GOD | YOUR IMMEDIATE REACTION | THE EVIL ONE = SATAN | SATAN'S INFLUENCE | OUTCOME OF YOUR REACTION |
|---|---|---|---|---|---|
| First Individual's Heart | The Word of God along the path | You have no interest in God's Word, as such no Understanding | Satan easily snatches away the message in the Word | Satan lies to you, causing you to disbelieve God's message in His Word | Unfortunately, God's Word has zero effect in your life: "It comes in one ear, and out the other ear" |
| Second Individual's Heart | The Word of God falls on rocky ground, which is shallow, there is no depth | You receive the Word with joy, but you are not "grounded" in God's Word; your daily decisions are not "filtered" through God's Word | Satan attacks your loyalty to God and tempts you | Satan uses people and circumstances and lie that God's Word does not work; you focus more on your problems instead of the promises in God's Word | Unfortunately, because of impatience, you give up and believe the lie that God's Word does not work. Thus you do not experience God's best for your life |
| Third Individual's Heart | The Word of God falls among thorns | You receive the Word, but are too concerned and worried about worldly, instead of spiritual things | Satan uses your worldly desires to distract you from giving God's Word its fullest attention | Satan uses your lust for worldly things such as wealth, busyness, etc, to prevent you from focusing on God's Word and growing | Unfortunately, because of the distractions and minimal focus on God's Word, you do not experience the desired results, and the Word of God is unfruitful in your life |
| Fourth Individual's Heart | The Word of God falls on good soil | You receive the Word and have good understanding of it (this person has been patiently studying the Word and is well grounded) | Satan still attempts, but he cannot steal from you because the Word is preeminent in your life and actions | Satan flees from you because you walk in the light. He will still attempt to plant his lies, but you can easily overcome it | This type of individual is the goal for all Christians; they are very fruitful for God's Kingdom, which is His will for us. |

This parable is very applicable and practical today. In fact, the four types of individuals the Lord discussed in this parable will be reading this book. After studying this book, each of you will walk away with totally different results. **Keep in mind that the Word of God is consistent, but the hearts of people are inconsistent, and God is not responsible for the condition of your heart; not even Satan is, you are the determining factor! Therefore, it is never the Word of God that does not work, it is us who do not know how to work the Word of God into our lives correctly.**

> *Keep in mind that the Word of God is consistent, but the hearts of people are inconsistent, and God is not responsible for the condition of your heart; not even Satan is, you are the determining factor!*

Your past, current circumstances, poor choices, wrong teaching, wrong friends, etc, might have hardened your heart towards God and His Word, therefore leading Satan to deceive and entrap you in his lies. But, as a child of God, your past is completely forgiven and "wiped out," and you have God on your side to enable you to overcome your current circumstances. So stop giving Satan the opportunity to harden your heart towards God, and work towards developing a sensitive heart to God and His Word.

In conclusion, developing a sensitive heart towards God requires diligent studying, meditating and practicing His Word, while overcoming doubt and exercising patience and staying consistent in prayer. As you invest time in studying the Word, your heart will start becoming sensitive to God's promptings, and you will start noticing some changes in your attitude, outlook in life, and your circumstances, etc. As you persist in seeking God through His Word, you will one day look back and realize how He had been slowly working in your heart all the while as you were studying, meditating and obeying His Word. That is how God works a lot of times: slowly but surely, in the background, as we seek Him earnestly—so do not give up, it is a process worth embarking on.

As you put God's Word into practice daily, prayer will become the key ingredient that will enable you to fertilize the seed (Word of God) planted in your soul. Practicing the Word daily means that you will, hopefully, depend on your prayers to sustain you. Turn now to the next chapter and learn the basic tools involved in the art of prayer.

# Summary Points

- Hearing and studying the Word of God without obeying it will yield minimal or no results;

- Although studying and knowing the Word of God is essential, putting it to practice is what brings the desired results. As such, only those who practice God's Word receive the blessings;

- God has a Covenant with Christians through Christ Jesus, to honor His written Word in the Bible when applied in our lives, by faith;

- God will not honor your actions outside His will, as expressed in His written Word;

- Satan's main goal is to cause you to doubt the Word of God and its integrity, thereby preventing you from practicing it and receiving its many blessings;

- The only and best antidote to the doubts and lies from Satan are the Truths found in God's Word;

- The Parable of the Sower teaches us that it is never the Word of God that is the problem. Rather, it is the condition of people's hearts and their subsequent reactions to the Word of God when they hear it proclaimed;

- God's Word is consistent, and will work the same for everyone [because God is no respecter of persons], when applied correctly. But, the hearts of people are inconsistent, and as such they fail to apply God's Word correctly, which leads to different and/or undesired results.

# Are You Moving Forward with Jesus?

## Chapter 9

# HOW TO PRAY THE WORD OF GOD

Prayer simply means communication with God, like you would talk with your friend. Unfortunately, many people have made prayer so complicated to the extent that it has become a spiritual calisthenics. I have ministered to many people who have told me that they do not know how to pray. That statement in and of itself implies they are looking for some kind of a formula, but none exists whatsoever. In what is generally called the Lord's Prayer (see the Gospels), the Lord Jesus offered a template (i.e., a guide, or a model) on how to pray, and not a formula, there is a big difference! Nonetheless, I often tell people that if they can speak, then, they can certainly pray.

In its simplest definition, prayer is simply a dialogue, whereby you communicate or talk with God, and you in turn, listen for Him to speak back into your heart. Sadly, there are those who embark in monologues during their prayer time rather than a heartfelt dialogue with God; as such, they do not give God a chance to talk back to them, and then they would quickly say, in Jesus name, Amen. How pitiful, because God is always talking, and willing to talk back to us, if we would be patient to listen to His still voice in our hearts during our prayer times. God desires to talk back to us because prayer is the primary channel by which we can have this dialogue with Him, and to ask for His will to come to pass. Hence, the primary purpose for prayer is to ask for God's will to be manifested on the earth, and in our individual lives.

There are those who are erroneously believing that there is no use to pray, because God's will will come to pass, regardless. Firstly , this line of thinking is not Scriptural, hence it is grossly wrong; secondly, God's will does not automatically come to pass in our individual lives, we have a role to play, such as obeying His instructions, living in obedience, etc. The Bible is clear that during the Old Testament era, the Israelites chronically disobeyed God's instructions, and as such, prevented His perfect will for their individual lives, and for the Nation of Israel from coming to pass (e.g., see the books of Ezra, Nehemiah, Isaiah, etc). So prayer is critical, and necessary in the life of a believer.

## Some Reasons Why You Should Pray

Although it may be obvious to some of you why you should pray, that may not be the case for others. Below are some reasons discussed in the Scripture why prayer should be an integral part in your life as a Christian.

I. The Bible teaches that we should pray because God wants to hear from us: Some examples of this can be found in 2nd Chronicles 7:14 and in 1st Thessalonians 5:16-18, etc. So when we pray, we can be certain that we are obeying God's will. In addition, God wants to hear from us. Even though He is Omniscient (i.e., He knows all things), He still desires for us to come to Him with our needs, concerns, fears, etc, through the channel of prayer (e.g., Genesis 20: 6-18).

In His grace, God will at times bless us even when we do not pray for certain things, because of our relationship with Christ Jesus, but there are other things that He will only bless us with when we specifically ask in prayer. We do not know why it is this way, but God works this way, and we accept it by faith. God desires to hear from us to the extent that when we are too weak or unable to pray, the Holy Spirit Himself prays and intercedes for us ( Romans 8:26-27).

II. Christ Jesus prayed to God the Father throughout His ministry, and taught His disciples how to pray. Some examples can be found in Luke 5:16; John 17; Matthew 26:36-40, etc. The Lord Jesus is our perfect example; and if He thought it was important to pray as exemplified in His ministry, then, as His followers, we certainly should pray as well.

III. The Lord Jesus taught His disciples how to pray. This shows that prayer is very significant; as such, it was necessary for Jesus to teach on this very relevant topic (Luke 11: 1-13).

IV. Prayer is one significant way to overcome the lies, doubts and deception from our enemy Satan (Ephesians 6:11-20), along with abiding in Christ, living in obedience, praise and worship, etc.

V. God answers prayers. We have a plethora of Scriptural evidence to this fact: prayer works (e.g., Genesis 20:17; 2 Chronicles 33: 1-13; Acts 12:5-17; Acts 16:25-34, etc).

VI. Prayer reveals your humility. When you pray, you willingly surrender your selfish desires and pray for God's will to manifest in your life. God honors humility and will reject the proud person (Proverbs 16:18; Proverbs 6:16-19). A proud person who foolishly thinks they " got it all figured out," would not pray, which is rather unfortunate because God's wisdom surpasses any human being's best decision. In fact, God did not create human beings to direct their own lives: we are incapable (Jeremiah 10:23), although some people are deceived by the devil, the world or their lustful desires, into thinking that they can control their lives, but they are wrong.

I am usually very concerned for those who think they "have it all together." In fact, I feel sorry for them, because the Bible is clear that there is no wisdom or human understanding or perception that can succeed against the Lord's (Proverbs 21:30). So as you humble yourself and submit your wishes to God through prayer, you will position yourself to hear from God, and in turn, make godly decisions.

VII. Prayer was a major part in the lives of biblical Saints mightily used by God. Some examples in the Old Testament include Abraham, Moses, King David, the Priests Ezra and Nehemiah, the Prophets Jeremiah, Elijah, etc. In the New Testament, prayer was an integral part in the lives and ministries of the apostles, such as the apostle Paul, Peter, John, etc. Since all Scripture is written to teach and instruct us about the ways of God (2 Timothy 3:16-17), these Saints serve as our examples. Hence, we should pray likewise.

Having a firm understanding of why we should pray is important. But, most importantly, it is essential that as God's co-worker, we pray in accordance with His Word, which is His will, because the Bible teaches that God answers such prayers. In the First letter of John chapter 5, the apostle John wrote, under the inspiration of the Holy Spirit that: "*This is the confidence we have in approaching God: that if we ask anything according to his will, he hears us. And if we know that he hears us—whatever we ask—we know that we have what we asked of him" (vv. 14-15)*, (emphasis author's).

Then, in Second Corinthians chapter 1, the Bible teaches that: "*For no matter how many promises God has made, they are "Yes" in Christ. And so through him the "Amen" is spoken by us to the glory of God*" (v. 20), (emphasis author's). So, the above Scriptures are teaching the importance of knowing God's will and praying in accordance with it, if you want your prayers to be answered. The greatest advantage of praying God's Word into your life is that you cannot go wrong, if you pray in faith and sincerity.

## How to Pray God's Word into Your Life

The Bible is "The Book of life," with answers to every problem you will ever encounter. Thus, praying God's promises into your life, in faith, is the best way to know you are not praying outside of His will. Praying God's Word into your life only requires one prerequisite: knowing the Word of God. The good news is that you do not have to be a professional student of the Word of God to do this. You can still pray whatever little you know about the Word of God into your life, expect, and receive results. So how do you pray God's Words into your life, you may wonder? Below I offer some helpful suggestions.

## Suggestions on How to Pray God's Word into Your Life

> Personalize the Scripture to Your Unique Situation

As an example, if you are struggling with any kind of fear at this time, there are hundreds of promises in the Bible promising divine protection from God to you, because of your relationship with Christ Jesus. Let us apply Psalm 91 as an example, which is one of those Scriptures. This Psalm begins with what I call a "disclaimer," pertaining only to those who have a covenant relationship with God through Christ Jesus, and are living in obedience to Him. Take a look at how the first two verses begin: *"Whoever dwells in the shelter of the Most High will rest in the shadow of the Almighty. I will say of the Lord, "He is my refuge and my fortress, my God, in whom I trust." Surely he will save you from the fowler's snare and from the deadly pestilence"* (vv. 1-3), (emphasis authors). If you are a Christian living in obedience, this Scripture is a promise to you. If you are currently not living in obedience, and/or you are practicing sin, then I suggest you repent, and be right with God, right now.

Psalm 91 is teaching that since you have made God your heavenly Father, you are under His divine shelter and protection from evil in this present world. The rest of the Psalm offers details about God's protective care to you. Below is the entire Psalm 91, on your left; then on your right, I offer a sample of a personalized devotional version I created as an example to add clarity, using the name Esther to represent an individual dealing with fear. The bolded words represent my additions:

*How to Pray the Word of God*

| Psalm 91 | A Sample Personalized Version |
|---|---|
| 1 Whoever dwells in the shelter of the Most High will rest in the shadow of the Almighty. | 1 **I, Esther,** dwell in the shelter **of God** and I will rest in the shadow **of my** God. |
| 2 I will say of the LORD, "He is my refuge and my fortress, my God, in whom I trust." | 2 **I, Esther** will say to the LORD, "**You are my** refuge and my fortress, **my God**, in whom I trust." |
| 3 Surely he will save you from the fowler's snare and from the deadly pestilence. | 3 Surely **my** God will save **me** from the fowler's snare and from the deadly pestilence. |
| 4 He will cover you with his feathers, and under his wings you will find refuge; his faithfulness will be your shield and rampart. | 4 He will cover **me, Esther**, with his feathers, and under his wings **I will** find refuge; his faithfulness will be **my protective** shield and rampart. |
| 5 You will not fear the terror of night, nor the arrow that flies by day, | 5 **I will** not fear the terror of night, nor the arrow that flies by day, |
| 6 nor the pestilence that stalks in the darkness, nor the plague that destroys at midday. | 6 nor the pestilence that stalks in the darkness, nor the plague that destroys at midday. |
| 7 A thousand may fall at your side, ten thousand at your right hand, but it will not come near you. | 7 A thousand may fall at **my** side, ten thousand at **my** right hand, but it will not come near **me**. |
| 8 You will only observe with your eyes and see the punishment of the wicked. | 8 I will only observe with **my** eyes and see the punishment of the wicked. |

| | |
|---|---|
| 9 If you say, "The LORD is my refuge," and you make the Most High your dwelling, | 9 **Since** "The LORD is my refuge," **and I have made God my dwelling,** |
| 10 no harm will overtake you, no disaster will come near your tent. | 10 no harm will overtake **me**, no disaster will come near **my** tent. |
| 11 For he will command his angels concerning you to guard you in all your ways; | 11 For **my God** will command his angels concerning **me** to guard me in all **my** ways; |
| 12 they will lift you up in their hands, so that you will not strike your foot against a stone. | 12 they will lift **me** up in their hands, so that I will not strike **my** foot against a stone. |
| 13 You will tread on the lion and the cobra; you will trample the great lion and the serpent. | 13 **I** will tread on the lion and the cobra; **I** will trample the great lion and the serpent. |
| 14 "Because he loves me," says the LORD, "I will rescue him; I will protect him, for he acknowledges my name. | 14 "…Because I, Esther loves the Lord, He will protect **me**…." |
| 15 He will call on me, and I will answer him; I will be with him in trouble, I will deliver him and honor him. | 15 **I, Esther, will call on God, and He will answer me; He, will be with me,… in my** trouble, He will deliver **me, Esther,** and honor **me**. |
| 16 With long life I will satisfy him and show him my salvation." | 16 With long life **He [God]** will satisfy **and bless me**…." |

As you can see from the table above, the two versions of Psalm 91 are emphasizing the same thing (i.e., God's protection to you), but the sample version I created is very personal and can be used as a devotional for meditation. To get the full impact of this, I recommend you pray the personalized version aloud, so that it will get very deep into your soul as you hear it. Doing this will strengthen your faith since faith comes by hearing the Word of God (Romans 10: 17). As you pray this Scripture aloud, you will be praying the will of God over your life, "owning" that Scripture and making it personal to your specific need; that is how God wants to personally protect you, as you trust in Him.

Personalizing a Scripture is very powerful. Once you get into the habit of doing this over a period of time, you will be amazed how the Holy Spirit will use Scripture to comfort and reassure you. **This is not to imply that the Holy Spirit will only speak to you when you personalize a Scripture: No, He will speak to you whether or not you personalize a Scripture.** But, the biggest advantage of personalizing a Scripture is that it [the Scripture] will target your specific need, and you will be praying God's promises over your exact problem. And since Bible faith is strengthened by hearing the Word of God, when you pray aloud a specific Scripture over your problem repeatedly, you will start believing (i.e., your faith will be quickened) the message in that Scripture, and it will change your perspective (i.e., this is what the Bible calls renewing of your mind, out of Romans 12:2) about your situation, and you will be better positioned to receive the answer to your prayer in God's perfect timing.

> Release Your Faith, Agree with God's Promises and Thank Him Before Seeing the Answer

Another way to pray God's Word into your life is to release your faith by thanking Him in advance for a particular promise in His Word before you see the physical manifestation. For example, If you are struggling with financial hardship, consider praying something like this:

*Dear God, I thank you that you are my provider and not my employer. I thank you that your Word promises me that you will provide all of my needs according to your glorious riches in Christ Jesus, and you have promised me that you will never allow me to go hungry. By faith, I stand in agreement with your infallible Word as I completely depend upon you. Heavenly Father, If there is any lesson for me to learn in this experience, teach me, as I am open to learning. Lead me, to the direction of abundance, show me what I have to do to come out of this financial hardship, and I will do it, whatever it might be. I need your supernatural wisdom, God. And by faith, I believe I am being strengthened, right now, by your Spirit, as He is leading me out of this situation. I thank you God that it is your will for me to prosper, so that I can be a blessing to others. Thank you God for delivering me out of this hardship. Your Word says whom the Son sets free is free indeed, so by faith, I am free from this problem as I rest on your promises, in Jesus name, Amen.*

A prayer like the one above is a powerful prayer of faith. As seen above, you do not beg God for what He has already promised you. Rather, you come into agreement with His promises to you, by faith, and you genuinely thank Him, in advance, because you believe in your heart that He has already answered your prayer [because He has], and then you wait for the manifestation to come, in His perfect timing. Like I said earlier in this book, anyone can praise God after he or she sees the results, which is not Bible faith at all; but believing in your heart that God's promises will manifest in your life, and rejoicing, and being expectant before you even see the results is a powerful display of faith; the type of faith that produces results. Remember what the Lord said, that we should believe at the time we pray, and not afterwards! (Mark 11:24).

> Confess God's Specific Promises Over Your Specific Situation

*You want to be precise with your request, but be open to God's response: think about this for a minute. Because God may not answer the prayer in the specific way you may want Him to, thus being open is necessary.*

Another example of praying the Word of God is simply confessing or speaking aloud God's specific promise(s) over your specific situation. The key word here is "specific" or what I call "targeted" prayer. **You want to be precise with your request, but be open to God's response: think about this for a minute. Because God may not answer the prayer in the specific way you may want Him to, thus being open is necessary.** Also, do not throw out vague non specific prayers: be exact, and then find the precise Scripture pertaining to your request. The Bible teaches that life and death is in the power of the tongue (Proverbs 18:21). So if you confess God's Word in faith, it will come to pass in God's timing, because God has promised us that His Words spoken in faith produces results (Isaiah 55:11; Matthew 8:8; Psalm 107:20). Using fear again as an example, consider praying something like this:

*Dear God: I thank you that your Word says " I should fear not." Today, by faith, and in the power and authority in your Word, I come into agreement with your promise, and I will not fear. I thank you for strengthening me with your Holy Spirit, and I refuse to fear because you are with me. I thank you that nothing shall separate me from you. I thank you that no weapon formed against me shall ever prosper because you are on my side, always; and since you are for me, no one can win any battle against me. I love you Father, because you first loved me, and your perfect love for me is my shield of protection and as a result, all fear must leave me, right now! You are my permanent shield, and I stand strong under your protection, as your angels surround me, watching over me, moment-by-moment. I thank you for such unfathomable love, care and protection, in Jesus name, AMEN.*

A prayer like the above is affirming God's Word to you, and is powerful because you are acknowledging and reminding yourself that God has already offered the solution; it is already done, and you are patiently waiting in faith for the physical manifestation. This type of attitude in prayer helps you to confidently approach God as an heir in God's Kingdom with Christ, rather than an orphan begging for the promises, there is a major difference. **You do not have to beg God to bless you. He has already blessed you through Christ Jesus; you just have to learn how to receive it by faith** ( 2 Corinthians 1:20); hopefully, this teaching is helping you. When you pray in faith like this, you will get an immediate response: the peace of God, which comes from the Word of God spoken over your situation.

> *You do not have to beg God to bless you. He has already blessed you through Christ Jesus; you just have to learn how to receive it by faith.*

The Bible teaches about various types of prayers. Regardless, all of them should be grounded in the Word of God. Following are some examples of various prayers taught in the Bible:

## Types of Prayers

### Prayer of Petition or Supplication

This is when you specifically ask God about your needs. Some Scriptural examples are (Luke 11:3; 2 Corinthians 12:7-10; Philippians 4:6-7; Psalm 5:1-3, etc). In this type of prayer, you would specifically present your specific request(s) to God.

### Prayer of Consecration

This type of prayer is also known as prayer of dedication, when you totally dedicate or consecrate something to the Lord 100%. A prayer of dedication is powerful, and it is my belief that God is especially pleased when we totally dedicate something to Him. Whatever we own belongs to God in the first place, so by dedicating it back to Him, we are just allowing Him to completely guide and direct our paths, which guarantees a much better outcome. In this type of prayer, we choose and allow God's will to take precedence rather than ours.

The one major issue with this type of prayer for many people is that they would consecrate something, such as their children to the Lord, then, they would attempt to manipulate the situation. For example, there are parents who still want to control their children's decisions as adults, rather than trusting and allowing the Lord to speak to them [their children] directly. Hence, before you consecrate anything to the Lord, be certain that you are ready to say "hands off," and trust God completely.

If you are unable to completely trust God, then do not pray this type of prayer yet, because your attempts at manipulating the situation will nullify it. If you are struggling with this type of prayer, ask God to strengthen you to totally dedicate "something" to Him first, before you proceed to pray this type of a prayer. A classic example of this type of prayer in the Bible is our Lord's prayer of consecration in the Garden of Gethsemane before His crucifixion ( see Matthew 26: 36-46), where He completely surrendered to God's will.

## Prayer of Intercession

This is when you pray on behalf of another person. Some Scriptural examples include (Exodus 32:11-13; Numbers 11:11-15; John 17: 6-25). With this type of prayer, be careful because you cannot pray against another person's will. For example, if you are praying for someone to receive their healing from God, but the individual you are praying for does not want to be healed, but rather, they want to die and go to heaven, your prayer will be useless. Or, if the person you are praying for does not believe it is God's will to heal them, your prayer will be useless as well.

God has given each of us a Free Will. God Himself is a "gentleman," and He will not violate anyone's Free Will, and neither should you! **So a <u>word of caution:</u> before you intercede for anyone in prayer, attempt to ask them what their prayer request is. Never assume what people want in prayer whether or not they are your children, husband, parents, family members, closest friends, etc, always seek to know their desires first.** If you were to study the ministry of Jesus, He often asked people what their requests were, before intervening, and we should do likewise by respecting people's choices.

## Prayer of Thanksgiving

This is when you thank God for His blessings, presence, favor, love, forgiveness, etc, in your life, even in times of problems. Thanksgiving should be an integral part of every type of prayer. This is so significant that when the Lord Jesus taught His disciples how to pray, He began the prayer with thanksgivings: He said:

*"This, then, is how you pray: "'Our Father in heaven, hallowed be your name, your kingdom come, your will be done, on earth as it is in heaven. Give us today our daily bread. And forgive us our debts, as we also have forgiven our debtors. And lead us not into temptation, but deliver us from the evil one"' (Matthew 6:9-14),* (emphasis author's).

As you can see from the prayer above, the Lord started the prayer by thanking God first, and then He proceeded to ask for God's will to come to pass on the earth, then He went on to teach about petitioning God for our daily needs, including our protection. Thanksgiving is an attitude of the heart: humility and submission. There are many people who have been mightily blessed by God in their finances, marriages, relationships, health, children, etc, yet they do not take the time to acknowledge and thank Him: what a pity, in my opinion.

God is very pleased to receive our praise and thanks from a genuine heart. Do not be like the 10 Lepers who where healed by Christ, and only [one] of them returned to offer thanks to the Lord ( Luke 17:11-19). Thank God daily for the blessings in your life, it could be worse. The book of Psalm is replete with examples of this type of Prayer, e.g., Psalm 93; 96; 103; 111, etc.

## Prayer of Praise and Worship

This type of prayer stemmed from the prayer of thanksgiving. With this type of prayer, you are primarily thanking, praising and worshiping God primarily because He deserves your worship as your Creator; then secondly, because of His goodness. In my view, praise and worship is the most powerful form of prayer, because it ushers you directly into the spiritual realm, God's presence. And while in God's presence in worship, totally focused on Him, all demons and personal problems must flee. Praise and worship is the best tool for spiritual warfare, because Satan is such a jealous person, he cannot tolerate you praising and worshipping God, hence he will flee from you.

**A word of caution: be certain that the lyrics you are singing during your praise and worship are 100% biblical. Do not only go by how good the music sounds, rather, go by how biblically accurate the lyrics are.** There are so many Christian music "out there" that sounds good, but upon closer attention to the lyrics, you would be disappointed, because they are not Scriptural. In fact, some of the lyrics are actually depressing, as if the Lord Jesus is still on the cross, but He is Risen! And we should celebrate and rejoice!

Alternatively, you can sing Scripture to the Lord as praise and worship; I do this all of the time. My favorite is Psalm 103, which I sing to the Lord during most of my praise and worship time, and I believe it blesses the Lord, and it edifies my soul as well. Some Scriptural examples of this type of prayer can be found in Exodus 15: 1-21; Acts 16: 25-34, the Psalms, etc. Praise and worship can also be in the form of adoration. An example of this is the prideful King Nebuchadnezzar who finally came to his senses, and in humility, had nothing else to offer God, but adoration for His majesty (Daniel 4:34).

## Prayer of Meditation

Meditation, as described previously, is a form of prayer. As you allow the Holy Spirit to speak directly to you and give you the revelation in His Word through meditation, your understanding is enlightened, your faith strengthened, and you will experience peace, which in and of itself, is an answered prayer. Personally, when I meditate on a Scripture and the Holy Spirit gives me the revelation of that particular Scripture, I would immediately switch to a prayer of praise and thanksgiving, as I experience His peace and affirmation.

## Prayer of Agreement

This type of prayer simply means that you and another Christian agree to pray together regarding a particular need. Many well meaning Christians often misquote Matthew 18:19–20 as the basis for prayer of agreement, which is incorrect. Because when you take a closer look at that Scripture in context, beginning with verses 15 through 18, the Lord Jesus was teaching about church discipline and not about prayer. But, this does not mean that two people cannot agree and petition God: they can. In my view, the best prayer of agreement, which I often apply to myself, is coming in agreement with God's Word and pray in agreement with the Scriptures in faith (Amos 3:3).

A <u>word of caution</u> here as well: if you choose to agree with someone in prayer, be certain that both of you are in agreement about God's will for the particular query you are petitioning God about. **If one of you is in disbelief or does not agree with God's will in the matter, then, your prayer will be nullified because of their [one of the person's] unbelief.** The biggest advantage of this type of prayer is the spiritual and moral support from the other person, because with or without the other person, God will still answer your prayer in faith, according to His will, and not because of the other person(s). So keep in mind that you, the Word of God, and the Lord Jesus, are enough for God to answer your prayer, period!

**Prayer of Repentance**

This is a specific type of prayer necessary once a person has sinned against God through their thoughts and/or actions, and they want to restore their relationship with Him. Repentance cannot be coerced; it must be genuine before God can accept it. Part of this involves acknowledging and accepting responsibility for the sin before God, and possibly to the person you have sinned against (if you have the opportunity to do so; at times you may not have the opportunity to apologize to the other person for various reasons, in that case, trust God and move on).

Just saying you are sorry after being caught is not a true repentance. A true repentance means you must (1) acknowledge your sin(s); and (2) stop practicing the sin and make a 180 degree change, away from the sin, while trusting the Holy Spirit to enable you; even before you are caught "in the act," lest you quench the power of the Spirit. Biblical examples of this type of prayer can be found in Psalm 51. This Psalm is King David's prayer of repentance after his sin with Bathsheba, as recorded in 2nd Samuel chapter 11. Other powerful examples of prayer of repentance can be found in Nehemiah chapter 9, when the Israelites realized, acknowledged and accepted their responsibilities for sinning against God (vv. 1-38), and they agreed to act accordingly, in order to make peace (see Nehemiah Chapter 10).

## Prayer of Spiritual Warfare

*It is important to be aware that a true Christian can never be possessed by the devil, because he or she is sealed by the Holy Spirit, although he or she can be oppressed by demons; there is a big difference between the two conditions!*

This type of prayer is primarily geared towards rebuking demonic attacks in your life or in the lives of others. Not all of the battles or struggles in the life of a Christian are related to demonic attacks. Many Christians blame the devil for every little thing, but most of their problems are self-inflicted, due to carnality. Conversely, there are many Christians who are oppressed by demons, and cannot discern it, thus, they are unable to resist. Regardless, we have an enemy in the spiritual realm called Satan, and when he strikes, we have to quickly discern it, and be ready to overcome his lies with the Truths found in God's Word. **It is important to be aware that a true Christian can never be possessed by the devil, because he or she is sealed by the Holy Spirit, although he or she can be oppressed by demons; there is a big difference between the two conditions!**

Rebuking demonic thoughts or other types of attacks can be as simple as refusing to entertain any ungodly or unbiblical thoughts or temptations. Second Corinthians 10 teaches that we should cast down (i.e., refuse to consider, ponder on) any imaginations (i.e., thinking patterns) that exalt (i.e., elevate) itself against the knowledge of God (meaning against God's Word); and we should compare those thoughts with the Truths found in Christ Jesus. That is to say, if the thoughts plaguing your mind are inconsistent with biblical teachings, then you should refuse to consider such ways of thinking (v.5).

*Satan can interfere with your prayers for various reasons, such as through your fears or the unbelief of others in your environment. It is not because Satan is stronger: NO! He is Not; God is stronger, and the Lord Jesus has already conquered him [Satan]. But your lifestyle can give Satan an inroad into your life, thus hindering your prayers.*

**Satan can interfere with your prayers for various reasons, such as through your fears or the unbelief of others in your environment. It is not because Satan is stronger: NO! He is Not; God is stronger, and the Lord Jesus has already conquered him [Satan]. But your lifestyle can give Satan an inroad into your life, thus hindering your prayers.** Or, there are times when Satan attacks a Christian for nothing he or she has done, but simply because the individual is a threat to him, because of his or her powerful witness for Christ. Regardless, we must stay alert and quickly discern if we are under attack, that way we can fight back with the Truths in God's Word, which is our best antidote. A classic example of Satan hindering a prayer is found in Daniel 10: 11-13.

A prayer of spiritual warfare can be as simple as you praying aloud something like this:

*Dear God, in the name of Jesus, I thank you that you have given me the power and authority in the name of Jesus to overcome Satan. I thank you that you have already defeated Satan, and I refuse for him to steal from me. By faith, I now enforce my authority against the evil one. In the name of Jesus, my Lord , Savior and Protector, Satan [call him by his name], I speak to you directly, I refuse to accept your lies, so depart from my mind, right now. I demolish your ungodly thoughts and I refuse to dwell on them. I curse you in Jesus name, so depart from me, now! Thank you God, that I am set free from the Kingdom of darkness, AMEN.*

Remember, Satan is already defeated, but you must resist his lies, and the best weapon for spiritual warfare is knowing and practicing the Truths in God's Word. Then, as you are living in obedience, when Satan tries to lie to you, you can quickly quote Scriptures, and he will flee from you, period! **You do not need to lock yourself up in a room for hours in order to bind and rebuke the devil, while yelling and hitting the wall, all that is not necessary as Christ Jesus shattered him "hands down" on the cross.** All you have to do is to live in the light (meaning abiding in Christ in obedience), and it will be much easier to resist and overcome Satan. Satan has no power or authority over you, except if you allow him through disobedience and sin. The name of the Lord Jesus spoken in faith will cause any demon to flee, as simple as that. Other spiritual weapons to use for this type of prayer are listed in Ephesians 6:10-20.

## Prayer of Fasting

This type of prayer is by far the most misunderstood, in my opinion, as people erroneously think that their fasting will impress God to love them more or act on their behalf, which is not true. God already loves you, that is His nature, He cannot love you less or more, period! God is love! And He is already impressed with you because of your relationship with the Lord Jesus, especially when you are living in accordance with His Word.

Fasting primarily benefits you, and not God. By fasting, you would be denying yourself a particular thing you like, for a period of time, in order to study, pray and meditate on God's Word. It could be denying yourself a particular food, one meal, two or three meals a day, or restricting certain fluids, abstaining from exercise, or from watching TV, etc, for a set period of time that you choose, for the primary purpose of getting closer to God to either: (1) hear His voice better for purposes of self-edification; or (2) to seek His wisdom and direction. The principle underlying fasting is that as you starve your flesh and reduce the stimuli from your physical environment by primarily focusing and feeding your spirit, it will be much easier to discern God's still voice in your heart and in His Word, as you draw closer to Him. This principle also applies when you are in constant prayer and totally focused on God.

Unfortunately, some people fast, but yet, they do not spend the time to study the Word, meditate and pray; in that case, that would not be considered fasting. **Keep in mind that your fasting will not cause God to react or act on your behalf. Rather, it will usher you into the spiritual realm, closer to Him.** God does not react based on your actions (which is called works), because He already moved on the cross over 2,000 years ago in the person of Christ Jesus, and He is always available. It is us who constantly move away from God; and by faith, fasting will enable you to clearly discern His inner promptings in your heart, as you move closer to Him.

The Bible offers no strict guidelines regarding the type or duration of a fast, although some people use the example found in the book of Daniel as a guide (Daniel 1: 8-14). Others attempt to fast for 40 days like the Lord Jesus did. Unfortunately, many people have died during fasting for prolonged periods of time because of a lack of wisdom. Due to space limitation in this book, I am unable to discuss details about fasting even though as a doctor, I could help many people in this area.

Suffice it to say that, I recommend that you seek medical advice from your Health Care Provider before embarking on any type of a fast, especially if you are taking prescribed medications, and are struggling with chronic diseases such as Diabetes, High blood pressure, etc. Usually, I advice my patients with metabolic diseases, such as Diabetes, to not undergo prolonged fast or to even attempt certain types of fasting.

**Prayer of Faith to Heal the Sick**

The Bible talks about this type of prayer in the book of James chapter 5 verses 14 through 15. This type of prayer involves anointing the sick person with oil, praying in accordance with the Word of God in the name of Christ Jesus, in addition to having the sick person willingly repent of any sins in their lives. The one offering the prayer and the sick person receiving the anointing must equally believe in God's willingness and faithfulness to heal.

**Prayer of Benediction**

This type of prayer is often heard in a church or other similar gathering after the service, or at times, at the beginning of a service. Usually, after the service or teaching of God's Word, the Pastor or Teacher would proclaim a blessing over the entire congregation. The Pastor may say something like this: "*I pray for the love of God to comfort your souls in Christ today, Amen*". It could be as simple as that. This sort of prayer can also be offered at the end of a Bible teaching book, such as this book. Some Scriptural examples of this type of prayer can be found in Numbers 6:24-26; Romans 1:7, 15:33, etc.

# PRACTICAL APPLICATION

Regardless of the type of prayer, the Bible teaches about certain key ingredients that must be met before we can approach God in prayer and expect results. Below are some major ones, although it is not an inclusive list.

## Key Ingredients For an Effective Prayer

### Purity of Heart

If your heart is impure towards the things of God, regardless of how long or hard you pray, you will not see the desired results (see Psalm 66:18-19). Thus, before approaching God, be certain your heart is pure and sincere. You cannot deceive God, He already knows your heart, so you might as well be honest (1 Samuel 16:7).

### Faith in God and His Word

Without biblical faith, it is difficult to receive anything from God (Hebrews 11:6). Remember how I discussed earlier that biblical faith involves believing first that you have already received the promise, and then you will see the manifestation later! The Lord taught this principle of faith to His disciples, which also includes us (see Mark 11: 22-24). And like I have said already, many people get this backward: they pray first, then believe later, which is wrong, and is actually unbelief, thus their prayers are hindered. **If you cannot first believe that you will receive whatever you are praying about, then do not pray yet. Instead, ask God to strengthen you, study His Word to quicken your faith in order to reach a place of**

**believing first, then proceed to pray in faith. Praying in doubt will yield no results! So you might as well not pray.**

Many people trust in God as they pray to Him, which is great, but exercising faith is a completely different matter. To exercise your faith after you first believe that you will receive the promise from God, you have to take the necessary steps through your actions as you are led by the Holy Spirit, in order to make your faith complete (James 2: 14-26). As an example, if you are praying and believing for God to prosper you financially, you would pray because you trust God as your provider. Thereafter, you would need to, in faith, start looking for a job, trusting that God would favor you as He directs your steps supernaturally.

If you were a manager at a large company that downsized and now you are jobless and believing God for a new job, do not sit around and wait for another managerial job right away. If an opportunity opens for a less paying or less desirable job, accept it by faith. And as you are faithful in that position, trust that God will honor your humility and faith, and eventually elevate you somehow. But for you to pray, then sit around and wait for a "high caliber" managerial job and refuse to accept a less honorable job is pride and foolishness; and is not biblical faith at all, this in fact will hinder your prayer, and limit God's favor in your situation.

I know someone who is in a similar situation right now. This person has a particular training in a specific area, and he has been believing God for a job in this area for over three years now, but it is not happening. In the mean time, he has had multiple opportunities to work elsewhere as a cashier, in sales, etc, but he has refused.

When this person sought my advice, I informed him to get a job anywhere, at a fast-food restaurant, grocery store or other similar retailers, etc, and he was upset, stating it would be a demotion, yet he is "believing God."

Finally, I told this person that his actions are not consistent with biblical faith, because God had opened various opportunities, yet he is determined to get a particular job. Guess what? This person is struggling financially and is not prospering. Likewise, do not sit around and expect exactly what you want, and in the specific way you desire it. Instead, trust God's timing and wisdom, regardless of how menial a job or task might appear to be on the surface; God may be molding and shaping you for something bigger, or even teaching you how to trust Him more. Take advantage of the opportunities He brings your way and grow in Him, overcome the test, and expect the best: this is biblical faith, which pleases God.

## Praying in Accordance with God's Will

*Even when God speaks to us through others, circumstances, dreams, visions, etc, it will be consistent with His written Word.*

A sure way to guarantee that your prayer will not be answered is praying outside of God's will, which is why I dedicated an entire chapter in this book teaching you the importance of praying God's Word, which is His will, into your life. God will not answer prayers outside His will, period! So the sooner you come into agreement with this, the better for you. God has limited Himself to operate in our lives within the confines of His Word. **Even when God speaks to us through others, circumstances, dreams, visions, etc, it will be consistent with His written Word.** It does not matter how much or how long you pray about something, it will not happen if it is outside of God's will, period!

Much more, neither the length of your prayer nor the amount of begging in prayer impresses God, if you are praying contrary to His Word, please take note of this Truth. **God is neither impressed nor does He act based on your pitiful countenance, begging, hitting and kicking the wall, or screaming when you pray; rather, He is moved by compassion towards those who are honestly praying to Him in accordance with His will.** The Bible teaches that when we pray according to God's will, we should expect results, which is why it is mandatory for you to know God's Word. The apostle John wrote, under the inspiration of the Holy Spirit:

*"This is the confidence we have in approaching God: that if we ask anything according to his will, he hears us. And if we know that he hears us—whatever we ask—we know that we have what we asked of him"* ( 1 John 5:14-15), (emphasis author's).

**This Scripture is powerful. Look at the last sentence "...*whatever we ask—we know that we have what we asked of him* (emphasis author's). This last sentence is implying that: (1) God will not say NO, to His promises; and (2) we should be confident that we already have the answer: Whoa!** How awesome is the God we serve through Christ Jesus, by the enabling of the Holy Spirit, thank you God!

I made this comment earlier, but it is worth stating again—stop begging God to help you or to answer your prayers; He has already done it through Christ; thus, learn to receive it by faith as you obey Him. God wants to bless you even more than you want it! Thus, no amount of begging, or your godly actions, apart from what He [God] might be asking you to do (i.e., acting in faith), will manifest the blessings sooner.

In fact, relying on your own good works, begging and pleading with God in order to impress Him, is called: WORKS (i.e., fleshy or carnal self-motivated tricks and efforts), which is offensive to God; you must approach God through Christ Jesus only, and give up your "WORKS," and learn to "rest" (i.e., trusting and waiting on Him by faith) on His promises as revealed in His Word. **God blesses us because of our covenant relationship with Christ Jesus and our obedience to Him based on His love and grace, and not because we deserve it or because of anything we do. None of us deserves God's blessings, which is why we are thankful for the blood of Jesus.** So stop trying to help God, He does not need your help! Just trust Him and rest in Christ after you pray —He has heard you!

There are times when God might lead you to take certain actions after you pray, which will help you to release your faith and enable you to grow. **If that is the case, then act in faith, and proceed to do whatever God places in your heart, but be certain that your actions are 100% consistent with Scripture. God will never lead you to act contrary to His written Word: We do not serve a God of confusion, but of order and peace** ( 1 Corinthians 14:33).

It is important to know that if you are praying in accordance with God's will and you are not seeing the manifestation, a few things could be happening: (1) it is not God's timing yet, and He wants you to grow so you can better handle and appreciate the blessing; (2) other people might be involved, and God may be doing a work in their hearts; (3) demonic hindrances could be in operation. If you are unsure why your prayer(s) is not answered, simply ask God for wisdom on how to proceed, and patiently wait for His response and direction. Every Christian, including myself, goes through this praying and waiting period in our journey with God. Personally, there are many things that I have been praying for, and I am still waiting for the manifestation; I am resting and trusting God's timing, I recommend you do likewise.

*Perseverance in Prayer*

This is a major factor in prayer, because God does not operate according to our timetable. Most of us do not like this, including myself, but this is something I am getting accustomed to. In my own life, there are things that I had prayed in accordance with God's will; and it took a few years to see the manifestation, and all the while, I stood in faith and never gave up. Those who inherit the promises of God have learned the art of perseverance or long suffering, which does not come naturally to human beings; it requires practice.

The Bible teaches about the importance of persevering in our faith (Hebrews 10:19-39; James 1:12; Romans 12:12). God is not mocked, when you persevere in faith, in due time, you will see the manifestation of the promise if you do not give up (Galatians 6:9), because God will always reward faith and tenacity. So while waiting for the manifestation, seek wisdom for direction. Besides, your spirit already knows the truth (1 John 2: 20-21), so pray for God to reveal it to you, and ask Him to redirect your prayer(s) as necessary while persevering. The Lord Jesus, your perfect example, exhibited much perseverance in His prayer life (Luke 6:12).

*Expectancy in Prayer*

I have already discussed how the Bible teaches that when

we pray according to God's will, we should be confident to see the manifestation (1 John 5:14). Expectancy brings into play another dimension: hope. When you are hopeful about the physical manifestation of your prayers, it helps you to endure, and it will edify you and foster growth in your relationship with God. **Biblically, hope is a person "Jesus Christ," thus your hope is based on known realities (the promises of Christ Jesus), rather than just an uncertain "wishing and a hoping" like the unbelievers do.** Hence, as a Christian, be hopeful and expectant! Unfortunately, there are those who pray, but do not even expect the results; in such cases, I have often wondered why they even bothered to pray in the first place. Be expectant whenever you pray, because it helps in releasing your faith.

## *Praying unceasingly*

Prayer is not something you do on special occasions only. Rather, the Bible teaches us to pray unceasingly (1 Thessalonians 5:16-18; Philippians 4:6; Ephesians 6:18; Colossians 4:2, etc). Praying unceasingly means you pray throughout the day: while driving, with your eyes open; while doing house chores; while at work, etc. In essence, prayer should become a routine part of everything you do. God does not want us to come to Him just on special occasions; He wants to be in constant fellowship with us, just like He was with Christ Jesus. Once you make it a habit of talking to God about everything throughout your day, just like you would with a close friend, you will be pleased how He will guide and comfort you moment-by-moment.

As an example, I talk to God throughout the day (which is praying unceasingly), regardless of how small the issue might be, and usually, at the end of my day when I reflect on how the day went, I am often amazed how I am able to discern how God had guided me throughout that day. Doing this encourages me, and makes me to appreciate my relationship with God much more, and most importantly, it causes me to be God dependent, which is what I want. I recommend you try it, you will not be disappointed. Praying unceasingly does not mean that you cannot set apart special times for lengthier prayers: you can. It is okay to spend "special moments" with God in lengthier prayers as you are led, but a moment- by-moment communication with God is essential, and is the best, in my opinion.

*Humility in Prayer*

Humbling yourself before God is essential as you approach Him in prayer. God Himself is humble (Philippians 2:5-8; Psalm 113:5-6; Isaiah 57:15), and this humility was well evident in the ministry of Christ Jesus. The Bible is clear how God hates pride and honors humility (Proverbs 6:16-19; Proverbs 8:13; Psalm 147:6, etc). **Never go to God in prayer and boast about all of your good works, and as such expect Him to bless you for that. God does not owe you anything; He loves you because love is His nature** (1 John 4:8). You can be certain that God will never bless pride and arrogance.

In the Gospel of Luke chapter 18, the Lord Jesus taught about self-righteousness (pride) and humility, using examples of two types of individuals who approached God in prayer: (1) the Pharisee (arrogant); and (2) the Tax Collector (humble). The Pharisee was so full of pride and when he was praying, he was arrogantly putting down others; but the tax collector, in humility, was afraid to even approach God because he acknowledged he was a sinner (vv. 9-13). The Lord concluded the story by saying that the Tax Collector was the one who received the blessing from God. Here is how the Lord Jesus concluded the teaching about humility in prayer:

*"... "I tell you that this man, rather than the other, went home justified before God. For all those who exalt themselves will be humbled, and those who humble themselves will be exalted"* (v. 14), (emphasis author's).

As you humble yourself and ask God for help, He will answer. Here is what He says in 2nd Chronicles chapter 7: *"if my people, who are called by my name, will humble themselves and pray and seek my face and turn from their wicked ways, then I will hear from heaven, and I will forgive their sin and will heal their land"* (v. 14), (emphasis author's). Are you ready to humble yourself before God in prayer?

*Praying in the name of the Lord Jesus is powerful and essential, in order for our prayers to be heard by God. But there is one catch to this: you must believe in Christ Jesus and in His redemptive work for this to be effective for you. Just ending a prayer with the name of Jesus does not mean that God will answer, especially, if you do not have genuine faith in Him.*

## Praying in the Name of Jesus Christ

Christ Jesus has overcome sin, death and the grave. He rose from the dead and is alive; He has been exalted and is currently seated at the right hand of God, interceding for us, His followers (Mark 16:19; Acts 7:55; Romans 8:34; Ephesians 1:20). The Bible teaches that every knee shall bow at the name of Christ Jesus (Philippians 2:10). The Lord Himself said: *"All authority in heaven and on earth has been given to me"* (Matthew 28:18), (emphasis author's). And in John 14, Jesus taught that when we pray in His name, He will honor our prayers, so God would be glorified (vv. 13-14).

So, It is obvious that **praying in the name of the Lord Jesus is powerful and essential, in order for our prayers to be heard by God. But there is one catch to this: you must believe in Christ Jesus and in His redemptive work for this to be effective for you. Just ending a prayer with the name of Jesus does not mean that God will answer, especially, if you do not have genuine faith in Him.** As an example, the Pseudo-Christian cults, such as the Jehovah's Witnesses and the Mormons can pray in the name of Jesus, but they deny His Deity (refusing to acknowledge that Jesus is God). Thus, based on their own false teachings of Christ Jesus, they are not His true followers. And the Lord said whoever rejects Him, rejects His Father, God (Matthew 10:33). Also, just ending a prayer in the name of Jesus does not automatically guarantee results, especially, if you are praying outside of God's will, and all of the key ingredients of an effective prayer listed above are not in operation when you pray.

**Other Recommendations For Your prayer Life:**

- ❖ You can pray anywhere, and at any time of the day, whenever you are led or desire to do so (Genesis 24:11-12; Acts 16:13; Psalm 63:6, etc).

- ❖ The length of your prayer does not determine the results. God answers short and lengthy prayers alike. Rather, God is after the sincerity of your heart when you pray. As an example, shouting HELP, in the name of Jesus is a very valid and powerful prayer, if prayed in faith and sincerity. In the Gospel account, the Lord Jesus prayed to calm the storm by simply saying: "Quiet! Be still!" And the wind died down and was completely calmed" ( Mark 4:39).

❖ You do not have to change your tone or sound very spiritual to impress others and God when you pray. Just pray to God as you normally talk; He is after your heart, and not after your sound or impressive speech.

❖ You can pray aloud (Ezekiel 11:13), or in silence (1 Samuel 1:13). Praying aloud has the added advantage that you will hear yourself. Since faith comes by hearing the Word of God, when you hear yourself praying God's Word aloud in faith, it will strengthen you.

❖ Your position when you pray is not as significant to God. God is not after the right or correct posture; rather, the purity and sincerity of your heart is what He will look at. Nonetheless, the Bible teaches about various positions when praying, such as kneeling, Ezra 9:5; standing, Nehemiah 9:5; sitting, 2 Samuel 7:18; lying prostrate, Matthew 26:39; hands lifted upwards, 1st Timothy 2:8; bowing, Exodus 34:8.

❖ You can pray alone (Matthew 6:6), or together with others (Matthew 18:20), as a church (Acts 4:23-31; ), in public (1 Corinthians 14:1-7), or as a family ( Acts 10:2).

It would be incomplete to close a chapter on prayer without talking on the subject of unanswered prayers. There are several reasons why a person's prayer may not be answered. Based on the key ingredients necessary for an effective prayer life as discussed above, I am sure you can easily discern why some of your prayers have not been answered.

**Personally, I believe that all prayers are answered by God: It is either Yes, No or Wait. A No, is a great answer, because**

**God loves you so much and He would not want to bless you with the least or with what is not best for you, in His wisdom.** I am so blessed for all of the times God had said No to me, because as I look back now, had God answered some of my selfish and thoughtless prayers, it would have brought much pain and suffering into my life.

There are other times when God had said Yes to my prayers, and then, I had realized it was not what I wanted after all. In those situations, I had quickly realized that, that answered prayer was God's permissive will for me, and not His perfect will, which is what I want. In such cases, I had quickly repented and asked Him for wisdom. I recommend that you change your perspective on how you respond when you do not receive the manifestation of your prayer; It could be a blessing in disguise.

## Major Reasons for Unanswered Prayers

There is a popular saying that "God's delays are not His denials"; this is very true, to the extent that you are praying in accordance with His will, and are including the key ingredients of an effective prayer discussed above. For purposes of clarification, below are some reasons that your prayers may be delayed or not answered at all. Below, are also some major reasons that some people often ignore or forget, as to why they do not see the manifestation they desire when they pray.

*Living in Sin*

The Bible is clear that when you are practicing sin, you sever your relationship with God, and He will not even listen to your prayer. The solution is simply a heart-felt repentance and restoration

*In God's view, sin is sin, non-negotiable, period! There are no big or little sins, the consequences are the same: unanswered prayers, and separation from God's favor and blessings.*

of the relationship. There are many people who do not regard this advice. I have ministered to many Christians who are outright practicing sin with no intention to stop, and they are deceived and erroneously thinking that they are not hurting anyone. Some of these Christians living in sin and disobedience are grossly deceived into thinking that because God loves them, He will answer their prayers regardless, which is a lie from the pit of hell, from the devil himself. You cannot manipulate God's love to get what you want, it does not work like this! (I discuss more of this in chapters 12 and 13).

**It is true that God loves everyone, even those who are practicing sin because His nature is love, but He will never approve such a lifestyle; and He will not bless anyone who is living contrary to His Word, because He will never contradict Himself nor His Word.** You must stop practicing sin and repent, before you can receive God's blessings and favor. If you believe your life is being blessed while living in sin, I can guarantee you that it is not God who is blessing you. It could just be your hard work or a disguised pseudo blessing from the devil in order to keep you in bondage. Remember, the Bible teaches that sin is pleasurable for a season (Hebrews 11:24-25), so do not be deceived, it [sin] will "catch-up" with you, and you will be miserable! And the Bible teaches that your sins will be exposed, eventually (Numbers 32:23); so, please STOP sinning against God who loves you!

Sin can be as subtle as unforgiveness ( Matthew 6:14-15), bitterness, hatred, etc, towards others, or it could be overt sins such as lying, gossiping, sexual immorality, stealing, laziness, etc. For those of you who are unsure, sexual immorality in God's eyes include having sex outside of marriage (whether or not it is with the same person), homosexuality, lesbianism, pornography, and all the various perverse forms of sex in the world today. **In God's view, sin is sin, non-negotiable, period! There are no big or little sins, the consequences are the same: unanswered prayers, and separation from God's favor and blessings. I want to clarify that if you are a genuine follower of the Lord Jesus, practicing sin will not prevent you from going to heaven, but you will get there sooner, because sin leads to death! You get the point?**

*Praying Outside of God's Will*

I have already discussed this topic to my satisfaction. If you are still unsure, I recommend you go back and reread this chapter. Suffice it to say that God has limited Himself to only answer your prayer according to His will, as expressed in His Word. And there is nothing you can do to change this, so accept this in faith and humility. This is not because God does not want you to enjoy certain things, but He loves you to the extent that He wants to only bless you with the best. A lot of times, we do not have the wisdom and foreknowledge to know the outcome of things we are praying for. But God, in His omniscience (i.e., all knowing nature), sees our present and future in a "snapshot," and He knows best what will be beneficial to us long term. So learn to accept and rest with this Truth about God.

## Wrong Motives

If your motives or intentions are wrong when you pray, God will not answer (James 4:3). By wrong motives, I am referring to ungodly, selfish, and lustful desires. God will not answer such prayers, thereby enabling your carnality and contributing to your self-harm; only Satan does something like that. If God were to answer such prayers, it would destroy you; so in His love, He simply says: NO! That way, you would grow out of it, if you are willing.

As an illustration, there are people who are praying and believing God for a beautiful home that may cost about six hundred thousand dollars ($600,000, USD) just to "show-off," which is pride and selfishness; yet, they cannot care for the three hundred thousand dollars ($300,000, USD) Condominium or Town Home they currently own. If God were to answer their prayers and bless them with a six hundred thousand dollar home, it will: (1) encourage their pride, which will be against God's nature; and (2) it will ruin them, because they will not be able to manage it, hence it will lead to much suffering. **Much more, God is in the business of blessing us and alleviating our suffering, and not in the business of initiating or promoting misery.**

## Doubting

Doubting God's promises can engender unbelief which is sin. Whenever you doubt the promises of God, you can be certain that you will encounter difficulty receiving from Him (James 1:6). God is very good and compassionate towards us. So if you are sincerely doubting some of His promises as expressed in His Word due to ignorance or wrong teaching, in His love, He will still be revealing Himself to you, and may even place others in your path to help you. But, if you know the Truths in His Word, and you are in disobedience and are willfully refusing to believe in Him, your doubting will definitely hinder your prayers from manifesting.

If you are struggling with doubt, I recommend you go back and reread the section of this book about overcoming doubt, and refer to the endnotes at the end of this book for further resources to assist you in this area. This is critical, so address this promptly, lest you will allow Satan to steal from you.

## Disobedience

When you live in disobedience, your prayers will go unanswered ( Proverbs 28:9). Disobedience is not necessarily sin, but it will hinder your prayers. For example, if God is instructing you, as clearly seen in His Word, to do some particular thing, such as forgiving someone, and you are not obeying, your actions of disobedience will be considered a sin, and it will prevent the manifestation of your prayers.

Another good example is in the area of finances. It is clear in God's Word that we should give and support churches and ministries that are furthering His Kingdom on the earth. And there are many Christians who are blessed by many churches and faithful ministries who are faithfully teaching them how to grow in the faith, yet some of these Christians refuse to support the ministries or churches with their finances; this is outright disobedience, and a major hindrance to your prosperity, favor and blessings from God. It is not the nature of God to bless or honor disobedience, period! Think about this for a minute: If God were to bless you while in disobedience, you will not mature in your relationship with Him, and that will hurt you long term. So in His love, God wants you to start trusting and obeying Him and to grow up!

*Pride*

I have already discussed why pride will hinder your prayers. Thus, you would be very wise to ask God to help you overcome this destructive emotion, if you are struggling with this sin, lest you cause more problems for yourself (Proverbs 16:19). Pride in God's eyes is also elevating yourself above others, such as your spouse, the poor, weak, illiterate, etc. Instead, the Bible teaches that we should humble ourselves and esteem others ( Philippians 2:3).

*Wrong Timing*

I have already discussed the issue of wrong timing. But suffice it to say that God works on His own timetable and not ours. So not seeing the manifestation of your prayer does not imply that it will not come to pass. As mentioned previously, if you are praying in accordance with God's will and all of the key ingredients of an effective prayer are in operation, rest (abide in Christ, stay focused) in the Lord; the manifestation will come, in His timing. The process of waiting for the manifestation of your prayer will yield great dividends, if you do not easily give up. God is patient and long-suffering, so keep in mind that whenever you have to endure in prayer, you will be allowing Him to shape and mold you into the image of Christ Jesus (Romans 8:28-29), which is God's ultimate plan for all of us, so waiting is good!

In conclusion, as Christians, we have a privilege that many others on the earth do not enjoy: the ability to talk directly to the

Creator of the heavens and the earth, who knows each of us by name, and wants to speak personally to us. True Christianity is the only faith in the world that has this personal relationship with the Only True God of the Bible. Therefore, approach your prayer life seriously; as it is quite an honor and a gift, because of the sacrifice of Christ Jesus: we are indeed blessed!

With so much discussion about prayer, I hope you now have a better understanding of this very complex topic. I now turn the discussion to another very relevant aspect of your relationship with God: His Church, with Christ Jesus in the center, and the presence of the Holy Spirit working in and through the Church.

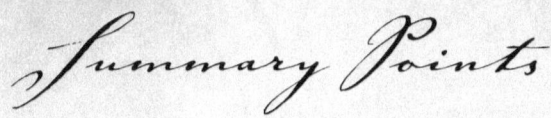

# Summary Points

- The primary purpose for prayer is to ask God for the manifestation of His will on the earth and in the life of the believer;

- A good way to be assured your prayers will be answered is to pray in accordance with God's will, as expressed in His Word;

- God is after the purity or sincerity of our hearts when we pray, and not after the length or eloquence of our prayers;

- An effective prayer can be as simple as shouting: HELP, in the name of Jesus;

- There is power and authority in the name of Jesus, who intercedes for us when we pray, but the prerequisite is that, we must have faith in Him [Christ];

- Some key ingredients for an effective prayer include, but are not limited to: faith in God's promises; correct motives; perseverance; praying in accordance with God's will; humility, etc;

- Some reasons for unanswered prayer or a delayed response to your prayers include, but are not limited to: wrong motives, wrong timing, praying outside of God's will, practicing sin, living in disobedience, etc;

- God always answers our prayers with either a NO; YES; or a Delayed response, which are all great responses in His wisdom.

Chapter 10

# KNOW THE BASIC TENETS OF THE CHURCH

The English word "Church" is a transliteration (i.e., the translation of a word from one language to another) from the Greek word: ekklésia, referring to an assembly, congregation or simply a group of people. With regards to Christianity, a church refers to a gathering of true believers who have placed their faith in Christ Jesus and as such, have a relationship with God the Father, and have been sealed by the Holy Spirit and baptized into the body of Christ (which is the Universal Church). The body of Christ refers to all those who have genuinely accepted to follow Christ Jesus as their Lord and Savior ( true Christians), regardless of their location in the world or denominational preference.

Christ Jesus is the cornerstone and the head of the church (Colossians 1:18; Ephesians 5:23). In Christianity, a church is not defined by the number of members. A true Bible believing Christ-centered church can be as small as two people, or as large as thousands of people; it does not matter, because the Lord will be in their midst (Matthew 18:20). This gathering of believers can take place in an individual's home, or in a building outside of the home; it does not matter, it will still be considered a church.

There are three main branches of true Christianity: (1) Roman Catholics ; (2) Orthodox; (3) and Protestants. In God's view, there is just one Universal Church: the "body of Christ," although we currently have different branches and denominations. Please note that this division or different branches of the faith was not initiated by God, but by human beings, due to various differences in certain theological expressions of the faith. So be assured that this division is not God's will for the Church.

After the ascension of the Lord Jesus, there was just one Universal Church for all Christians, which started in the first Century, as noted in the book of Acts in the Bible. But the initial division of the Church came about around the 10th Century AD, when the Orthodox church separated from the Roman Catholics. Then, around the 15th Century AD, the Protestant movement began after a former Roman Catholic Priest, called Martin Luther, protested against certain Roman Catholic beliefs, rituals, and Man-made doctrines which were inconsistent with the Holy Scripture. This protest led to the birth of the Protestant branch of the Church.

With the Protestant movement came thousands of Protestant denominations, with over 4000 in existence currently. By the printing of this book, it is likely that more Protestant denominations will have emerged. It is beyond the scope of this book to provide details about the various reasons for the Church division, etc. Suffice it to say that, in heaven there is just one Universal Church — those who

*Unfortunately, there are thousands of people who will die and go to hell because they were counting on church membership as their ticket to heaven. If you are unsure where you belong: visible or invisible church, please settle this matter today, right now, by accepting to genuinely follow the Lord Jesus.*

have sincerely placed their faith in the redemptive work of the Lord Jesus.

I have repeatedly emphasized throughout this book that belonging to a local church or regular church attendance will never convert a person into Christianity: A person must be born again to be a true follower of the Lord Jesus. **In this life, we have the <u>visible church</u>, referring to all those who physically attend church and profess to be Christians; then, there is the <u>invisible church</u>, referring to all those who also attend church, but are true followers of the Lord Jesus: only God knows the heart. Unfortunately, there are thousands of people who will die and go to hell because they were counting on church membership as their ticket to heaven. If you are unsure where you belong: visible or invisible church, please settle this matter today, right now, by accepting to genuinely follow the Lord Jesus.**

God is very concerned about counterfeit Christians in the church as evidenced by the Lord's warning in Matthew 13. In this teaching, the Lord Jesus warned that His true followers and counterfeits coexist in this present world and in the church. As such, it may be difficult for us, as finite humans, to tell the difference between the two, but in His second coming, He will separate them (vv. 24-30). Again, if you are one of these people, meaning, a counterfeit Christian (i.e., you attend church regularly but you have not accepted Jesus Christ as your personal Lord and Savior), I highly recommend that you humbly repent and make a genuine confession of faith to follow the Lord Jesus. If you wait until you die, it will be too late.

Let me give you an idea of how you can tell if you are just a church attendee and not a genuine follower of Jesus Christ: if you are uncertain or unsure whether or not there was a point in your life that you asked Christ to come into your life, I recommend you do an honest self-evaluation! Right now! You might have been going to church all of your life, but have never asked the Lord Jesus to come into your life; if that is the case, ask Him right now, and He will! This is so important because asking Jesus to come into your life is such a momentous event that most people will remember a point in their life when that decision was made.

That decision to follow Christ is a "second birthday" and most people do not forget that moment in their life, just like they would not forget the date, month, and/or year of their physical birthday. Even those who have attended church as children reach a point in their lives as adolescents, teenagers or adults, when they personally would ask Jesus to come into their life as their Lord and Savior! So, again, if you are unsure, invite Jesus into your life, right now, and settle this matter once and for all!

> *The Jehovah's Witnesses and the Mormons are not a part of the true body of Christ, because they deny the true doctrines of true Christianity as expressed in the Bible.*

**<u>A word of caution</u> is necessary here: The Jehovah's Witnesses and the Mormons are not a part of the true body of Christ, because they deny the true doctrines of true Christianity as expressed in the Bible. Furthermore, they reject the Deity of Christ Jesus and His essential teachings, and they profess that He [Jesus Christ] was a "created human being," which is absolutely false because Christ Jesus called Himself God, who always existed and is eternal.** The Lord Jesus was very clear that if anyone rejects Him as God, He will also reject them before His Father, God (Matthew 10:33), and the Bible is very clear that whosoever rejects the Lord Jesus also rejects God the Father (1 John 2:23).

Much more, the Bible teaches that if anyone rejects the Lord Jesus as God in the flesh, that person is an antichrist, and will not inherit the Kingdom of God (1 John 4:3). So the very doctrines of the Jehovah's Witnesses and the Mormons are contrary to those of the Lord Jesus. Thus, their own teachings and beliefs speak volumes, as they reject themselves as true followers of the Lord. These are not judgmental statements, but are statements of Truths, based on the teachings of Christ and His Word, hence I am making a righteous evaluation here.

As Christians, God has called each of us to speak His Truths in love, with hopes of giving individuals the opportunity to choose wisely, because only the Truths of God will set people free. Thus, knowing the major, absolute and essential core beliefs of true Christianity is necessary in detecting a counterfeit church or individual.

## The Essential Doctrines of True Christianity

The best way to detect a counterfeit is not to study the hundreds of counterfeits out there; that would be humanly impossible to do, since there are too many. Rather, by becoming extremely familiar with the real thing, in this case, God's Truths, you will be able to easily detect a "phony." The Bible teaches that people perish due to a lack of knowledge (Hosea 4:6), thus knowing the essential doctrines of the faith is critical to your relationship with God through Christ.

There are hundreds of relevant doctrines taught in the Bible which the Universal Christian Church espouses, such as the doctrine of baptisms, giving, eschatology (end times), prayer, worship, etc, but all of these are not pertinent to your salvation and eternal security. <u>First things firsts</u> — you must be grounded in the essentials, which, depending on your decision, will either send you to heaven or hell. Then, as you grow in the Lord, you will become familiar, and hopefully grounded, in the various other doctrines taught in the Bible, which are absolutely necessary for your growth and proper relationship with God.

Below, I briefly discuss, in no particular order, the non-negotiable essential doctrines of true Christianity pertaining to your salvation and eternal security. Because I have already discussed these doctrines throughout this book in passing, I will just mention them here and refer you to previous chapters for details.

✓ *The Deity of Christ*

As true Christians, we believe that the virgin Mary supernaturally became pregnant through the working of the Holy Spirit and gave birth to God Himself in the flesh (i.e., the incarnation), in the person of Christ Jesus. I have already explained throughout this book how the Lord Jesus was 100% God and 100% human being, please refer to chapters 1 and 2 for details. Numerous Scriptures teach us this, but some examples include ( John chapter 1; 5:18; Colossians 2:9; Revelation 1:17–18; Matthew 2:11; 4:10, etc). Other Scriptures that explain the humanity of Jesus Christ include, but are not limited to (Hebrews 4:15 ;Matthew 8:20 ;1 Peter 2:23; John 3:14, etc).

This essential Truth about our Lord Jesus is something that all of His true followers accept by faith, primarily because Christ Jesus called Himself God, and backed it up with verifiable miraculous evidence, which no other human being in the history of the world can refute or has ever come close to performing. Denying the Deity of the Lord Jesus leads to eternal damnation (i.e., hell, which is separation from God in all eternity), Christ Jesus said this Himself (see the Gospels). Sadly, pseudo-Christian cults (i.e., any religious group that distorts the Truths of God as found in the Bible), such as the Jehovah's Witnesses, Mormons, etc, reject this absolute Truth of the Deity of Christ.

✓ *Salvation in the Lord Jesus is Only Because of God's Grace Through Faith*

No human being can ever earn their way into God's Kingdom; you must accept the redemptive work of Christ Jesus on the cross by faith, which God has provided for each one who is willing, because of His infinite love for us (Ephesians 2:8-9). And there is absolutely nothing you can do on your own effort to add or take away from the sacrificial work of Christ. The Jehovah's Witnesses and/or Mormons are teaching that a person has to perform additional works to be accepted by God, which is a lie from Satan. The last words of our Lord Jesus on the cross says it all:

*"Later, knowing that everything had now been finished, and so that*

*Scripture would be fulfilled, Jesus said, "I am thirsty." A jar of wine vinegar was there, so they soaked a sponge in it, put the sponge on a stalk of the hyssop plant, and lifted it to Jesus' lips. When he had received the drink, Jesus said, "It is finished." With that, he bowed his head and gave up his spirit"* (John 19:28-30), (emphasis author's).

**Looking at the Lord's Words (i.e., Scripture) above, how can anyone miss it. It is so clear that, only Satan, working through cults, can deceive people and keep them in such deception**. But today, I have presented this Truth to you, so make a decision for God.

- ✓ *The Atonement of Christ Jesus*

The Hebrew word "Kaphar", means atonement in the English. According to the Strong's Concordance, the word atonement describes an act of reconciliation of the guilty party by divine sacrifice. In the Bible, atonement means to make amends by removing the guilt of a person who has sinned against God. As discussed elsewhere in this book, in the Old Testament, the High Priest offered animal sacrifices for the sins of the people, including his own sin. But the sacrificial death of the Lord Jesus and His resurrection met God's standard of perfection 100%, and paid for the sins of the world plus the penalties for each sin (1 John 2:2).

Animal sacrifice is no longer needed. Which means it is only through Christ Jesus that anyone's sins can be atoned for, thus granting them a relationship with the Only One True God of the heavens and the earth, the God of the Bible. It is rather unfortunate that certain individuals and cults still offer animal sacrifices for their sins; God will never accept that. You either accept the precious blood of the Lord Jesus, or you reject it, no in-between, you must decide, then deal with the consequences of your own choice in this life, and in the life after! Hopefully, you will decide to accept Christ.

✓ *True Christianity is a Monotheistic Faith*

In chapters 1and 3 of this book, I delved into this matter, please refer there for details. But suffice it to say as true Christians, we worship one God in three distinct persons: God the Father, God the Son, and God the Holy Spirit. And the God of the Bible condemns polytheism (see Isaiah 43:10 ;44:6; Exodus 20:3–6).

✓ *The Resurrection of Christ Jesus*

As true Christians, we believe that God the Father rose the Lord Jesus from the dead after three days as prophesied. He is alive, and seated at the right hand of God the Father, interceding on behalf of the Saints, which include all those who have placed their faith in Christ (Acts 2: 29-36; Romans 8:33-34; Hebrews 7:25). Without the resurrection, our faith as Christians and our hope of eternal security is useless. But indeed, Christ Jesus was raised from the dead (1 Corinthians 15: 14-22), and all those whose faith are in Him will also be resurrected on that last day (1 Thessalonians 4:13-20).

✓ *The True Gospel Message of Christ Jesus*

The true Gospel of Christ Jesus is essential in understanding the heart of true Christianity. Distorting the simple but profound Truth of the Gospel message will definitely lead to heresy (false teaching). First Corinthians chapter 15 clearly defines what the Gospel is:

*"Now, brothers and sisters, I want to remind you of the gospel I preached to you, which you received and on which you have taken your stand. By this gospel you are saved, if you hold firmly to the word I preached to you. Otherwise, you have believed in vain. For what I received I passed on to you as of first importance: that Christ died for our sins according to the Scriptures, that he was buried, that he was raised on the third day according to the Scriptures, and that he appeared to Cephas, and then to the Twelve. After that, he appeared to more than five hundred of the brothers and sisters at the same time, most of whom are still living, though some have fallen asleep. Then he appeared to James, then to all the apostles, and last of all he appeared to me also, as to one abnormally born" (vv. 1-8),* (emphasis author's).

Here is what the Bible teaches about anyone proclaiming any other Gospel message apart from the above:

*"But even if we or an angel from heaven should preach a gospel other than the one we preached to you, let them be under God's curse! As we have already said, so now I say again: If anybody is preaching to you a gospel other than what you accepted, let them be under God's curse"* (Galatians 1: 8-9), (emphasis author's).

As you can see from the above Scriptures, denying or distorting the true Gospel message will mean rejecting the entire ministry of the Lord Jesus, which will lead to eternal damnation. Much more, distorting the true Gospel message could potentially hinder the work of the Holy Spirit in convicting unbelievers of their sins. Because, without the true Gospel message being proclaimed, how would an unbeliever hear the good news that Christ died for their sins, thus giving them the opportunity to accept His sacrifice?

The Bible teaches this very important truth about the Gospel in the book of Romans chapter 10. Under the inspiration of the Holy Spirit, the apostle Paul wrote:

*"For there is no difference between Jew and Gentile—the same Lord is Lord of all and richly blesses all who call on him, for, "Everyone who calls on the name of the Lord will be saved." How, then, can they call on the one they have not believed in? And how can they believe in the one of whom they have not heard? And how can they hear without someone preaching to them? And how can anyone preach unless they are sent? As it is written: "How beautiful are the feet of those who bring good news!"* (vv. 12-15), (emphasis authors).

The apostle went on to declare in verse 17: *"So faith comes from hearing, that is, hearing the Good News about Christ"* (New Living Translation), (emphasis authors). Hopefully you can see how critical it is for the correct Gospel message to be proclaimed, and why the Bible condemns anyone who distorts this Truth. This brings up an important issue that is common among many Christians, which is the erroneous belief that a person can pray for an individual to obtain salvation without the Gospel message being proclaimed. This is not possible, because it is not Scriptural!

You cannot pray for someone or anyone to be saved without that person hearing the Gospel message, that will be a wrong prayer. You know why? Because Christ Jesus already died for the sins of the world, including the sins of the friend or loved one you are praying for. Rather, pray a prayer of faith, such as thanking God that He has already died for their sins and loved them more than you do; then ask God to place someone along their path who will proclaim the

Gospel message so that they can hear it, and then make a choice to believe it and decide; individuals must be given a choice to decide!

Or, if the person has been exposed to the Gospel message and is still resisting and rejecting it, pray and ask God to open his or her heart to the Truth, and pray for God to remove the blinders or strongholds in his or her heart from Satan, so that he or she might receive the Truth and decide to follow Christ. Then, trust God to use that seed (Word of God he or she had heard) to convict him or her of their need for a Savior, Christ Jesus. **A person must perceive his or her need for God, and desire to be delivered from his or her ungodly lifestyle before a genuine confession and acceptance to follow the Lord can be made; it has to come from the heart, in order to be a genuine conversion.** And this sincerity to follow Christ cannot be coerced, so be steadfast in prayer, until that conviction happens.

> *A person must perceive his or her need for God, and desire to be delivered from his or her ungodly lifestyle before a genuine confession and acceptance to follow the Lord can be made.*

One of the worst things you can do is to pray for someone who has never heard the Gospel message to become a genuine Christian and be saved. How is that going to happen? And in whom would you want them to believe in? And believe in what? So it is important to refer back to Romans chapter 10 to fully comprehend the necessity for the Gospel message to be proclaimed. Many of you may be wondering about all those people who died before hearing the Gospel message? Or about little children or mentally challenged individuals! Well, there is hope! God is just and He will judge these people fairly. Due to space limitation, I am unable to provide answers to these very important questions in this book, but if you want to study more in this area, we have some resources that will help you. <u>Please refer to the end notes for our 5-Part audio CD teaching titled "True Christianity: The Gospel Message of Jesus Christ," for details</u>.

I remember a gentleman who came to me about a year ago requesting that I pray for his dying father to accept Jesus Christ; his father was battling end stage brain cancer. I asked the gentleman if his father had heard the True Gospel message before, he was unsure. So I asked him if he would be willing to proclaim the Gospel to his dying father, and he told me he was afraid of rejection. I went on to explain to him the necessity of hearing the Gospel message as taught in Romans chapter 10; he was quite surprised, and he agreed to do that once he got home.

When he accepted the truth about the Gospel message, instead of praying for his father, I prayed for the Holy Spirit to enable and strengthen him [the gentleman] with power, in order to proclaim the Gospel to his father without fear of rejection. I also prayed for the Holy Spirit to give him the correct words to say to his father, at the right time. With regards to his fear of rejection, I reassured him that our primary role as Christians is to proclaim the true Gospel message, and totally surrender and trust the Holy Spirit with the outcome.

We are not to worry about the results or the rejection after proclaiming the Gospel. As much as we want everyone to be saved once we proclaim the Gospel message, we are not responsible for what happens in their hearts, that is God's job. We must learn to rest and trust Him [God] with the results. The Bible teaches that when the true Gospel is proclaimed, signs and wonders, such as people accepting Christ, will follow, so we must learn to trust that (e.g., see the Gospels, book of Acts). Also, remember that people may not accept Christ in front of you, they may do that later, when alone, away from your presence. So just proclaim the Gospel and trust God with the results. It is only when we get to heaven, when we will find out exactly how many people we took with us.

This gentleman I was ministering to was so strengthened and encouraged as he left my presence. Likewise, when you have an opportunity to proclaim the Gospel, pray for strength, direction and the right words or approach to take, then step out in faith and proclaim the good news, rather than sitting around and praying for someone to be saved who has never heard the Gospel. You have to plant the seed first (the Gospel message), then fertilize it with your prayers, Amen!

Regrettably, many world religions have rejected the essential doctrines of true Christianity outright - which is considered blasphemy (i.e., rejecting the conviction of the Holy Spirit), and the Lord taught that blasphemy is the only unpardonable sin (Matthew 12:31). Nonetheless, there is always hope for repentance as long as a person is still alive. So, if you have been rejecting the Lord Jesus, today is an opportunity for you to accept Him and receive life.

*Wrong doctrines will definitely lead to wrong perceptions about God, which will in turn lead to wrong expectations, lifestyle practices, and much frustration and the inability to enjoy the abundant life Christ died for us to enjoy.*

Many people unfortunately reject the Lord Jesus due to wrong doctrine (i.e., teaching) about His True identity. **Wrong doctrines will definitely lead to wrong perceptions about God, which will in turn lead to wrong expectations, lifestyle practices, and much frustration and the inability to enjoy the abundant life Christ died for us to enjoy.** The primary way to learn these doctrines is directly from the Bible, and much teaching from your local church; which is why belonging to a local church is necessary.

Because the Godhead is living on the inside of each true Christian, we do not only have to worship God in a physical building called church or in other similar gatherings: we can do that anywhere and at any time. The Bible also teaches that we are to become a living epistle (meaning a book to be read by all), in order to reflect God's glory to the world (2 Corinthians 3:2), and attract others to Him and to His Church (the body of Christ).

Because the Triune God indwells every true Christian who represents the Church to the world, many Christians are regrettably not members of a local church, citing the excuse that they can worship God outside of a physical building. While this is true, the Bible admonishes us not to forsake the assembly (church) of believers (Hebrews 10: 23-25). So by belonging to a local church, you will be obeying God's will. So what is the purpose of a church, you might be wondering? This is an excellent question, and the answer might be different from what you think! Let us examine this issue further.

## Purpose(s) of the Church

The purpose(s) of the Church (referring to all true Christian churches globally, i.e., the Universal Church) are varied, and include to:

- **Worship God**: Although each Christian can worship God at their convenience and at any time individually, the Bible encourages and offers multiple examples of worshipping God as a group (corporal worship). An intricate part of this includes praying together as a Church (see the book of Acts).

- **Proclaim the Gospel**: It is the primary responsibility of the church to proclaim the Gospel message of Christ Jesus to the dying world (i.e., evangelism). Each individual Christian also has this responsibility as well, according to the Lord Jesus ( Matthew 28:18-20). Part of this responsibility includes sending out missionaries across the world for purposes of helping the underprivileged, and in turn, proclaiming and spreading the Gospel.

- **Grow Spiritually in Doctrinal Truth**: A major purpose of the church is to teach new and mature followers of the Lord Jesus the correct biblical truths, in order to prevent them from falling into error, counterfeit teachings and various bogus philosophies of Men, thereby preventing them from falling into the hands of false teachers (2 Timothy 2:1–2; Ephesians 4:12; Matthew 28:18-20). The church ought to do this by equipping them (i.e., teaching and discipleship) with biblical Truths, and preparing them for good service for God through Christ. Notwithstanding, each Christian has the responsibility of studying the Truths found in the Scripture for themselves, thereby positioning themselves to easily discern counterfeits.

- **Offer Fellowship**: The Webster Dictionary defines fellowship as a friendly relationship among individuals who share similar interest or feelings. The church can provide the ideal environment for its members to fellowship, share into each other's lives, and grow spiritually as a team. True biblical fellowship is not a casual "get together for coffee," but offers biblical teachings, sharing of testimonies for the benefit and edification of others, praying, worshipping of God, etc, and eating, if necessary.

- **Support its Members**: Another purpose of the church is to support its members with their various emotional and physical needs, such as financial, counseling in various matters pertaining to living godly lives, etc; in addition to providing a forum whereby members could use their respective God given gifts and "callings" (i.e., specific vocations) to help others.

- **Support its Community**: A significant purpose of the church is to support its immediate communities. This include getting involved in things such as prison ministry, elder ministry, local school programs, etc, and making a positive spiritual impact in other surrounding businesses, schools, homes, etc. In an ideal world, a neighborhood which has a local church should experience less crimes, and enjoy much prosperity and tranquility.

- **Unity in Christ**: One purpose of the church is to foster unity in Christ and adherence to His teachings among the believers. Part of this involves providing a Christ-like leadership team for members to emulate. Such leadership will enforce church discipline as taught by Christ (Matthew 18:15–17;1 Peter 5:1–3), thus avoiding much contention, division and factions in the local church.

> *One of the biggest problems present in some churches today is the unfortunate reality that the ministry of the Holy Spirit has been quenched, due to various unbiblical erroneous teachings, as such, they are attempting to operate in their own power, which is futile.*

While some of you may perceive the above purposes as not realistic; it is indeed, with the help of the Holy Spirit, who is ever present in every Christ-centered church globally. **One of the biggest problems present in some churches today is the unfortunate reality that the ministry of the Holy Spirit has been quenched, due to various unbiblical erroneous teachings, as such, they are attempting to operate in their own power, which is futile.** The Lord Jesus is very clear about this: He said apart from Him, we, as individuals, and/or a church, can accomplish nothing (John 15:5).

Now that you understand the major purpose(s) of the church, I present below some major reasons why belonging to a local church is beneficial.

## PRACTICAL APPLICATION

**Some Godly Reasons For Belonging to a Local Church:**

Church attendance in and of itself is not sufficient, although it helps. However, becoming a member of a local church is God's will for each of His children. Below are some of the reasons:

- **It is a Step of Obedience**: When you become a genuine member of a local church, it pleases God, because it is a step of obedience. God wants you to enjoy the benefits of your salvation, which often involves others in the body of Christ. Besides, the Lord Jesus Himself and all of the apostles attended their local synagogue (i.e., place of worship or church) frequently as recorded in the Gospel accounts, book of Acts and other epistles in the New Testament. So modeling their examples will be pleasing to God.

- **To Worship God with Fellow Christians**: God is always pleased whenever you worship Him in Spirit and in Truth (John 4:24). This means, you can worship God anywhere because as a Spirit, He is always present with you everywhere and at all times. And you worship Him in Truth because of the sincerity of heart, in accordance with His written Words. Each of us can, and should worship God individually, and we will still bless God and receive His blessings from the experience. Nonetheless, worshipping God as a group or as a body of believers in a church setting has its own special anointing and manifestation of God's presence.

- **To Fellowship with Like-Minded Christians:** Belonging to a local church will foster fellowship with your fellow brothers and sisters in Christ, possibly leading to Christ-centered meaningful relationships that would be difficult to find in the world with unbelievers. God knows that when you fellowship with your brethren (other brothers and sisters in Christ), you will be edified and encouraged in the faith, which pleases Him. It is absolutely essential to surround yourself with other like-minded believers who can stand with you while believing in God's promises, and offer spiritual support during those "tough" times when it appears as if nothing is working.

You cannot live the Christian life in a "vacuum;" all alone, that will not be God's will for you. Other benefits of fellowship include: (a) sharing your testimonies with others while listening and learning from their testimonies as well; (b) offering accountability, whereby your fellow brethren can quickly correct you in love and grace if you start slipping into sin, or when your actions are inconsistent with the faith; (c) sharing Scriptural truths and revelations with others and bouncing off ideas as you grow in your relationship with the Lord; and (d) the possibilities for other out of church networking. Your fellow Christians can introduce you to individuals or organizations outside of your church who may provide opportunities for a new job, career, etc, plus much more.

In a perfect world, fellowshipping with other brethren would foster such Christ-centered relationships whereby everyone would profit, and God would be pleased. But unfortunately, we live in a "fallen" imperfect world, with individuals in the church whose hearts are not genuine, so you have to apply godly wisdom in any relationship with your fellow "Christian." Because counterfeit Christians are currently coexisting with genuine believers in the body of Christ ( Matthew 13:24-30), keep in mind as you fellowship, that not everyone in the church is a genuine follower of the Lord Jesus.

- **To Support Your Local Church:** Without Christians supporting their local churches with their finances, prayers, attendance, gifts and talents, their churches will struggle to carry out God's specific will for them, because most of the time, God desires to work through the members in the church. The Bible teaches that each of us has been blessed with a unique gift for purposes of benefitting others in the body of Christ. Ideally, your local church should provide the forum for you to use your gifts, in order to mold and shape them for the betterment of the body of Christ. Some people are blessed with gifts of administration, singing, helps, teaching, leadership, etc ( 1 Peter 4:10; Romans 12:6-8; Ephesians 4: 10-14). Without volunteering to serve, some of the positions in the local church would be vacant, and you would miss the opportunity to grow in your gift.

Additionally, the church has to pay its staff, electricity, support the poor, etc. Thus without your financial support, the church will not be able to meet its financial obligations and help the underprivileged in the world and in the body of Christ. Furthermore, there are thousands of non-church members who walk into hundreds of local churches daily, needing financial help, perishable foods, etc; thus, the church relies on your financial support to truly function.

Most importantly, the pastoral staff needs the continuous prayers from church members as they step out in faith to accomplish God's will for their respective churches.

With the aforementioned purposes of the church and reasons to belong to a local church, it is necessary to briefly mention <u>some reasons not to attend or become a member of a church.</u> This might surprise some of you that I would even mention this, but indeed, you would be amazed at some of the ungodly reasons why people actually join a church. Let us examine some of them.

## Some <u>Ungodly Reasons</u> <u>Not to</u> Belong to a Church

I discuss these primarily to warn you, **not to use them as** *reasons to join a church.*

- ○ **To Go to Heaven**

<u>Having a relationship with the Lord Jesus is what takes you to heaven and not church membership.</u> *<u>I have explained throughout this book that church membership will not save you or take you to heaven; you must be born again and become a genuine follower of Christ Jesus</u>*. While attending church will hopefully expose you to the Gospel of Christ Jesus (i.e., depending on whether or not the local church actually preaches the true Gospel), you still have to independently ask Christ to come into your life as your Lord and Savior. This is critical because there are many churches, unfortunately, who do not even proclaim the True Gospel of Christ. <u>Once you become a genuine follower of Jesus Christ, then, as I have already explained, attending church is necessary.</u>

- **To Assuage Your Guilty Conscience**

    I have heard of many stories about people who commit heinous crimes during the week, then attend church on Sundays, and give large amounts of money to the church in order to "feel good" about themselves. **You cannot buy God's love or forgiveness. No amount of giving or church attendance will cleanse you from your sins, guilt-ridden conscience, deceits or lies: you have to completely stop the sin, and genuinely repent in the name of the Lord Jesus, then He will forgive, accept and sustain you with His Truth and peace.**

- **To Please Others**

    There are those who "play church," by regularly attending church in order to impress others about their godliness, which is an affront to God. You can deceive others, including yourself, but you cannot deceive God, who sees you inside and out, and knows your thoughts (1 Samuel 16:7; Jeremiah 17:10). Anyone who does this is a "fool," in my opinion, because he or she is joking with their eternity: this is a matter of life or death, heaven or hell, so if you are doing this, please STOP! Repent and accept Christ Jesus as your personal Lord and Savior.

- **To Deal with Loneliness**

    Many people join a church for purposes of fellowship because they are lonely. While fellowshipping for the right reasons as discussed above are godly, it is rather horrible to join a church primarily for this reason. Church membership, attendance and fellowship will not take away your loneliness, or provide you with what you can only receive from God. Only God can occupy that "empty place" in your heart, thereby replacing the loneliness with a purpose, when you genuinely accept Christ Jesus as your Lord and Savior. In addition, **you cannot experience the fruit of a relationship with Christ (true meaning in life that transcends your loneliness), without being attached to the root, (having a relationship with God through Christ and abiding in Him).**

> *You cannot experience the fruit of a relationship with Christ (true meaning in life that transcends your loneliness), without being attached to the root, (having a relationship with God through Christ and abiding in Him).*

- **To Have their Personal Needs Met**

    Many people go to various churches to beg for money, food, etc. While a church is the right place to receive all of these, it is unfortunate that there are those who abuse the love and kind gifts from churches. If you do this: STOP, and ask Christ Jesus to help you with your needs, rather than manipulating the church. Trust God, and if He wants the church to continue helping you, it will be done with the right motives. The apostle Paul even admonished the Corinthian church members who were attending church services and abusing the meals (see 1 Corinthians), likewise, we should refrain from such behaviors. If you are not a Christian, accept the Lord as your Savior, and He will meet your needs appropriately.

- **To Look For a Spouse**

    This should not be the primary reason to belong to a church. God can still put the right husband or wife in your path outside of the physical building of a church. Whenever I hear a person say they attend church in order to meet their future spouse, it always reveals to me their limited view of God. God can do the impossible! He can orchestrate events in your life to happen in such a way that you can meet your future spouse at a gas station, grocery store, shopping mall, or elsewhere. Nothing is impossible with God!

- **To Deceive the Gullible Christian**

    It is unfortunate that there are many people who are not true Christians, but join a church for ulterior motives. These individuals are wolves disguised in sheep clothing, and at the right opportunity, they will take advantage of the gullible Christian who is easily trusting everyone who attends church (Matthew 7:15). I recommend you use godly wisdom in all of your dealings with anyone in the church. Much more, ask the Holy Spirit to guide you before beginning any sort of business with any church member, or before engaging in any sort of business related activity that makes you vulnerable.

- **To Fulfill their Curiosity**

    **While this may not be a bad reason, I mention it here because I do not want you to be an "outsider" for the rest of your Christian life.** There are Christians who chronically attend church because they are curious! I have often wondered what they are unsure and curious about? In the early stages when you are searching for a local church to join, a genuine curiosity is necessary, but a time must come when you have to make a decision and join a church.

Others are looking for a perfect church. **Regrettably, all of the churches are made up of imperfect people, including the pastor and church leaders, who are all finite human beings seeking God themselves. So the moment you find a "perfect" church and become a member, it will become imperfect because of you, who is not perfect.** So stop the "church hopping," and be grounded in a local church for all of the reasons explained in the preceding section.

> *Regrettably, all of the churches are made up of imperfect people, including the pastor and church leaders, who are all finite human beings seeking God themselves. So the moment you find a "perfect" church and become a member, it will become imperfect because of you, who is not perfect.*

With three branches of true Christianity and thousands of Protestant denominations, some of you may be wondering how to decide on which church to join! This is such a relevant question that deserves an entire book on its own, but I will broach this topic briefly here. Many individuals become members of a local church because their parents attended that particular church, or because their friends go there, or because the music is good. Other reasons I have heard include the mega size of the church, its apparent wealth, appearance, wealthy attendees and members, beautiful women, etc. All of these are not biblical reasons to belong to a church, and as such, will not be beneficial to your spiritual growth.

**God does not bless a church based on its appearance; rather, He blesses a church based on the biblical Truths proclaimed by the church, and their godly services within and above the church building. Thus, a mega church does not necessarily imply that the church is anointed by God.** Unfortunately, some churches attract large crowds and quickly grow into mega churches because they "water down" the Truths found in God's Word (i.e., they do not proclaim the complete Truths), which often attract certain personality types. But with time, sadly, such churches will eventually quench the Holy Spirit, and as such dwindle in membership, because those who are genuinely hungry for God's Truths would quickly realize their lack of spiritual growth and go elsewhere. With that in mind, below are some major questions to keep in mind before joining any church as a member.

## Some Recommendations for Selecting a Local Church

Before you make a final decision regarding which church to join, consider asking the recommended questions below in your research process.

o *Is the Church Christ-Centered?*

By Christ-centered, I mean, do they acknowledge Christ Jesus as their Lord and Savior, the cornerstone, and head of the Universal Church, and in their local church? Is Christ and His teachings elevated and upheld in their local church? The fact that a church has the name Jesus Christ on their bulletin, church website or other informational material does not mean much. Find out if there is any evidence that Christ Jesus is actually the center of the church? This is easy information to know by just visiting the church a few times and being observant. Since you have the Spirit of God indwelling you, He will confirm this knowledge to you when you visit the church, trust Him.

I have been to churches or similar so called "Christian" gatherings whereby during the service, my spirit was distressed (i.e., God was warning me), and I had to depart. Be certain to take some time and invest in the research process before deciding, as there are many pseudo-Christian churches (i.e., cults) that have attached the name of Jesus Christ on their website and informational material, but they do not submit to His teachings, but theirs [which are all Man-made and as such keep people in bondage].

o  *Is it a Bible Believing Church?*

By this, I mean, do they believe in the essential doctrines of true Christianity as espoused in the Bible, and as already explained earlier in this chapter? This is very crucial. You must be absolutely certain about this issue. Also, is the Bible (i.e., the teachings in the Bible) the final authority of the church? Or, is it their church or denominational doctrine that is their authority? I cannot emphasize this issue enough! There are many churches out there that elevate their own doctrines rather than those taught in the Bible; I would not recommend that you join such a church, because the Holy Spirit will be quenched there! Christ Jesus taught that the traditions of men (i.e., church doctrines and various legalistic practices) will quench the power of God's Word (Mark 7:13), so be warned not to heed human traditions. Rather, let the teachings of the Bible be your final authority! This is very important, lest it will negatively affect your relationship with God, and how you receive His blessings.

- *Do they Practice What they Preach?*

If a local church espouses to believe in the core doctrines of the faith, this is great! However, do they practice it? These are two different issues! For example, there are churches that claim that the Bible is their authority, yet they ordain homosexual ministers as Pastors, Priest, etc, which is grossly contrary to the Scriptural position. Likewise, there are churches that espouse to believe in the teachings of Christ, yet they are unforgiving to those who have undergone a divorce, or they poorly treat those who are ex-murderers, convicts, etc; essentially, they do not practice the love of Christ. These are major issues to consider because sooner or later, a church like this will mislead you, leading to a "snag" in your relationship with God.

- *Is the Church Involved in Various Ministries to Improve their Local Communities?*

While this may not affect your salvation, it is crucial in your service to the Lord. As Christians, we are called to serve others, just like Christ Jesus came to serve us. When it is all said and done, and when we die and go to heaven, the Lord will honor us based on our good service to Him while alive, so good Holy Spirit led good service with the right motives are paramount to your relationship with God. So, if a local church does not practice servanthood (i.e., good service to others as unto the Lord), that church would not be furthering God's will for the Universal Church. If I were you, I would not join such a church, because good service is relevant to God.

- *Is the Church Involved in the Great Commission of Christ Jesus?*

This involves discipleship and evangelism in order to equip its members and spread the Gospel of the Lord Jesus across the world. If a local church is not involved with equipping the Saints and spreading the Gospel, then that church is not obeying the Lords' commandments, and I would not join such a church, if I were you.

- *Does the Church Provide the Opportunities for You to Serve and Use Your gifts?*

Any church that does not provide the forum or opportunity for you to utilize your God given gifts and talents, may pose a potential problem for you, especially if you are desiring to serve God. Notwithstanding, you can always serve God elsewhere besides your local church, but the local church should be the ideal environment to begin.

It may seem like a lot of questions just to join a church. But it is relevant, because having these answers will enable you to make a godly decision, before you subject yourself under the teachings and leadership of any church. While the aforementioned recommendations may seem like a lot, do not be discouraged! There are many awesome, Bible believing churches around, but you will have to invest some time in searching, and the Holy Spirit will help you.

## How to Begin Your Search For a Local Church

The process of searching and selecting a church takes time. So I recommend you begin by reading about various churches from their website, ask others, visit the churches and pray about it, while remaining sensitive to the promptings of the Holy Spirit as He guides you. Do not be in a hurry to join any church; be certain in your heart, and allow the peace of God and His confirmation to guide your selection.

Regardless of how you approach this, seriously or casually, keep in mind that the church you attend will have a great impact on your growth and relationship with God consciously and subconsciously, so please choose wisely. Once you decide on which church to join, there are some questions that I recommend you ask yourself in order to evaluate your perspective and expectations. As an example, ask yourself the following:

- How can I improve this church with my gifts and talents and make a difference?

- Am I willing, and ready to serve? And in which ministry within the church?

- Is it important that the Pastor or church leaders know me personally?

- Do I have a Christ-like attitude about serving others?

Answering the above questions honestly will enable you to evaluate whether or not your perspective is godly. You want to strive to uphold a godly perspective as you begin this journey with a local church. For example, there are those who would be easily upset if the Pastors or church leaders do not recognize them by name; this is ridiculously selfish, and a self-centered ungodly attitude. Others would be upset if they are not recognized when they serve; again, another self-serving selfish ungodly attitude that does not please God. Hopefully, answers to these questions will help you to renew your thinking to be aligned with God's Word and the true purpose(s) for a church.

**Keep in mind that you do not attend church or serve in order to please the Pastor: you do it for the Lord Jesus. Once you gain and maintain this godly perspective, you will not be easily upset when you are not honored by church members for your service. God is the one to honor you, and not the Pastor or others. Granted, it would be encouraging if the church would acknowledge your service, but do not count on that as a reason to serve.** God is watching, and He will honor and elevate you in due time. I can give you dozens of examples in my own life and service to God in regard to this issue, but due to space limitation in this book, I am unable to do so. But suffice it to say that God has honored my service to Him in unexpected ways, when those whom I directly served did not recognize it, so focus on God and serve for Him! The Bible teaches that Christ Jesus served with gladness and never complained even though He was rejected, we are to do likewise.

Before I end this chapter, I want to briefly talk about dealing with denominational differences. With thousands of Protestant denominations, and the various branches of Christianity, eventually, you will run into another Christian, from another branch of the faith or another denomination, who will not agree with some of your "positions" about Christianity. This can be very frustrating. Nonetheless, the sooner you learn to avoid arguing with your fellow brother or sister in Christ, the better it will be for you. I believe it is

Satan's goal to use our denominational difference and cause much strife, thereby preventing us from working together in furthering the Gospel of Jesus Christ.

## Dealing with Denominational Differences

As a Bible teacher for over 10 years now, I have learnt that the majority of arguments among Christians of different denominations are focused on the "non-essentials" of the faith. By non-essentials, I am referring to things such as the method of preaching and proclaiming the Gospel, choice of music, length of the service, methods of baptism, dress code, speaking in tongues, etc. Although these different methodologies might negatively or positively affect your relationship with God, they are irrelevant with regards to your salvation and eternity. So while these non-essentials can be important in how you live out your Christian faith and receive God's promises, do not waste your time debating and arguing about them. Rather, invest time in studying the Scripture and seeking the Holy Spirit for revelation, and focus on your growth in Christ.

On the other hand, there are other doctrinal Truths that pertain to your salvation, such as the Deity of Christ, salvation by grace, and all of the essential doctrines of the faith discussed above, that are worth debating about, in love and grace. Hence, apply wisdom and debate wisely. Below are some recommendations for dealing with doctrinal differences:

1. Find a "common ground", Christ, and focus on that. If you and your fellow brethren agree about the Deity of Christ, then ignore the other non-essential issues;

2. Focus on the clear essential doctrines of the faith that pertains to your salvation, and seek unity in love and overlook the non-essentials;

3. Seek to understand the other person's position, even though they may be non-essentials. None of us has 100% revelation of God, you may learn from the other person. Besides, each of us is in a different "place" in our relationship with God, so be merciful towards your fellow brethren;

4. Do not be dogmatic about your non-essential position, you could be wrong, besides, it is a non-essential anyway;

5. Focus on the "big picture," the True Gospel of Christ, which is eternal, and is the only hope for the world. At the end of the day, the Gospel Message of Christ is the final authority regarding our final destination upon death: "hell and heaven";

6. Walk in forgiveness and love, and move on;

7. Learn to peacefully agree to disagree in love and gentleness.

In conclusion, focusing on how you could serve the Lord through your local church, rather than focusing on what the church could do for you, will help you to focus more on Christ. And, as God becomes a priority in your life, make it your goal to develop an intimate relationship with Him, by presenting yourself to Him daily as a living sacrifice, which will enable you to experience more of His presence. With this thought, let us now proceed to the next chapter for details about presenting yourself to God daily as a living sacrifice.

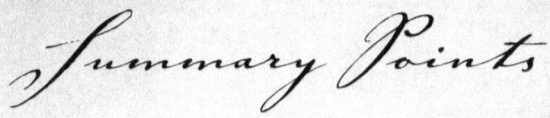

# Summary Points

- Jesus Christ is the head of the Church;
- A church is simply a gathering of believers who have a relationship with God through Christ;
- The primary purpose for the church is to proclaim the Gospel of Christ Jesus to the lost world, in addition to making disciples and evangelism ;
- Regular church attendance or joining a church does not imply you are a Christian, and will not take you to heaven: you need a personal relationship with God through Christ Jesus;
- Knowing the essential doctrines of true Christianity will prevent you from being deceived by the numerous pseudo-Christian cults and false teachers in the world;
- The primary purpose for you to belong to a church is because, it is God's will for you;
- Some ungodly self-serving reasons for going to church include but are not limited to: looking for a spouse, manipulating others to help you, seeking approval from others, impressing others, etc;
- In dealing with denominational differences, find a common ground: Christ Jesus, and focus on the essentials of the faith, rather than the non-essentials.

# Are You Moving Forward with Jesus?

## Chapter 11

# HOW TO BECOME A LIVING SACRIFICE

Accepting to follow Jesus, knowing the Word of God and putting it to practice in your life and sustaining in prayer, in addition to all of your good service to the Lord are critical. But, when it is all said and done, God is after "your heart." He desires a personal relationship with you primarily: everything else is secondary. It is out of a genuine relationship with God that everything you will do for Him will be based on. And, it is in the context of such a relationship that you will be well positioned to appropriate God's best for you. Hence, your relationship with God is preeminent.

Given the significance of a vibrant relationship with God through Christ, the next three chapters will discuss various aspects of developing such a heartfelt relationship. This chapter begins with the initial step towards such a relationship: becoming a living sacrifice. Then, the next two chapters will expound on how to develop an intimate relationship with God, and how to avoid extremes in that relationship.

During the Old Testament dispensation, the High Priest would offer animal sacrifice to the Lord in order to atone for his sins, and the sins of the Israelite community. While this system of sacrificing animals to appease God was important, He made it clear that obedience from the heart was much desirable (Psalm 40: 6-8; Amos 5:21-24; 1 Samuel 15:22). But as New Testament believers, we have become the living sacrifice instead of animals, because of our relationship with God through Christ. Here is what the Bible teaches regarding that:

> *Becoming a living sacrifice implies that you lay aside your personal wishes and desires daily, in order to follow the Lord and allow His desires to take precedence in your heart. This also implies focusing your entire energy, plans and resources to the Lord, and trusting Him to guide your life daily, step-by-step, moment-by-moment.*

*"Therefore, I urge you, brothers and sisters, in view of God's mercy, to offer your bodies as a living sacrifice, holy and pleasing to God—this is your true and proper worship"* (Romans 12:1), (emphasis author's).

This Scripture is teaching that, in light of God's unconditional love for us, which led Him to sacrifice Himself on the cross on our behalf, we should willingly offer ourselves to Him daily and wholeheartedly by faith without reservation. Doing that in and of itself, is an honorable worship to God, which is pleasing to Him. Thus, **becoming a living sacrifice implies that you lay aside your personal wishes and desires daily, in order to follow the Lord and allow His desires to take precedence in your heart. This also implies focusing your entire energy, plans and resources to the Lord, and trusting Him to guide your life daily, step-by-step, moment-by-moment.**

Becoming a living sacrifice is the initial step towards developing a deeper relationship with God, and, it is a step of humility and gratitude towards Him, who will in turn bless you. Becoming a living sacrifice does not mean that God does not want you to enjoy this life. Rather, He wants you to seek His wisdom and direction, so that He can help you to enjoy the best in this life, since He did not create you with the infinite wisdom and abilities to rule or control your own life (Jeremiah 10:23; Proverbs 3:5). Even though God has given you the Free Will to make your own choices because of His great love, He still wants you to ask Him for guidance because He knows what is best for you. Besides, as a Christian, purchased from the Kingdom of darkness by God with the blood of Christ Jesus, God has become your Master and Owner anyway, thus, you are no longer in control of your life.

## Why Become A Living Sacrifice

The only way to enjoy the best life God has predestined for you is to become a living sacrifice. People become Christians for various reasons, but I believe one of the major reasons is because they realize the emptiness in their lives without God, or they came to the realization that they are unable to lead their own lives,

> *Some people erroneously think that the initial surrender to God is sufficient for a meaningful Christian life, but it is not. True Christianity is a lifestyle, and not an event.*

thus they come to the end of themselves and surrender to God, which is awesome. But unfortunately, **some people erroneously think that the initial surrender to God is sufficient for a meaningful Christian life, but it is not. True Christianity is a lifestyle, and**

**not an event.** In order to experience God's perfect plans for your life, you will have to deliberately allow Him to direct and lead you daily; and the only way to do that is to become a living sacrifice. I once heard a minister explain how becoming a Christian is an instantaneous event, but living as a Christian is a process. I totally agree with this statement, which is why it is essential to become a living sacrifice.

Many Christians are not enjoying their relationship with the Lord, and are not living in His blessings because they are not fully committed to Him. That is to say, they have accepted Christ Jesus as their Lord and Savior, yet they have not fully surrendered every area of their life under His Lordship. I believe the primary reason for this is uncertainty and fear, because they have not experienced God's faithfulness; and as such, they are unable to completely trust Him. The only way you will experience the full benefits of your relationship with the Lord is to become a living sacrifice daily. God is not impressed with half-hearted commitment; He wants you to surrender to Him 100%. It is only when you reach this place of 100% commitment, that you will start experiencing the full extent of God's peace, joy and overall contentment in every area of your life.

The Lord Jesus said in order for a person to gain his or her life, the individual must first lose it (Matthew 16:25). What Christ Jesus is referring to is the same concept of a living sacrifice, whereby you completely commit your life to God; and as you do that, you will start to experience the real purpose of life. If you are a Christian who has never made a 100% commitment to the Lord, you can start right now. On the other hand, if you are a new Christian, this is the best time to make this commitment before you make many ungodly decisions and suffer major consequences.

## PRACTICAL APPLICATION

## How to Become a Living Sacrifice

Deciding to become a living sacrifice is not something that happens naturally and automatically. This has to be a conscious decision, requiring perseverance in prayer. Below are some recommendations.

### Some Recommendations For Becoming a Living Sacrifice

*1. Seek First the Kingdom of God*

It is very disappointing and shocking to know that some of those who profess to be Christians do not desire the things of God; I have met such "Christians." They are barely existing and waiting to go to heaven when they die, and are not enjoying the journey. This is a pity, because Christ Jesus died for us to enjoy and overcome in this present world (Galatians 1:4).

The first step in becoming a living sacrifice is to put God first in everything you do. This includes making Him Lord in every area of your life, such as your finances, relationships, marital life, career endeavors, job preferences, etc. For example, seek His wisdom in prayer, be patient and obtain direction from His Word before making decisions. There are certain things you may desire that have specific answers in the Bible; if that is the case, pray for wisdom and obey His Word in faith. For those things you are unsure, pray and allow God to guide you, then obey, as He leads you. But there are other basic things such as what to eat, wear, etc, that God trusts you to apply practical wisdom and decision making without much effort.

As you seek God first in everything you do, you will be presenting yourself to Him daily as a living sacrifice, and you will be very pleased how you will experience His presence and peace. God will honor your decision to seek Him first by blessing you in various ways, including meeting all of your needs, etc, in His perfect timing (Matthew 6:30-35); that is His promise, He is faithful, you can count on that!

It is rather unfortunate that there are those Christians who are chronically chasing after the blessings of God, rather than allowing the blessings to chase them! Do you know why? Because they are neglecting this simple principle taught by Christ Jesus in the Gospel of Matthew: " *But seek first his kingdom and his righteousness, and all these things will be given to you as well*" (6: 33), (emphasis author's). The "all things" that the Lord is referring to include, "all things," such as our basic needs and other issues we might be dealing with in every area of life. When your entire focus is on seeking God, His blessings will chase you effortlessly; this is the best antidote for stress and worry.

There is a biblical principle that if you sincerely seek God with all of your heart, He will honor your desire (Matthew 7:7; Jeremiah 29:10-13), so seek Him first. The interesting thing is that, as you become focused on seeking God first, your problems will start to disappear without you attempting to figure things out; it is supernatural how that works!

Seeking God first also requires godly actions in every area of your life, and approaching all of your earthly responsibilities with godly standards, as unto the Lord. For example, you would do your best to become the best employee, the best sales man, the best teacher, professor, doctor, dancer, etc, and exhibit the best conduct in carrying out your business dealings. As you do this, God will promote you, and you will gain honor and respect from others.

As a doctor in private practice, I do not advertise my business or solicit for new patients like most doctors in private practices do; rather, I focus all of my energy in treating every patient with godly care, respect, and love. As a result, my patients are referring friends, relatives and others to me on a regular basis, and I do not have to worry about patient census. I have learnt to trust the Lord with my patient census, and He has always been faithful, as I make a conscious decision daily, to live as a living sacrifice.

I proudly tell others that God is my "boss," and my sole provider, and not the contracts I have with health insurance companies, or the patients who come to seek medical care from me. With this perspective, I do my work diligently "unto the Lord" and not "unto man"; thus God is blessing my practice without me stressing out, and I have to turn-down some new patient referrals because I only work part time due to my full time ministry calling. I have used this testimony to encourage many of my business associates, and they have been thankful for this godly wisdom. Hopefully, it encourages you as well.

## 2. Abide in Christ Daily

A daily abiding in Christ is mandatory, in order for Him to mold and shape you and bring out the best in you. Essentially, you have to become 100% God dependent. I have already discussed elsewhere in this book how Christ Jesus is the "root" (i.e., source of power and life) that enables us to produce the "fruit" (i.e., godly results). Abiding in Christ does not imply that you study the Bible throughout the day or become a professional minister. Instead, it means that, you "hide" His Word in your heart through studying and meditating on the Scriptures as a lifestyle, and you give it preeminence in everything you do (refer to the chapters on meditation and practicing the Word), while allowing the seed (Word of God) to be grounded in your soul. As you spend time in the presence of God studying His Word, fellowshipping with other believers, fasting, praying, engaging in Holy Spirit led godly services for the Kingdom of God, etc, you will be abiding in Christ and offering yourself daily to God as a living sacrifice.

**You cannot have the fruit without the root. Since Christ is the source of the fruit: not abiding**

*You cannot have the fruit without the root. Since Christ is the source of the fruit: not abiding in Him means, no fruit, period! This is non-negotiable, and there is nothing you can do to circumvent this principle of God.*

**in Him means, no fruit, period! This is non-negotiable, and there is nothing you can do to circumvent this principle of God**. There are those who are searching for the fruit (i.e., results), but are refusing to abide in the source (i.e., Christ). They are wasting their time and chasing after the wind, it will never happen. In the natural world, most people can relate to the fact that it would be stupid to go to a garden to harvest tomatoes if you did not plant tomato seeds, right? Likewise, in the spiritual realm, it is equally stupid to believe and expect God's blessings and evidence in your life, if you are not attached to the source— Christ Jesus. Hopefully, you can relate to this simple analogy.

## *3. Consecrate Yourself to the Lord Daily*

Becoming a living sacrifice requires a deliberate act of consecrating yourself to the Lord daily. Our natural tendencies as "fallen" human beings is to practice our selfish desires, thus rebelling against the things of God. A lot of times, we do this naturally and subconsciously without first thinking of God; so becoming a living sacrifice is not going to be easy for most people. It will require some effort on your part, as your spirit and flesh would be at war against each other (Romans 7: 14-25). A good way to start is to begin with prayer. I recommend you begin each day with praying something like this:

*Dear God, I thank you that You are willing to lead and guide me today. On my own I am unable to do this. I ask for you to fill me with Your Spirit today, and enable me to live for you. Strengthen me God, so that I can live for you today, and yield to your promptings and guidance. I surrender all of my plans today under your Lordship, direction, and wisdom. I am open and willing to obey you today, as I step out in faith to do whatever it is that you want me to do, help me Lord, in Jesus name, AMEN.*

If you pray something like the above sincerely, the Lord will honor that. The good news is that the Holy Spirit indwelling in you will enable you to consecrate yourself daily to God as you are willing to surrender and trust Him. Over 2000 years ago, the apostle Paul told the Christians in the church at Galatia that his former lifestyle before Christ was dead, gone, never to be remembered anymore. And as a new creature, the apostle told the Galatians how he allowed Christ to live through him daily (Galatians 2: 20); this is an excellent example of a consecrated life. Likewise, when we consecrate our lives to God as a living sacrifice, we have to allow Christ Jesus to live through us.

As an example, if you are struggling with forgiving someone who has seriously hurt you, instead of struggling to forgive them on your own effort, ask the Lord to do it through you. Consider praying something like this: *Dear God, on my own, I am struggling to forgive this person but I want to obey you. So I ask you to love them through me, as I take a step of faith to forgive them right now, and express kindness towards them, thank you Lord Jesus, Amen.*

As you act in faith while trusting God to work through you regardless of the circumstance, you will be offering yourself as a living sacrifice, consecrating yourself to Him, and He will honor you above and beyond your wildest imagination.

## 4. Obey God

Seeking God first in everything you do, abiding in Christ and consecrating yourself to Him daily will be futile if you do not obey Him. I know people who seek God, pray unceasingly and yet do not carry out His instructions. Personally, I cannot relate to that. Why seek God in prayer, worship, fellowship, etc, and not obey what He tells you to do? Obeying God's instructions as outlined in His Word, in addition to His inner promptings in your heart are essential in becoming a living sacrifice, lest you will not reap the results you are desiring.

There are certain things God will not release in your life until you carry out certain instructions; so obedience leads to abundance. **A word of caution** — I said this earlier, but it is worth repeating here — **The primary way God will speak to you is through His written Word, and not through a vision, dream, circumstances, people, etc. If God uses these things to speak to you, it will be consistent with His Word.**

## 5. Perseverance

Becoming a living sacrifice is a process; it requires perseverance. Perseverance is not a human quality, it requires supernatural strength from God. God understands this, which is why perseverance or long-suffering is a Fruit of the Spirit (Galatians 5:22-23), which every born again believer has through faith. Becoming a living sacrifice does not imply perfection; Christians will never reach the state of perfection in this life, that will only happen in heaven when we are glorified. Thus, in your journey as a living sacrifice, you will make many mistakes. The Bible teaches that even though a righteous man (referring to those who have placed their faith in Christ Jesus), falls seven times, that individual will rise again ( Proverbs 24:16). You know why? Because the Lord Jesus is with them.

So do not be very harsh on yourself when you make a mistake. Be very patient with yourself. If you make a mistake, quickly recognize it, genuinely confess and repent, then ask the Holy Spirit to fill you again. Make it your goal to learn and grow from each mistake, no matter how horrible it is; move on, and do not repeat the same mistake. God is patient with you, He knows your heart.

I know Christians who have made major mistakes in their journey, and are unable to persevere through it and forgive themselves even though their repentance was genuine. In such cases, they have been unable to appropriate God's grace and persevere through their failures; yet, God has forgiven them and He does not even remember the transgression anymore (Psalm 103; 1 John 1:9). But the Master thief, Satan, has blinded and deceived them from accepting God's forgiveness. If you are one of those Christians, please, in Jesus name, move on; God has forgiven you if your repentance was genuine. So go and bless someone else with your testimony and put the devil to shame!

Furthermore, living as a sacrifice does not mean that you will automatically see all of the fruit or desired results immediately. You need to be patient. But, if you have sincerely dedicated your life to the Lord as a living sacrifice, you will immediately start experiencing His peace and joy, because your mind will be focused on Him daily (Isaiah 26:3). It takes many years of walking with the Lord to experience certain results. But while persevering, God will be molding and shaping your character for the best (Romans 5: 3-5). God knows exactly what you need and at the right time, so do not give up. While persevering, continue to seek Him for wisdom and direction, abide in Christ, be steadfast in prayer, and live in obedience. And as you do these things, the Lord will infuse you with supernatural strength (Isaiah 40:31), and you will definitely reap the spiritual blessings (Galatians 6:7-9).

As an example, I have been walking intimately with the Lord now for a long time, and I started teaching Bible studies around 2006. Then, sometime in late 2013, I started to dedicate my life to the Lord daily as a living sacrifice even though I had been abiding in Him all those years, serving, and seeking Him first. The difference was that in 2013, I made a non-negotiable decision that I wanted to experience more of God's presence, blessings and favor in my life, especially if I was going to be a fruitful Minister. It was amazing how in just a few weeks of making that decision, I noticed more peace, contentment, closeness to God, confidence in my relationship with Him, and a general sense of security about everything in my life. Many others, including my patients, noticed "something" different about my demeanor and they have asked me what changed? Of course, I told them that it was my wholehearted commitment to the Lord.

Then about one year after that decision, sometime in 2014, the Lord clearly spoke to my heart that my life was just beginning. Can you imagine that? After all those years! Nonetheless, I was happy to know that God had honored my decision and actions, and the best is yet to come. Still, I continue to persevere daily as a living sacrifice. It may not take such a long time in your case, but regardless, never give up, God is watching, keep on persevering. Who knows? Someday we may be reading your testimony!

In conclusion, becoming a living sacrifice is the initial step of developing a solid relationship with the Triune God, rather than approaching Him from a list of Do's and Don'ts. With that, let us proceed to the next chapter where I discuss some key ingredients in developing an intimate relationship with God.

## Summary Points

- Becoming a living sacrifice simply means you willingly commit your life to the Lord 100% without any reservation;
- It is God's will for each of us to willingly become a living sacrifice;
- The best way to experience God's best is to become a living sacrifice;
- Some examples of how to become a living sacrifice include, but are not limited to: seeking God first in everything you do, abiding in Christ, and obeying His commandments as expressed in the Scriptures, etc.

# Are You Moving Forward with Jesus?

## Chapter 12

# HOW TO DEVELOP AN INTIMATE RELATIONSHIP WITH GOD

In the previous chapter, I discussed how becoming a living sacrifice is a necessary step towards developing an intimate relationship with God. You may be wondering how intimate you can know God? The answer is simple: very intimate, because that is His will. One of the deepest desires of The God of the Bible is to have an intimate relationship with each of us, His children, whom He has adopted into His kingdom. God is love, and as such He wants each of us to freely reciprocate His love and desire to know Him more — He does not want a causal relationship with you, but an intimate one.

The Lord Jesus portrayed His intimate relationship with God throughout His ministry by calling God His Father (see the Gospels). And the Bible teaches that as God's children, we have His Spirit in our hearts crying: Abba Father (Romans 8:15; Galatians 4:6), which is an endearment, expressing intimacy, all pointing to how much God desires an intimate relationship with us.

Knowing God intimately will equip you with a solid foundation in your journey with Him. **Sadly, many Christians know of God from bits and pieces from others, but they do not know God personally through their daily experience.** Without personally knowing God, you will miss out from the best He has to offer, and from a vibrant exciting journey with Him, which is His desire.

In the Old Testament era, the Jews could not address God as their Father, because of the distant relationship they had with Him, which explained why they accused Jesus of blasphemy because He called God His Father, and claimed equality with Him [God the Father]. But as New Testament believers, we have the honor and privilege of calling the One True God of the universe our Father. How awesome!

Also, true Christianity is the only faith in the world which espouses this type of intimacy with God. No other religion in the world today can claim such intimacy with their deity or deities, because they are religious systems invented by mere human beings. On the other hand, true Christianity focuses on a personal relationship with The Only True Living God through Christ Jesus. Before I discuss how to develop this intimate relationship with God, let us briefly examine why true Christianity is a relationship and not a religion; that way you will have an understanding of why you should make it your goal to pursue a personal relationship with God, rather than religious do's and don'ts.

## True Christianity Is Not a Religion

To further expound on this, I want to examine the definition of religion. Webster Dictionary defines religion as: (1) "The belief in a god or in a group of gods"; (2) "An organized system of beliefs, ceremonies, and rules used to worship a god or a group of gods"; (3)

"An interest, a belief, or an activity that is very important to a person or group".

According to the above definitions, religion emphasizes various rules (do's and don'ts) in their attempts to worship and please a god or deity. In the various world religious systems today, adhering to these ritualistic do's and don'ts are considered absolutely necessary in order to be accepted by a god or gods. However, true Christianity rejects polytheism (the worship of multiple gods), and is not based on a set of rules and regulations to adhere to. Also, true Christians do not focus on activities, but on their relationship with God through Christ.

True Christianity is beyond all of the above definitions because: (1) Christ Jesus already fulfilled God's perfect standard of righteousness or holiness ( the ritualistic Mosaic Law of the Old Testament do's and don'ts); (2) A true Christian is already accepted by God because of the redemptive work of the Lord Jesus, and no extra do's or don'ts are required; and (3) through the working of His Spirit, God is in the continuous process of sanctifying the true Christian as he or she yields to Him. Conversely, all pseudo world religions are man's creation and attempts to reach a god. **True Christianity is not a religion—it is based on a relationship with God through Christ.**

It is unfortunate that some Christians, and even some denominations are still attempting to adhere to do's and don'ts in their relationship with God, which is an affront to Him. The Bible describes these useless and vain attempts at approaching God as "good works" or self-righteousness, which are pervasive in the various pseudo world religions today. God dislikes these man-made religious systems and their self-righteous attitudes, because of their futile attempts to circumvent His perfect standard of righteousness: Christ Jesus. God's heart in this matter is clearly seen in the book of Galatians.

The apostle Paul had founded the church in Galatia in the region of Asia, back then, then he left and proceeded with his other missionary work. After his departure, the Judaizers (certain Jewish converts to Christianity) came into the church and were falsely teaching the new Christians how they still had to observe the Mosaic Laws (the Jewish do's and don'ts, such as circumcision, observance of the Sabbath, etc), in order for them to be accepted by God. These false teachers were essentially teaching that Christianity was an extension of Judaism, and as such, espousing that the sacrifice of Christ Jesus was insufficient. They were deceiving the new converts that their "good works" were necessary for a relationship with God. And to this false teachers, the apostle Paul wrote under the inspiration of the Holy Spirit:

*"You foolish Galatians! Who has bewitched you? Before your very eyes Jesus Christ was clearly portrayed as crucified. I would like to learn just one thing from you: Did you receive the Spirit by the works of the law, or by believing what you heard? Are you so foolish? After beginning by means of the Spirit, are you now trying to finish by means of the flesh?" (Galatians 3:1-3),* (emphasis author's).

It is obvious how irate God was with the Galatians for trying to live out their Christian faith by do's and don'ts. Likewise, God is still irate today, when Christians approach Him in a legalistic, self-righteous, do's and don'ts manner. The Scriptures teach that we accept to follow Christ Jesus by faith only, a free gift from God, without any do's or don'ts or "good works" (Ephesians 2:8). Thus, in the same way that we accepted Christ (i.e., by faith), we should likewise live out our relationship with God (i.e., by faith), as we abide in Christ and obey the Word of God, and not by do's and don'ts (Colossians 2:6-12). Suffice it to say that the Bible is very clear that true Christianity is not a religion, but a true relationship with God through Christ, and the enabling of the Holy Spirit.

So how do you cultivate this relationship with God, you may wonder? You do it by first becoming a living sacrifice (already discussed in the previous chapter), while seeking to know God intimately through His Word. Without knowing someone, it will be difficult to develop any sort of a relationship with them, this is the same with God. Hence, once you consecrate yourself to God as a living sacrifice, the next logical step would be to grow in your knowledge of Him, right? Let us now proceed to examine how you can know God more and develop an intimate relationship with Him.

## PRACTICAL APPLICATION

### Knowing God Intimately

The only way to know anyone is to spend time with that person, right? I am sure most of you would say YES! It is unfortunate that many Christians know their spouses, children, parents or even certain friends much better than they know God; this ought to be the opposite. We are supposed to know God more than we know anyone else, especially, as He has revealed Himself to us in His Word. For those of you who are married, you probably dated your husband or wife for quite some time before you decided that he or she was marriage material, right? You just did not get married a few months after you initially met! I hope that was not the case.

So let me ask you this: you spent considerable amount of time with your fiance(é) in order to know them right? You probably went out shopping, visited other friends, went to the movies, etc, right? You probably spent hours on the phone talking or communicating in some other way, right? During the process of doing these activities, you would agree that you gradually started to know your fiance(é), right? Such as their favorite foods, movies, car, TV show, author, their likes and dislikes, etc, right? So, by the time you got married, you had developed trust in him or her, and you knew enough about him or her to be comfortable to spend the rest of your life with that individual, right? I am sure you would agree with me that it was a process getting to know your spouse, right? Well, guess what? It is likewise with God. Knowing God intimately and developing a relationship with Him is the same process you would undergo in developing any other meaningful earthly relationship with a fellow human being, as explained above.

In fact, your relationship with God is the cornerstone to your success in any other earthly relationships. You know why? Because, without a solid relationship with God, it will be difficult, if not impossible, to express unconditional love, compassion, etc, towards others. You may not like this statement, but it is a biblical principle — <u>It is only when you are attached to the source of love (i.e., God), and allow His loving qualities to flow through you, that you will be able to reach out to others in like manner.</u> So developing an intimate relationship with God should be the ultimate goal for everyone, especially a Christian.

## Some Recommendations For Developing an Intimate Relationship with God

### ➢ Spend Time With Him

*As you saturate yourself in God's presence through studying His Word, you will begin to know how to discern His still voice in your heart. The more time you spend in the Word, the easier it will become to know when God is directly speaking to your heart, compared to the many other voices in your life or environment.*

You cannot know God without knowing His Word, it is impossible. There are two types of knowing: (1) Intellectual ; and (2) Experiential knowing. Intellectual knowing is "head " knowledge of God, which is a beginning point. But unfortunately, some people end here. Make it your goal to take it one step further: experiential knowing, whereby you experience the presence of God in tangible ways in your life, such as His joy, peace, supernatural love and care for you personally! Some of you may be shocked to know that this is possible: yes indeed, it is! And how do you experience God in this manner? By spending time in His presence, studying and meditating on His Word. Some people do not like this, because it means they have to study the Scriptures, but I am sorry to say that, this is the <u>primary</u> way you can know God more.

**As you saturate yourself in God's presence through studying His Word, you will begin to know how to discern His still voice in your heart. The more time you spend in the Word, the easier it will become to know when God is directly speaking to your heart, compared to the many other voices in your life or environment.** With consistent practice and patience, you will reach a level where God's voice will become very clear in your heart when He speaks to you (i.e., you will become very sensitive to His still voice and promptings), and you will be able to easily discern the voice of a stranger. This is what Christ Jesus meant by saying His sheep knows His voice, and they would not follow a stranger (John 10:5; 10: 27). Sadly, many loving Christians have not mastered the art of discerning God's still voice and promptings, hence they are easily led astray.

**By discerning the voice of God, I am not referring to an audible voice [although God can still choose to speak to people in an audible voice. Nothing is impossible with God], but in the context of this book, I am referring to an inner knowing in your heart when God speaks to you.** For example, it is like a lady being blindfolded and walking in a room with about a hundred people talking, yet, she would still be able to discern her husband's voice in a whisper from the rest, because she knows him very well. This type of knowing is not difficult, because it is God's desire for you to know Him, but it will require some effort and patience on your part.

Saturating yourself in God's presence does not necessarily mean you take time off from your job to study His Word, or spend extended periods of time studying daily. For the most part, you can do this by simply meditating on His Word as you proceed with your daily activities. However, there are occasions when you will need to spend extended periods of time in His presence by studying His Word.

As an example, in your relationship with your spouse, children or other loved ones, you have periods of brief gatherings, and special times for lengthier gatherings where you might go to a movie, eat at a fancy restaurant, go for a long walk or just "hang out" and talk, right? Likewise, developing an intimate relationship with God requires the same kind of quality and quantity time and attention. There may be days when you may spend a brief time in His presence, and other days that you invest lengthier time studying, meditating and worshipping Him.

I am reluctant to mention any specific time frame because it depends on various factors, and I do not want some people to become legalistic about the amount of time spent with God. But, as an example, for those who are just starting to do this, 45 to 60 minutes a day may be a good start, with gradual increase of the time spent with Him. Remember, most of you would spend this time watching "junk" on TV anyway, you might as well invest it in your relationship with God!

Personally, there have been days when I have designated a specific time frame to spend with God, then as I started studying, meditating and worshipping Him, I would end up spending twice as much time as originally planned, because I was experiencing much benefit from it. So give yourself enough time, that way you do not have to abruptly stop, especially when He is ministering and speaking to you directly through His Word. It does not matter what time of the day you do this, although early mornings are usually the best time, because your soul and physical body are well rested and more sensitive at that time of the day. Also, it is a good habit to anchor your soul with God's Word before you begin your day. But for those of you who work the night shift and sleep during the day, upon awakening in the evening, you could do the same, as you will be more rested and hopefully sensitive at that time.

I also recommend you take specific days off, maybe one or two days, if possible, about every few months or so, away and alone somewhere, with limited distraction, for purposes of studying, meditating, fasting and praying. Doing this will enable you to minimize environmental distractions, and train your five senses to easily discern God's inner promptings in your heart. As you experience much benefit from the time invested with God, you will be encouraged, and would want to spend more time in His presence.

I remember the first two years of fighting cancer, I barely worked, as such, I put that time into perfect use by spending about 8 to 10 hours a day with God; it transformed my life radically. My faith became tangible, to me, and God's presence in my life became a reality, and it was extremely difficult when I had to transition back to work and was unable to spend that much time with Him. I am not implying that you need that much time to experience God's presence: NO. But the principle is the same — The more time you invest in God's presence, the more benefit you will get out of it, period! It is really up to you! The Biblical principle is that when you seek God with all of your heart, soul and mind, you will experience His presence, and you will be nourished (Matthew 22:37).

> ### Test His Word

Another great way to know God and develop an intimate relationship with Him is to test His promises. **I am not referring to putting God to test out of selfish motives or to prove that His Word does not work, that would be stupid. <u>By testing His Word, I am referring to you taking a stance to walk by faith and apply His promises in your daily life, in order to experience His presence, which will quicken your faith</u>.** Talk is cheap. Anyone can talk; and in fact most people talk and never deliver the "goods." Most of you would agree that you would not trust anyone who talks and does not act, right? In your earthly relationships, you would want to have a meaningful relationship with a friend or loved one who is consistent and lives up to his or her word, right? And the best way to know this is to observe the individual over a period of time, to ascertain he or she comes through with their promises, right? And you would do this by putting friends and other loved ones in your life through a test; and if they pass the test, you would then elevate them one notch up in your level of trust and dependability, right? I believe most of you would agree with me on this! Guess what? This process of testing and building trust in your earthly relationship is the same progression you would undergo, in developing an intimate relationship with your heavenly Father, God. And you would do this by putting His promise to test in your life and observing His faithfulness, you will be pleased with the outcome—because God is 100% faithful.

Many Christians do not have a trusting relationship with God because they have not tested His promises. Some of them have heard bits and pieces about God's faithfulness, compassion, unconditional love, dependability, forgiving nature, etc, from others, but they have never experienced any of these for themselves. In Malachi chapter 3, God said we should test and observe if He does not come through with His promises (v. 10). Although this principle is specific to tithing in the Old Testament, it can be applicable in other areas in our lives as well.

Test God's promises by applying them in your life, and do not add or delete from them; then, observe what happens. For example, the New Testament principle of giving is that you give out of love, as you are led by God in your heart (2 Corinthians 9:7). Thus, if God places it in your heart to give, say, $1000 (One thousand dollars, USD) to a Ministry or Church, you would, hopefully, gladly obey and do it without grudging. If you do that, I can guarantee you, based on the authority of His Word, He will bless you back in many ways. I have seen this principle work in my own life countless times. I do not know exactly how this works in the spiritual realm, and I do not think anyone knows exactly how; but it works, and I have heard hundreds of other similar testimonies to this effect. The blessing may not necessarily be financial, it could be in any other area in your life, but it works!

As another example, if you make a sincere decision to develop an intimate relationship with God, and you do your part in investing quality and quantity time in His Word, you will definitely begin to sense His presence in your life in supernatural ways; doing this will be part of testing His promises and experiencing His faithfulness. I am not referring to a physical manifestation [although nothing is impossible with God], but rather, a confident sense of knowing that God is with you. And as you experience more of His presence, it will strengthen your faith, trust and dependability on Him, and you will be emboldened to make comments such as "I personally know God; He is my friend." This kind of confidence and trust will provide an unshakeable foundation in every area of your life, and that is God's will for you.

## ➤ Be Consistent in Your Prayer Life

I have already discussed prayer in chapter 9, so refer to that for details. But I want to add that a great way to test God's promises is by praying according to His will as expressed in the Bible, then evaluate the manifestation. As you receive answers to your prayers, keeping in mind that a yes, no or wait, are all valid answers, you will be reassured, and your perception of His faithfulness will become a reality to you, which will foster an intimate relationship.

## ➤ Be Consistent in Your Fellowship with Christ-Centered Individuals

Another sure way to know God and develop an intimate relationship with Him is to make it a habit to fellowship with other like-minded Christians, such as those who genuinely love God and are seeking to know Him more, and are consistent in their witness. This is where "the rubber meets the road"; because many people say they are Christians, but their lifestyles portray a completely different picture. The Lord said we shall know His true followers by their "fruits", referring to evidence of His presence and work in their lives. The Lord also taught that a bad tree, referring to a counterfeit Christian, cannot produce good fruit (i.e., godly evidence in their lives); likewise, a good tree, referring to a genuine Christian, cannot produce bad fruits (i.e., ungodly evidence in their lives) (Matthew 7: 15-20). This is such a simple analogy that I often wonder how people can miss this; probably because they ignore the evidence and want to be deceived, or they are outright ignorant of the nature of God and evidence of a godly lifestyle.

The people you spend the most time with will definitely influence your decisions and overall lifestyle, this is a very clear biblical principle. The Bible warns that bad company, such as ungodly friends, will corrupt godly manners (1 Corinthians 15:33). In previous chapters, I had discussed the biblical principle how bad company can corrupt godly manners, but it is fitting to talk more about this very relevant issue here. Some of you may not accept this godly Truth, but it is true, and you would be wise to heed this advice. Friends who do not appreciate or love God may not cause you to practice overt sin, I hope not, but they will cause you to lose your excitement about God. You will "cool off" and become lukewarm and dull about the things of God, such as spending more time in His presence or participating in godly services, etc.

These signs [becoming lukewarm towards the things of God] are usually gradual at the beginning, and before long, you will end up becoming so hardened or insensitive to the things of God and lose the benefits of a vibrant intimate relationship with Him.

In this condition, some people may just say "it is no use to pursue God," and they might quit seeking Him, because they would not be experiencing His presence and blessings. This would not be because of anything God did, but because of their ungodly lifestyle and fellowship with those who dislike the things of God. Even though they will not lose their salvation if they were genuinely saved, they will lose the benefits of that blessed intimate relationship with God in this life — so do not do that; that would be a shame! God wants to bless your life now, in this life!

My recommendation is that you limit, or even avoid close friendships and/or fellowship with those who do not love God. This does not mean that you do not talk with them; you must, because as Christians, Christ Jesus said we are the "salt and light" of the world (i.e., we should allow our witness for Christ and Godly lifestyles to positively impact the lives of unbelievers in this dark world). So we must keep an "open door" policy, and have some kind of contact with ungodly people, in order to have opportunities to minister to them, and for our lifestyles to hopefully, convict them about their ungodliness, thereby bringing them to God. Thus, we ought to pray for them and walk in love, and let them know that we are always open to sharing the love of Christ with them whenever they are ready ( Matthew 5:13-16). But there are times when we have to cut off contact with people who are willfully abusing us, refusing and rejecting the Gospel message, and are argumentative and causing strife, that way, we could invest our time in the lives of those who are sincerely open to God ( Matthew 7: 6). Abuse is never acceptable. You can pray from a distance for those who are rejecting the message of Christ and causing trouble, and trust God for other opportunities to witness to them.

Or, it may be that God would use someone else and not you: Again, your job is to "plant the seed" (i.e., proclaim the Gospel Message) while allowing and trusting God to bring the harvest. Do not take these things personally, because you are not ultimately responsible for anyone's salvation, except yours. If you take these things personally, you will be attempting to usurp God's position; just trust Him and move on to the next person, in Jesus name. Therefore, be certain to spend time with godly friends, attend Bible studies with them, share your testimonies, and learn from their examples. As you do these things, you will be developing an intimate relationship with God.

> **Be Patient With God**

It is amazing how people are patient with their children, spouses, and close friends, but when it comes to God; they want to see immediate results. God is not an automatic ATM machine. Just like any other relationship, developing an intimate relationship with God requires time and patience; it will not happen overnight. You have to invest quality and quantity time and some effort; the same principles I discussed in chapter 11 about becoming a living sacrifice are very applicable here.

To illustrate, when a farmer plants a strawberry seed, he or she does not go to the garden every week or so, to uproot the seed to ascertain whether or not it is growing, right? Rather, the farmer plants the seed and fertilizes it regularly, then one day, at the appropriate time, the seed will start sprouting; and the stem will be noticeable, then, before long, the full grown strawberry fruits will be ready for harvest. This principle is obvious and acceptable in the physical realm, but in the spiritual realm, many people often struggle with this and they are impatient with God.

Just like the farmer who allowed enough time for the strawberry fruit to sprout, similarly, you will have to allow enough time for your relationship with God to grow. Just like the farmer who did not uproot the seed during the waiting period; instead, he fertilized it. Likewise, you have to protect and nourish your relationship with God by remaining consistent in fertilizing it with: (1) Seeking Him; (2) Studying and meditating in the Word; (3) Testing His promises; (4) Praying; (5) Godly fellowship; (5) Godly service; (6) Living in Obedience; (7) Witnessing, etc. **It is not that God is withholding His friendship from us in order to put us through the torture of waiting: No. Rather, we are the ones who need to renew our minds and change our perspective about God, in order to start receiving from Him**. Unlike our earthly relationships, God is always present and available to those who desire to know Him more, and the process of knowing anyone, including God, takes time, period!

### ➢ Avoid Activities That Do Not Please God

Just like you would not engage in behaviors or activities that displeases your spouse, children and other loved ones, do likewise to God. Do not practice sin, even things such as gossiping, jealousy, lying, etc, that most people may not perceive as big sins to God. **In God's Kingdom, sin is sin, there are no little or big sins. He does not grade sin on a curve, the consequences are the same, period!** Like I have expressed throughout this book, when you practice sin, you become a slave to Satan, who is the author of all sins, and that lifestyle leads to spiritual death such as darkness in your soul (i.e., anxiety, fear, worry, depression, insomnia, etc), and separation from God's presence, blessings and fellowship (Romans 6:16).

This spiritual death in turn leads to a host of other physical problems such as High Blood Pressure, various Stomach diseases, Heart Diseases, etc, and subsequent premature physical death: So avoid sin and live godly for your own benefit. The Scripture warns us to avoid things that will place a heavy burden on our relationship with God (Hebrews 12: 1-3), and interfere with our consistent fellowship and growth with Him.

## Consistently Minister to the Lord

Ministering to the Lord is an area where we often forget or totally miss. God has needs just like we do. The difference is that God is self-existent and self-sufficient , and does not need us, but He chose us. On the other hand, we need Him to sustain and survive as human beings. Even though God is self-existent and self-sufficient, because of His nature of love, He desires fellowship with us, His creation. Because of His humility, He will not force Himself onto anyone; He has given us a choice to humbly reciprocate His love. One way to reciprocate God's love is to make it a habit to consistently minister to Him out of a genuine heart. Reciprocating God's love is similar to what we do in our earthly relationships when we give special attention to our loved ones and buy them gifts. With regards to giving your gifts to God, an excellent way to do that is to offer your financial support, in addition to regular prayers, as you are led by the Holy Spirit, to faithful churches and ministries that are advancing His work on the earth.

Imagine how depressing it would be if you genuinely love someone who does not acknowledge or express any appreciation whatsoever for your love, you would be hurt! Most of us will agree that when we love someone, we express our love in various ways such as staying in touch, buying gifts, spending quality and quantity time with them, and going out of our way to support them, etc, in order to nurture and sustain the relationship — ministering to God is no different!

Knowing and developing an intimate relationship with the Lord entails a daily willful decision to express your thanks and appreciation to Him, for His goodness, thus ministering to Him, just like you would to your loved ones. As an example, you can verbalize thanks to God without mentioning your personal needs; praise and worship Him for His goodness; majesty and love with undivided attention, etc.

**The key ingredient when ministering to the Lord, just like any other thing in God's Kingdom, is sincerity of your heart. If you are not sincere about ministering to the Lord, then do not waste your time and efforts because it will not bless Him or profit you.** If you genuinely desire to minister to Him but you do not "feel" like doing it, do it anyway, out of love and not based on your emotions. Because, like everything else in the Christian journey, we do not act based on our emotions, but by faith. And as you start ministering to Him by faith, your emotions would gradually switch towards desiring to do it. You know why? Because your body will start releasing chemicals, such as oxytocin and endorphins, which will change your mood and perception.

It is interesting how ministering to the Lord in turn blesses us. I remember when I attended a service at an Orthodox church locally, and for about 30 to 45 minutes, their worship was primarily focused on ministering to the Lord. It was amazing how the presence of God permeated that church, and I left that service feeling more blessed by the Lord from ministering to Him, than the Lord Himself; I believe, as His joy, peace, life, etc, enveloped me that entire day. Throughout the Scripture, we are told to bless the Lord and minister to Him; I encourage you make it a lifestyle to do so (e.g., see the Psalms).

In conclusion, developing an intimate relationship with God is a life-long process. No one can ever say they have saturated the depths of God, because God is infinite by nature and we, as human beings, are finite. The goal therefore, is to start, and be persistent in seeking and knowing God as a friend who cares and loves you. Now that you are aware about the basic tenets of developing an intimate relationship with God, let us turn to the next chapter where I discuss how to avoid extremes in your relationship with Him.

## Summary Points

- True Christianity is not a religion, but rather, a relationship with God through Christ Jesus;
- Even though God is self-sufficient, given His nature of Love, He desires an intimate relationship with each of us;
- Developing an intimate relationship with God will not happen accidentally, you will have to invest quality and quantity time in His presence, just like you would with any other meaningful earthly relationship;
- Some recommendations on how you can develop an intimate relationship with God include, but are not limited to: spending quality and quantity time with Him through His Word; testing His promises by putting His Word to practice; engaging in godly services; fellowshipping with godly believers; avoiding sin, and consistently ministering to the Lord.

# Are You Moving Forward with Jesus?

# Chapter 13

# HOW TO AVOID EXTREMES IN YOUR RELATIONSHIP WITH GOD

As you work on developing an intimate relationship with God, be certain to avoid extremes. God is humble. He is quite a "gentleman," who is interested in a day-to-day fellowship and intimate relationship with you. Being too extreme in your approach to Him will lead to some major problems. There are two possible extremes that many godly Christians might unfortunately fall into: (1) legalism; or (2) abuse of God's grace. Either one of these is spiritually fatal, and the Bible addresses both of these issues. Let us take a closer look at these extremes.

## The Pitfall of Legalism

The word "legalism" is traditionally used by Christians to describe a very strict doctrinal position whereby some believers, unfortunately, adhere to various rules and regulations (do's and don'ts) for their spiritual growth, and even to matters pertaining to their salvation. I briefly discussed the notion of legalism in the previous chapters, but here, I want to offer a detailed discussion on this problem, with hopes of teaching you how to avoid it.

Those who hold a legalistic position about various Christian doctrines essentially miss the true essence of why the Old Testament Mosaic Law (rules and regulations or do's and don'ts ) was given in the first place. Before Christ, God gave the Mosaic Law to the Jews during the Old Testament era, in order to serve as their "guardian," "teacher," "protector," or schoolmaster" in the ways of righteousness (Galatians 3:24). The Old Testament Law, which reflected God's righteous standard was actually meant to reveal to the Jews how impossible it was for them to keep it, hence they needed a Savior (see chapter 5 of this book).

In fact, because the Old Testament Law represented God's righteous standards, it revealed the Sinful Nature of Man, and brought death instead of freedom (see the book of Romans; 2 Corinthians 3:7-11), due to the frustration and impossibilities of keeping it. But one person, Christ Jesus, fulfilled the entire Old Testament Mosaic Law perfectly. Hence we, as New Testament believers, do not have to approach God in a legalistic fashion.

But, if you, a New Testament believer, insist on approaching God from a legalistic position, you will definitely experience the same frustration and death that the Old Testament Jews experienced. In the book of Colossians, the Bible warns against living out our Christian faith in legalism. The apostle Paul wrote under the inspiration of the Holy Spirit:

*"Since you died with Christ to the elemental spiritual forces of this world, why, as though you still belonged to the world, do you submit to its rules: "Do not handle! Do not taste! Do not touch!"? These rules, which have to do with things that are all destined to per-*

*ish with use, are based on merely human commands and teachings. Such regulations indeed have an appearance of wisdom, with their self-imposed worship, their false humility and their harsh treatment of the body, but they lack any value in restraining sensual indulgence"* (2:20–23), (emphasis author's).

As you can see from the Scripture above, the saddest thing about legalism is that it gives the appearance of godliness which is often outward. As such, those who are legalistic have a sense of pride, as they are deceived into thinking that their self-righteousness and outward appearances will win them favor with God, which is false; because God is after the heart, and not after outward appearances. The legalistic individuals' self-righteousness may win them favor with their fellow men, but not with God Who is not impressed, and will never bless or honor self-righteousness. <u>Worst case scenario, legalism will prevent people from allowing God to change them from the heart, resulting in them missing out on God's grace and divine plans for their lives.</u>

Legalism was the major problem the Lord Jesus experienced with the legalistic Jews of His day, the Pharisees and Sadducees (see the Gospels). These legalistic group of people gave the Lord the hardest time because of His humility, heartfelt love, compassion and fellowship with ordinary people. And in return, the Lord expressed the harshest words towards them, calling them "hypocrites," "white washed tombs," "dead men bones," etc (see the Gospels). Today, in the body of Christ, we still have what I call the "Pharisees and Sadducees Syndromes" as evidenced among some believers. While some Christians may not be applying those same do's and don'ts as seen in the Mosaic Laws, they have come up with hundreds of other sophisticated rules and regulations that are hindering many others from enjoying a genuine heartfelt intimate relationship with God, thus impeding their growth. Below are some examples of what legalism sounds like:

**Legalistic Christians often Make Comments Such As :**

- "God will not answer your prayer if you do not go to church," which is FALSE.

- "You should attend church on a particular day, such as Saturday," which is FALSE.

- " You can only eat certain foods to please God," which is FALSE.

- "You can only listen to Christian music," which is FALSE.

- "You cannot wear makeup to church," which is FALSE.

- "You must cover your hair and wear long pants to attend church," which is FALSE.

- "You have to study the Bible [X amount of times per day, they would specify the exact times] in order for God to answer your prayer," which is FALSE.

- "You have to pray [X amount of times per day, they would specify the exact times] in order for God to answer," which is FALSE.

- "If you drive such and such a car, God will not be pleased," which is FALSE.

- "If you do not scream, and yell and hit the wall when you pray, God will not answer your prayer," which is FALSE.

- "God helps only those who help themselves," which is FALSE.

- "Women cannot preach, teach or proclaim the Gospel of Jesus Christ," which is FALSE.

- "If you do not belong to a certain denomination, you are not a Christian," which is FALSE.

- "Catholics are not true Christians," which is FALSE.

- "Those who do not adhere to certain denominational teachings are not Christians," which is FALSE.

- "Those who are not filled with the Holy Spirit, as evidenced by speaking in tongues, are not true Christians," which is FALSE.

- "You are not saved, if you do not perform additional works to please God," which is FALSE.

- "If you do not attend church, you cannot be a true Christian," which is FALSE.

- On and on it goes.............., all rules and regulations, which are all FALSE.

The list of self-imposed rules and regulations is endless. Christ died to give us the freedom or liberty that the Old Testament people never experienced. As an example, while it is important to dress modestly and presentably, God is after your heart. Because if God can change your heart, you will, without any one telling you, start changing your outward appearances and mannerisms effortlessly, through the power of the Holy Spirit.

> *The more you entangle yourself in legalism in order to please God, the more you will end up despising and disliking your relationship with Him, and you will in turn view the Christian life as too difficult. In fact, it is impossible to live out your faith by rules and regulations.*

**True change can only come from within [through God], and not from without [outwardly on your own efforts]. The interesting thing is that once you allow God to change you from the heart, you will be set free to live out your Christian life primarily to honor and glorify Him because you love Him, and not because of obligation (i.e., do's and don'ts), in order to gain His favor; there is a big difference. But the legalistic Christians are primarily performing out of obligation to win God's favor, which is neither from their heart nor out of love for Him**. The irony is that, the legalistic Christians are so blinded that, they completely forget or ignore the simple truth that God sees their hypocrisy openly! In their blindness and pride, they approach God as they approach their fellow human beings, in pride and deceit.

Make it a goal in your relationship with God to avoid legalism, because it will ruin you. Legalism will prevent you from enjoying the freedom Christ Jesus died for you to have. Because **the more you entangle yourself in legalism in order to please God, the more you will end up despising and disliking your relationship with Him, and you will in turn view the Christian life** as too difficult. **In fact, it is impossible to live out your faith by rules and regulations**. So, avoid legalism and enjoy your relationship with God?

Besides legalism, another extreme to avoid in your relationship with God is that of abusing His grace. Let us examine this issue closely.

## The Pitfall of Abusing God's Grace

God's grace is multifaceted. Simply put, it refers to God's favor, love, kindness, compassion, and blessings towards us, including His offer of eternity to us, even though as "Fallen" human beings, we do not deserve it. Part of God's grace is His mercy towards us, referring to God's choice to withhold His punishment towards us, even when we deserve it.

Just like King Solomon expressed in the book of Ecclesiastes, there is nothing new under the sun (1:9). It appears that practicing sin is the primary way that people abuse God's grace. Way back over 2000 years ago, there were those who specialized in taking God's grace and mercy to the extreme, essentially abusing it by living in sin (see the book of Jude). Likewise today, in the body of Christ, there are those who profess to be followers of the Lord, yet they are unashamedly practicing sin and proudly expressing how God still loves them, regardless.

In fact, those abusing God's grace are so deceived into thinking that God is approving of their sinful lifestyle because they claim to have "peace," which is absolutely impossible, if you are a genuine Christian. Just like the apostle Paul said in the book of Romans, let God's Word be true and everybody else be a liar (Romans 3:4)! It is impossible for a person to live a life contrary to God's Word, in gross disobedience and sin, and enjoy the peace of God at the same time — impossible! This deceit is from Satan, keeping those people in bondage by placing blinders in their "souls."

> *God is perfectly holy and righteous, and cannot, and will not, no matter how you want to say it, fellowship with anyone who is practicing sin.*

**Practicing sin and God's peace are mutually exclusive — hence, you cannot have both at the same time, impossible. God is perfectly holy and righteous, and cannot, and will not, no matter how you want to say it, fellowship with anyone who is practicing sin!** This is the nature of God, and there is nothing you can do to circumvent this. So if you foolishly believe such nonsense from Satan, then God's Word has proven that you are a liar, and I choose to believe God and not you, period! End of discussion.

Of course, God still loves a person who is living a sinful life and abusing His grace, because He is love in His core nature. **God does not give love, or love you less or more based on your actions! He is love! And He is stable and consistent. But our actions or lifestyles will do one of two things: separate us from God's presence (i.e., getting us further away from Him, in addition to hindering His blessings, favor and protection in our lives), or draw us closer to Him, which will position us to receive His abundant blessings.** We are the determining factor and not God or even Satan.

God is always present, but it is up to us to allow His presence to manifest in our lives. And one thing that will definitely separate us from God's presence and quench the work of the Holy Spirit in our lives is sin. So please, do not allow Satan to deceive you that God is pleased with you [because He, God, is love] when you are living a sinful lifestyle. Thus, abusing His grace and living in sin is outright foolishness and stupidity: STOP IT! I believe you are wiser than that. **God did not die for you, and raise you up so that you would remain in bondage by Satan. He has set you free through the blood of Jesus, so STOP the sin! I find it very ironical that the same people who abuse God's grace actually end up going without it, because they allow Satan to devour them — this is deep, meditate on it!**

I heard a story recently about a woman who is professing to be a "Christian," but she is unashamedly practicing sexual sin, living and engaging in sexual relationship and cohabitating with her sister's estranged husband. This lady is stupidly going around telling everyone how God is blessing the relationship; but even a child can figure out that this behavior is wrong and ungodly. This is such a lie from the "pit of hell," and the kind of deception that Satan can get people into. This lady is so deceived by Satan; she will not repent, yet, she spends hours "studying the Bible and praying", believing she is right with God.

When confronted, she had the audacity to say that Christ has freed her to live her life, thus no one should judge her because God loves her!—what a pity, and a disgrace to the name of the Lord Jesus and a horrible advertisement for God. These are the kind of people whose sinful behaviors would turn innocent people, who are genuinely seeking God away from Him. Hopefully, you are learning right now, from this book, that God will never condone any form of sin, period! So do not allow such lies from Satan to turn you away from your pursuit of God!

Who knows if such a person, like the woman I described above is even a genuine Christian! Like the Lord asked, why would anyone bother to call Him Lord, if the individual refuses to practice what He teaches? (Luke 6:46). As already mentioned in previous chapters, the Lord warns that a good tree cannot produce bad fruit, and a bad tree cannot produce good fruit; thus, by people's fruits (i.e., their actions), we can tell if they are His true followers. Furthermore, Jesus warned that not everyone who calls Him Lord is His true follower. So for those of you who may be thinking that I am judging this lady, these are the Lord's Words and not mine (see Matthew 7:21-23). Thus, if my comments about this lady bothers you, I recommend that you take your concerns to Him [Christ Jesus] directly. In this situation described above, it is either this lady has not sincerely made Christ her Lord, or she has, but she is living in disobedience; and neither one glorifies God.

To those abusing God's grace, be very prepared to deal with the consequences, because all sin and disobedience have subsequent consequences. **God is not mocked, a man must reap what he sows (Galatians 6:7).** This is a principle of God that cannot be circumvented. Grace abusers often forget about this principle, because they are blinded and deceived by their lustful passions and selfish desires, but a day of "reaping" will come, very soon. In the natural world, it would be stupid to plant Pineapple seeds but then expect to harvest Mangoes, right? Likewise, in the spiritual realm, you cannot abuse God's grace by living in sin and expect to see godly results. It will not happen!

There is a popular saying that goes like this: "garbage in, garbage out." That is to say, if you allow "garbage" (i.e., ungodly thoughts, habits and practices) to get into your soul, it must come out into the physical realm somehow. For most people, it comes out in the form of unexplained restlessness, anxiety, fear, worry, insomnia, chronic frustration, strife, all sorts of diseases, etc, which are all forms of spiritual death. This does not happen because God is punishing you for abusing His grace and living in sin; rather, your actions of obeying Satan and giving him direct access into your life will lead to the suffering and death. Satan's main objective is to kill, steal and destroy you completely (John 10:10); thereby, destroying your testimony and turning others away from God. So do not give him access to your life!

## PRACTICAL APPLICATION

It is God's will for us to avoid legalism and to appreciate, and appropriate His grace accordingly, rather than abuse it. So what are some things you can do to avoid falling into the pitfall of legalism? Below I offer some recommendations:

### Some Recommendations on How to Avoid Legalism

- Agree with God's Word that you cannot live out your Christian faith based on rules and regulations;

- Agree with God's Word that He is after your heart, and He desires an intimate relationship with you;

- Agree with God's Word that He wants you to approach Him as you would a friend, with sincerity and love, rather than from a do's and don'ts perspective;

- Ask the Holy Spirit to change the intentions of your heart, so that your actions, worship and services to God will be primarily based out of love for Him, and a sincere desire to please and glorify Him, rather than attempts to "show-off your self-righteousness";

- View your fellow Christians as God views them, with unconditional love and acceptance, and not from your self-righteous perspective;

- Keep in mind that each individual is in a different "place" in their relationship with God, thus be considerate in your dealings with others;

- With the exception of heresy (i.e., false teachings), do not judge another person's ministry, relationship with God, or growth process based on your standards; you cannot perceive the heart. And you do not have the ability to know what God might be doing in someone's heart;

- Learn to be patient with people and observe God's work in their lives;

- Do not "put down" others who are not as "holy" in appearance, mannerisms, or speech as you might think you are! That attitude is not pleasing to the Lord;

- Remember the absolute Truth that God never blesses us based on our good performances or works, but because of our position and relationship with Christ. Although good services as led by the Lord are necessary to further the Kingdom of God on the earth, all such services should be based out of love for God and from a genuine heart;

- Remember that you already have favor with God because of the Lord Jesus, and you cannot add or delete anything from that; so relax and enjoy the "ride": REST in Christ;

- Approach your relationship with God with simplicity and humility. Do not try to impress Him! He is already impressed with you because of Christ Jesus, He already loves you indefinitely, and there is nothing you can do to make Him love you more or less!;

- Do not allow anyone to dictate to you specific days that you can attend church or worship God; or allow others to impose other specific rules to you such as what to eat, wear, etc, in your approach and relationship with God;

- Obey God's Word, abide in Christ, and allow the Holy Spirit to lead your actions and relationship with God. Refuse to allow others to dictate to you their legalistic ways on how you should please God. You have been set free by the blood of Jesus to have an awesome relationship with God, express your liberty and freedom in Christ ( I talk more about freedom in Christ later in this chapter).

I could add more on the above list, but hopefully you get the point. **Most importantly, do not get legalism mixed up with "good service" for the Kingdom of God. Every Christian is a co-worker of God in order to foster His Kingdom on the earth; as such, God expects us to engage in good service for Him. But we must perform these good services willingly, out of love and compassion for the lost and the underprivileged as we are led by the Holy Spirit, and not out of obligation or legalism in order to win God's favor.** The Old Testament do's and don'ts (rules and regulations) were merely a shadow of the real thing: Christ, and He has already fulfilled all of them ( see the book of Hebrews).

As mentioned earlier, the other extreme a person can fall into in his or her relationship with God is that of abusing God's grace, which is an awful shame and disgrace. Let us now examine how to avoid this pitfall.

## Some Recommendations on How to Avoid Abusing God's Grace

- Study the Scriptures and ask the Holy Spirit to enable you to have a revelation of God's grace, which will help you to better understand His unconditional and unfathomable love for you. Without this revelation, you will struggle with this issue, because a true revelation of God's grace is the impetus to preventing and avoiding ungodliness and sin (Titus 2:11-14). It is my belief that if you actually get a revelation of God's grace towards you, you will not want to hurt Him [God]. As an example, it would be difficult for you to hurt your spouse, friend , or another loved one who continuously expresses his or her love towards you, and does not hurt you, but goes out of his or her way to please you, right? Likewise, why would you want to hurt God, who has done nothing wrong to you, except love you and died on the cross to redeem you from Satan?

Like the apostle Paul said, how can we, Christians, continue to sin in order for God's grace to abound? It cannot be so! That was his answer, because Christ has redeemed us from the Sinful Nature and propensity to practice sin, thus, sin has no dominion over us. Through the enabling of the Holy Spirit, you can overcome sin. I have said this throughout this book, but it is fitting to say it here again: If you are practicing sin now, I recommend you (1) ask God to forgive you, right now; (2) stop the behavior completely; and (3) accept the consequences without excuses, and trust God's forgiveness and cleansing.

- View God's grace from a godly perspective —in light of His unconditional love and your freedom in Christ.

The freedom we have in Christ is not to abuse God's grace by living selfishly and practicing ungodliness, but rather to love and serve one another (Galatians 5:13-14). It is freedom to serve and worship God from your heart without the constraints of the Old Testament rules and regulations. It is freedom to make the right decisions to honor God, and to worship Him anywhere, and in any style suitable to your temperament. It is also a freedom to address God as your Father, and to go to Him directly with your petitions and have the assurance that He hears you. Much more, it is a freedom to personally know the Truths of God as revealed in His Word, and the ability to personally discern His voice in your heart.

Freedom in Christ also implies surrendering yourself to Him willingly, and allowing Him to direct your paths. This type of freedom promotes a general sense of psychological, physical and spiritual well-being and contentment in your relationship with Christ. This type of freedom is so liberating that it causes you to want to say something like: "*I am proud of who I am in Christ, and there is nothing anyone can do to shatter my new identity.*" Freedom in Christ will also promote confidence and foster stability in all of your earthly relationships, as you will become "rooted" in the source of love: Christ Himself.

Additionally, freedom in Christ is energizing, as it will propel you to engage in godly services and gain a deeper appreciation of God. Most importantly, this freedom will enable you to better appreciate God's grace, which has brought salvation to all people, and has delivered you, from the Kingdom of darkness (Titus 2:11). Hallelujah! Praise the Lord!

In conclusion, loving God from your heart and serving Him will lead to much peace and liberation in your life. God is always willing to bless you abundantly, but legalism and abuse of His grace will definitely quench His presence and blessings. Therefore, in your approach to God, make it a daily effort to live in the freedom you now have in Christ, and allow His grace to change your heart. Now that you have a solid understanding of how to develop a relationship with God and avoid extremes, let us proceed to the next chapter, where I focus on the necessity for continuous growth as a Christian.

## Summary Points

- At the end of the day, when it is all said and done, God is primarily after your heart, because He desires a personal relationship with you;

- All of your good service to the Lord has to be grounded from a genuine heartfelt relationship with Him, primarily because you love Him;

- If you have a genuine love for God, you will approach Him as a friend, rather than from a list of do's and don'ts;

- Approaching God from a legalistic approach is futile; you will be frustrated and miss the blessings of God;

- Those who abuse God's grace by practicing sin will definitely quench the presence of the Holy Spirit in their lives, thereby giving Satan direct access into their lives to kill, steal and to destroy them;

- Because of God's grace, true Christians have the freedom and/or liberty through Christ and the enabling of the Holy Spirit to know God personally, and to fellowship with Him as they desire;

- It is the grace of God that should energize and propel us to love and serve Him more;

- A lack of revelation of God's grace is one reason why some people abuse His grace.

## Chapter 14

# How to Grow in Your Relationship with God

Just like we expect an infant to someday grow as a toddler, then adolescent, teenager, and finally as an adult, God expects us to likewise grow as His Children. In my view, one of the most tragic things is for a Christian to remain a "baby Christian" the rest of their earthly lives. It is a shame to be a follower of the Lord Jesus, yet be stunted in the knowledge and blessings of such a great salvation. I liken it to someone who receives a free scholarship to attend a very expensive and prestigious University; yet, he or she does not take the time to read the requirements for completing the application, either due to ignorance or just "plain laziness"; and as such, the individual proceeds to borrow large sums of money to pay for the tuition: this would be a tragedy! Unfortunately, this example is very similar to what "baby Christians" do—the Lord has done everything for them, including offering His Word as a guide for their lives; yet, they refuse to invest the time to study, grow, and experience His blessings.

Imagine how disgusting it would be for a parent(s) if their toddler child reaches adulthood, but refuses to behave like an adult; and instead, lounges on the "sofa" all day watching TV and playing video games, expecting the parent(s) to do everything for him or her. I am certain that this kind of behavior will be repulsive to any loving parent(s) who desires to see their young child grow into a responsible adult making contributions to society. If such an adult does not change quickly and start behaving like a mature responsible adult, eventually, he or she will be 100% stunted in every area of life, which will pave the way for a host of physical, emotional, and spiritual issues. Likewise, a "baby Christian" is an "open door" for a host of physical, emotional and spiritual attacks from Satan, due to stunted knowledge about his or her identity in Christ.

## Why Growth is Essential

As a new Christian, or a Christian who has not been properly taught (i.e., discipled) about his or her true identity in Christ, you are an easy prey to your enemy Satan, because you are not well grounded in the Truths found in God's Word. Satan could not prevent you from becoming a Christian, but now that you have accepted to follow the Lord, he [Satan] will do everything he can to plant lies and doubts in your mind about your salvation and relationship with God. He may even introduce and plant thoughts in your mind to the notion that "you are not really saved," which is a lie. And he may even bring to your remembrance a lot of your past sins, which God has completely forgiven. Or worse, Satan may even lie to you that your salvation was too easy, thereby lying to you that you have to perform extra "works" in order for God to accept you; which is a lie! All of these thoughts are lies, which is why growing as a Christian is absolutely essential.

Growing in your true identity as a child of God will also prevent you from becoming easily tossed back and forth by every new false doctrine or philosophy of the world, which all originate from Satan (Colossians 2:8). Nowadays, every time you turn around, there is a New Age Spiritualist with a bestselling book about some new way to be happy, make money, know some god, fulfill all of your dreams, etc. These New Age Spiritualists are not inventing anything new, it is the same lies packaged under a different name. The book of Ecclesiastes says, there is nothing new under the sun (1:9); it is the same devil, with a new wrinkle. But God is consistent and predictable— the same yesterday, today and forever (Hebrews 13:8), so growing in your faith will definitely foster stability in your pilgrimage as a Christian.

The Bible teaches that God has given us, His children, everything we need to live godly lives as Christians and grow in the faith (2 Peter 1: 1-3). And throughout this book, I have explained how God lives [in the form of His Spirit] on the inside of each believer; and we have His Word, which is like a roadmap to live out the Christian life. Much more, because of God's love and grace, He has given us His promises [found in His Word] so that we can become partakers of His "divine nature", thereby freeing us from the wickedness of the world (2 Peter 1: 4). But, it is our responsibility to appropriate God's promises and grow in our faith and journey with Him, through the power of His indwelling Spirit.

Accepting to follow Christ Jesus is a free gift, but some effort is required to grow in Him. After the initial expression of our "saving faith" (i.e., the faith required to initially accept Christ Jesus as Lord and Savior) at the time we decide by faith, to follow Jesus, we must continuously engage in godly activities that will enable our faith to be quickened and strengthened. I have said throughout this book how becoming a Christian is an instantaneous event, once we make a genuine confession of faith; but growing in the knowledge of Christ is a process, over the remainder of our lives.

The Bible teaches that growth "in Christ" takes place as we become virtuous, knowledgeable, self-controlled, patient, godly, and exhibit brotherly affection and love in our pilgrimage on the earth. The good news is that, it will be the indwelling Triune God enabling you to exercise these qualities as you allow and obey Him. And as you do these things and grow in your faith, you will then become productive and bear much fruit for God's Kingdom, which is His will for you (2 Peter 1:5-8). Let us now examine each of these responsibilities for our growth, even though I have discussed most of them in preceding chapters.

## PRACTICAL APPLICATION

### How to Continuously Grow in Your Faith

> **Become Virtuous**

To be virtuous means you have "good character," or you are a person with "good qualities" or "good worth." Essentially, you are a person of "high caliber", with highly desirable qualities by others. In regards to Christianity, it implies that you exhibit Christ-like qualities that are immediately obvious to others. You cannot cause these qualities to manifest on your own effort; they will only emanate from you if you are abiding in Christ (John 15:1-8). So, it goes without saying that abiding in Christ is absolutely essential for your growth. If you are still unsure how to abide in Christ, I recommend that you reread this entire book, especially focusing on chapters 2; 3; 12 and 13.

> **Become Knowledgeable**

The correct knowledge about the Triune God is critical for your growth. I am not referring to just a "head" or academic knowledge; rather, a deeper revelation or experiential knowledge of the true nature of God and the Truths of who you are in Christ. I have explained throughout this book the importance of knowing the true nature of God and His available power to you through the Holy Spirit. Knowing the true nature of God is the only antidote against heresy. **There are many so-called truths out there, but you only need to focus on knowing The Truth —the Truth about God as revealed in His Word.** The only way you will overcome the trials, temptations and hardships in this life is to be rooted, and be grounded in the Truths found in the Bible. You will do this by consistently studying and meditating on the Scriptures, fellowshipping with "like-minded" believers, engaging in good service, and witnessing to others about your faith in Christ. If you are still unsure how to do these things, I recommend that you reread this entire book, paying particular attention to chapters 2 through 10.

> *Even though Christ Jesus has set you free from the Kingdom of darkness, it is your choice whether or not you experience that freedom daily.*

**Even though Christ Jesus has set you free from the Kingdom of darkness, it is your choice whether or not you experience that freedom daily. In the Gospel of John chapter 8, the Lord taught that if we are faithful in applying His teachings in our lives, then we will become His disciples (i.e., students), and it is only then, that the Truth will set us free (vv. 31-32). Many people often misquote and take that Scripture out of context by emphasizing the part that says "*...the truth shall set you free (v.32)*". But the Lord had a prerequisite to that (i.e., being faithful to His teachings, applying them into our lives and becoming His disciples). So the truth in and of itself does not set any one free—you must apply the Truths of Christ in your life in order to experience its liberating ability.**

Therefore, to experience the kind of freedom the Lord is talking about, you have to consistently study, meditate and apply His teachings in your life; and as you do that, His teachings will become experiential knowledge to you, which will then supernaturally transform your life and set you free from the darkness and deceit this world has to offer. I recommend that you reread and meditate on the teachings found in chapters 7 through 9 of this book, and learn how to allow the Truths of Christ to take precedence in your life and transform you moment-by-moment.

*Wrong knowledge about God will lead to wrong ways of praying, worshiping, living, expecting and receiving from Him, along with a host of other problems and frustration in this life.*

Never underestimate the power of knowing the correct knowledge about God and your salvation. In the book of Hosea, God said that His children perish due to a lack of knowledge about Him (4:6). **Wrong knowledge about God will lead to wrong ways of praying, worshiping, living, expecting and receiving from Him, along with a host of other problems and frustration in this life.** You can avoid all of these problems by just investing some time in knowing more about your great salvation and the Triune God.

Much more, the Bible admonishes us to be always ready to explain to others why we have such unfathomable hope in Christ (1 Peter 3:15). The best way to do this is by gaining the correct knowledge about Christ. And you will do this by diligently studying and meditating on the Truths found in the Word, in order to be edified, grow in your faith, and be well equipped to educate and explain to others the blessed hope you have in Christ.

> ➤ **Display Self-control**

Your growth involves exhibiting self control, which is an

evidence that you are manifesting the Fruit of the Spirit. You do this by asking, and relying on the Holy Spirit to enable you to exhibit control in every area of your life, such as not overdoing or under doing anything. You must maintain godly boundaries. For example, do not overeat, overwork, oversleep, etc, and do not under eat (i.e., starve yourself to be thin), under serve God, or become lazy and/or passive in anything you do. Self- control also entails allowing the Holy Spirit to regulate (i.e., teach you how to control or manage) your emotions, speech, finances, shopping, marriage, raising of your children, other relationships, or other areas in life you might be struggling with maintaining godly boundaries.

Without proper self-control, you will open the door for your enemy Satan, to attack you. I like the way the Amplified Bible (AMP) puts it: *"Be sober [well balanced and self-disciplined], be alert and cautious at all times. That enemy of yours, the devil, prowls around like a roaring lion [fiercely hungry], seeking someone to devour"* (1 Peter 5:8), (emphasis author's). Just like everything else in life, self-control is a process, so be patient.

> **Become Patient**

Another quality required for your growth is the ability to be patient with God, yourself and others. I have already discussed this issue at length in the preceding chapters. But suffice it to say, **the life of a Christian is a life of learning how to be patient, while trusting God**. We are finite beings, and God's timing and ways are often different from ours. Often, most of us only gain a godly perspective and appreciation for our "patience" once the manifestation of God's promises is evident in our lives. But, if you endure your race with a godly perspective from the beginning, it will advance your growth and mold your character much faster.

I have already explained how godly patience ultimately leads to hope, which is energizing, so keep this in mind. By godly patience, I am referring to an attitude of continuous growing in the faith, while studying and abiding in Christ with expectancy to inherit His promises as written in The Word. Many people claim to be patiently waiting for the Lord, yet they engage in ungodly conducts in attempts to circumvent things; this will not glorify God, and He will definitely not bless such compromised behaviors.

> ➢ **Exhibit Godliness**

Growing in godliness (i.e., righteousness, holiness, etc ) involves all of the other responsibilities I have discussed above and throughout this book. I explained early how righteousness is imputed to us at the time of salvation because of our position in Christ. But the experiential aspect of this (i.e., practical righteousness) implies that you become responsible in living holy and in abstaining from practicing sin through the indwelling power of the Holy Spirit, thereby maintaining your purity (1 John 3:3). Growth also means that you become continuously aware not to allow your actions to quench the Holy Spirit by any means; rather, you become steadfast in allowing Him to mold and shape you into the image of Christ, so that you will manifest His godly qualities (Galatians 5: 22-23).

> ➢ **Exhibit Brotherly Affection**

Expressing a genuine and, an unselfish (i.e., selfless) attitude, care and concern for your fellow Christian, or any other human being is essential for your growth as a child of God. God is unselfishly caring and compassionate towards us: Christians and non-Christians alike. But the difference is that, He has a covenant relationship with the Christian through Christ, and no such relationship exists between Him and the unbeliever. But He loves each of us, because that is His nature. But as His children [those who have a covenant relationship with Him], He wants us to grow and manifest these same qualities of selfless care and concern, etc, towards Christians and non-Christians alike. Our natural tendency as "fallen" human beings is to be selfish (i.e., focus primarily on our own needs and problems), which is a recipe for depression and anxiety. But, as a new creature in Christ and abiding in Him, God wants you to grow and become more selfless in your actions, which is the best antidote for depression, anxiety, loneliness, fear, worry, and a host of other toxic disease-prone ungodly emotions that people experience when they are self-absorbed.

The best way to overcome your selfish desires is to simply refuse to act on them (i.e., dying daily to your flesh), and focusing on the needs of others through the enabling of the Holy Spirit. As you do that, God will supernaturally take care of your own needs (Proverbs 11:25). I do not know exactly how this works spiritually, but it does. As a minister, I have experienced times and days when I was physically and emotionally exhausted from ministering to others; but I was strengthened supernaturally, and thus I continued to minister to others even when I thought I would not be able to—that was God meeting my needs, as I met the needs of others.

> **Exhibit Love**

Growing in your ability to exhibit God's kind of love is essential. The cardinal way others will discern you are Christ-like is through your unconditional love for others (John 13: 34-35). Briefly, there are four major kinds of love: Eros (i.e., passionate and sexual love); Phileo (i.e., friendship love); Storge (i.e., love for family); and Agape (i.e., God's kind of love). In this chapter however, I will only focus on agape love, which is God's kind of love.

Agape love is unconditional, selfless love in action; it is the only type of love with the highest level of satisfaction and stability. As an example, God displayed this type of love for His creation when He died on the cross. Agape love is not based on your emotions, but rather, on a decision to love someone, whether or not they deserve it. This type of love is supernatural, and you cannot express it to others without abiding in Christ, who is the source of the love. This kind of love also requires corresponding actions to make it complete; it is not "mere talking"!

The Lord Jesus said that if we love Him, we should obey Him and practice what He teaches (John 14:15, 23-24). Obeying God is good evidence that we love Him and are growing in our relationship with Him. Nonetheless, "talk is cheap," and anyone can profess to love God; but, if the individual's lifestyle is inconsistent with God's Word, such a person is a liar, period!; and no further discussion is necessary! As you mature in Christ, be certain to make decisions primarily based on what the Word of God teaches, and not based on your emotions or what everyone else is saying or doing. I have highlighted throughout this book how we live out the Christian life by faith in God and His Word, and not by how we feel (2 Corinthians 5:7). Therefore, do not wait to "feel" agape love. You will never be able to exhibit agape love if you wait to be led by your emotions! Instead, act in love and trust God with the results!

For example, expressing Agape love means you make a decision to love those people around you who you might perceive as unlovable for various reasons that only you know; and you learn to become compassionate towards others, because God loves them. If God can love them in spite of how unlikeable and unlovable you might perceive them to be, who are you not to accept and love them? Personally, what enables me to love those individuals who have hurt me is to simply ask the Lord Jesus to love them through me; and I constantly remind myself that God loves them as they are, even though He does not condone their ungodliness and selfish behaviors. With that perspective, I would ask the Holy Spirit to strengthen me as I approach my relationship with them from that Godly perspective; it works, consider trying that approach.

Furthermore, Agape love means that you easily forgive, and you offer yourself to help others in need, without being asked first. Additionally, agape love means you serve (i.e., doing godly service for Christ) without grudging or complaining; you support the body of Christ through your prayers and finances; you become the best employee or employer, etc, all of which are essential for your growth as a Christian. **Agape love is not**

> *Agape love is not difficult to practice as you abide in Christ and allow Him to flow through you. The problem is that many people are attempting to express agape love on their own efforts — it is impossible.*

**difficult to practice as you abide in Christ and allow Him to flow through you. The problem is that many people are attempting to express agape love on their own efforts — it is impossible. You must be attached to the source of the love: Christ, and have experienced the love for yourself, in order for that love to flow through you to others.** You probably have heard the popular saying that "you cannot give what you do not have," this is so true in regards to agape love. But, as you spend time in God's presence and grow in your journey with Him, you will start experiencing His love for you, which will then enable you to express His supernatural love towards others.

It is God's will for you to grow, and as such, He will be faithful in enabling and encouraging you in your pilgrimage, so that your lifestyle will glorify Him. On the other hand, refusing to grow will cause you to become blinded to the fact that you have been cleansed from your past, and this blindness could lead you astray, and right back into the old lifestyle and habits which Christ delivered you from (2 Peter 1:9). But, the good news is that those who embrace these responsibilities and grow will not "fall away" (i.e., relapse), or become blinded to the Truths about their new identity in Christ (2 Peter 1:9) —the choice is yours!

As you can see from the above qualities required for our growth as Christians, they require some kind of action on our part. **This is not to imply that actions are required before you are accepted by God: NO, that is not what I am saying.** Even though you become born again with absolutely no "works" on your own, the Bible teaches that "good works or services" are indeed necessary to grow in your faith and to become Christ-like. And a genuine conversion to Christianity will produce good "works" to glorify Christ. It is our responsibility therefore to allow the Holy Spirit to mold and shape us into the image of Christ, as we abide in Him with reverential fear of God, while avoiding all ungodliness (Philippians 2:12).

We must make it a daily habit to grow in the faith and be strengthened, as we obey God. The apostle James, under the inspiration of the Holy Spirit emphasized that faith without corresponding action is essentially "useless," because a genuine conversion to the faith will produce good "works" for the Lord (James 2:14-25). Again, this has nothing to do with how you obtain salvation in Christ; but rather, the apostle James is teaching on the importance of acting out our faith (i.e., putting to practice what we believe) as we are led by God. It implies stepping out in faith and doing whatever the Bible teaches, or doing whatever the Lord might be prompting you to do in your heart, which will be consistent with His written Word. When it is all said and done, God will reward us in eternity based on our good "works or service" to Him (see the book of Revelation).

As an example, as a Christian, you believe it is God's will to pray and "lay hands" on the sick in order for them to recover, right? Thus, if you know someone who is sick and requires you to pray for their healing, it will be God's will for you to pray for them! But if the Lord is prompting you to physically "lay your hands" on them and pray that way, yet you refuse to do so, your faith will be incomplete. In this case, to make your faith complete, you would pray for the individual, plus physically "lay your hands" on them, in order for your faith to have full impact. Carrying out

God's instructions in this manner is necessary for your growth and the quickening and strengthening of your faith in Him.

As a minister and a doctor, I have the opportunity to interact with hundreds of Christians and non-Christians alike in any given week, and some of their testimonies are very empowering. I want to share just one of such edifying and encouraging testimonies, pointing to how tenacious we have to be in our growth as Christians. I saw one of my elderly dearest patients last week, who is exemplary of a true Christian who is continuously growing in the faith. She is 96 years old, and became a Christian in her early twenties.

Throughout her journey with Christ, she has experienced tremendous pain, suffering, and unexplained hardships. Just after a few years of marriage, her beloved husband was murdered, execution style and she was an eye witness to that horrific scene. Then, as a single mother, she struggled through much poverty to raise her three boys. Notwithstanding, while she was still dealing with the grief and major loss of her husband, one of her children became mentally ill and was committed into a mental institution, with very limited privileges for her to visit him. Because of financial issues and transportation, she was lucky if she saw him [her son] once a year. Then, her eldest son, as a young adult, became an alcoholic and ended up dying in his early fifties from Liver Cirrhosis.

Through all of the hardships, the family was torn apart, and the siblings were not communicating due to much strife and other family conflicts. As a result, she was not able to spend time with one of the sons until after the death of the other son. In spite of all these emotional and financial hardships, she kept studying the Word, and remained steadfast in prayer while growing in her faith. Over the last 50 years or so, she would get up around 4:30AM every day to spend about two to three hours with God, in His Word. Additionally, she was heavily involved in good service for Christ and frequent fellowship with other believers in her local church community.

In spite of her challenging trials, she exhibits no anger, resentment, or frustration, and has no complains whatsoever about her relationship with God through Christ. She told me how she is very grateful that God brought her through her trials and hardships. She acknowledges that her son killed himself by drinking, but she has forgiven him. Finally, with much prayer, the family is now together, and they have overcome the bitterness and strife.

Whenever I spend time with this patient, I always walk away feeling so blessed and encouraged, because there is much tranquility in her presence; I could sense that God is with her. At her age, she looks like she is only 75 years old. Today, she continues to spend time with God daily, attend church, grow in her faith and is steadfastly expressing agape love towards others.

Friend, God has not promised us, His children, a perfect ride (i.e., a trouble free existence as Christians) in this world, but He has promised us a perfect landing (i.e., heaven). In fact, the Lord Jesus warned that in this life, we will encounter hardships, but we should be comforted because He has overcome the world (John 16:33). As we abide and grow in Christ, we should remain unshakable, in spite of the trials, tribulations and hardships round and about us, and exhibit tenacity in our

*Your maturity as a Christian is solely dependent on you, and not God, the devil or anyone else.*

faith, just like my 95 year old patient did and still does.

In conclusion, I hope you make a daily decision to grow in your faith regardless of the circumstances. **Your maturity as a Christian is solely dependent on you, and not God, the devil or anyone else**. God has given you the free gift of salvation, now live it out with reverential fear and boldness in Christ. God wills for each of us to mature in the faith and be established in our unique gifts in order to bless and improve the lives of others. Nonetheless, **before we can impart to others what God has revealed to us, we must be "rooted" and be confident in our own identity in Christ; hence, continuous growth is mandatory for the true Christian**. I now turn to the last chapter in this book to discuss another very critical aspect of your growth — witnessing for Christ.

# Summary Points

- Becoming a Christian is an instantaneous event, but growth "in Christ" requires time and some effort on your part;
- Baby Christians refuse to grow in the faith, and are in great danger of being attacked by the enemy, Satan;
- Growth is essential in order to prevent the possibility of "falling away" from the faith;
- Key aspects of your growth involves becoming virtuous; knowledgeable; patient; godly; exhibiting God's kind of love, and the ability to witness for Christ;
- Before we can impart to others what God has revealed to us, we must first be "grounded" in our own identity in Christ, thus continuous growth as a true Christian is mandatory.

Chapter 15

# HOW TO BE AN EFFECTIVE WITNESS FOR CHRIST

Telling others about Jesus Christ is something that the Lord requires us, His disciples, to do, in addition to teaching others about His Truths [discipleship] (see Matthew 28:16-20). Telling others about your faith in Christ is usually described as witnessing. The Strong's Concordance describes the word witness as the act of "bearing a testimony to something." In the case of Christianity, it implies an act of sharing your testimony about Christ Jesus with others, Christians and non-Christians alike. You would do this by telling others about your personal experience as a Christian,

*Every Christian has a testimony of how they came to know Jesus Christ —every life is a story of God's unconditional love and grace!*

and informing them of the things God is doing in your life, in hopes of encouraging and building their faith in God. **Every Christian has a testimony of how they came to know Jesus Christ —every life is a story of God's unconditional love and grace!** So share your story with a Christ-like confidence and boldness!

Among Christians however, sharing your testimony is for the primary purpose of edifying and strengthening your fellow brethren, in order to quicken their faith and foster hope. But the primary goal for sharing your faith with non-Christians is for purposes of helping them, through the enabling of the Holy Spirit, in order for them to perceive their need for a Savior: Jesus Christ, who can deliver them from their Sinful Nature. The focus of this chapter is on witnessing to unbelievers. Witnessing can also be described as evangelism (i.e., spreading the Gospel Message of Christ; although by definition, Evangelism is slightly different).

Witnessing is God's will for each Christian, and not just for the "professional ministers." In fact, sharing your faith with others is another great way to foster your growth as a Christian. This is so because as you witness to others, they might ask relevant questions about your faith which will, hopefully, lead you to study more to ascertain the answers; and through the process of studying and searching for answers, you will grow in your knowledge about the faith. You do not need much knowledge about your salvation and new identity in Christ to be a witness. All that is necessary is for you to tell someone why and how you accepted the Lord, and how He has changed your life; then trust the Holy Spirit with the results.

It is my belief that the primary reason why people do not want to witness for Christ is because they do not understand some basic principles about witnessing, and as such, they become afraid and/or are intimidated by others. With this in mind, let us examine some of these basic principles and recommendations for witnessing effectively.

# PRACTICAL APPLICATION

## Some Recommendations on How to Be An Effective Witness For Christ:

### You Must Be Abiding in Christ in Order to Witness to Others

First things first: you cannot give what you do not have. As already explained throughout this book, Christ is the vine [source of our power] and we are like the branches [flowing out of Him]. Christ Himself describes this analogy in the Gospel of John chapter 15. Thus, if you are not abiding in Christ, you will not be able to be an effective witness for Him. Hence, a continuous filling of the Holy Spirit is absolutely mandatory in order for anyone to be an effective witness for Christ (see chapter 3).

In fact, after His resurrection, Jesus Himself warned His disciples not to witness for Him until they had received the infilling of the Holy Spirit (see Acts chapter 2). This implies that only those who are filled with the Holy Spirit can effectively witness for Christ. One unfortunate problem we have today in the body of Christ is that many Christians are attempting to witness for Christ without the power from the Holy Spirit — this is futile and will not yield results. This leads me to the second most important principle and recommendation.

### You Should Never Witness on Your Own Power and/or Efforts

Like I said above, you must be a Spirit led or Spirit filled Christian in order to witness effectively for Christ. This is primarily because when you witness for Christ, you become the vessel for God to work through to reach others. Keep in mind that your primary role is to be willing and available to step out in faith and tell someone about what Jesus Christ has done in your life, or about the circumstances that led you to make the decision to follow Him as your Lord and Savior. And when you tell your story, be honest. Do not lie or exaggerate in an attempt to convince anyone. Trust God with the results. At times "too much talking" will turn individuals off, just speak the truth with confidence and allow God to work in their hearts.

## You are Not Responsible For the Final Outcome of Your Witnessing to Others

This is an area where I could write an entire book about. Many loving Christians who have deep compassion for the "lost" (i.e., unbelievers) and are committed to spreading the Gospel message, including myself, have made this mistake — attempting to be responsible for another person's decision for Christ. This is the job of the Holy Spirit, and not ours. I used to be very disappointed and saddened for days, when someone rejects Christ after I had spent hours witnessing to them. But as I mature in witnessing to others, the Holy Spirit has been teaching me how to "let go" and not to take it personally.

I am still very troubled when someone rejects Christ as their personal Lord and Savior, but I have learnt how to accept that rejection and just move on, knowing that I have done my job by planting the "seed" (i.e., the Gospel Message), and trusting God with the final outcome. But most importantly, I continue to pray for those people. It is a biblical principle that someone may plant the "seed" [Word of God], and another person may be the one to reap the harvest (i.e., leading a person to accept to follow Christ), but ultimately, God gets the glory (1 Corinthians 3:6). So whatever you do in the act of witnessing, be certain not to take people's rejection of Christ personally: pray for them and move on!

## Briefly Get to Know the Person You are Witnessing to First

It is wisdom to be friendly with someone first, expressing your love and concern (i.e., agape love) for them before you start witnessing to them. Even when the Lord leads you to witness to someone, start by first asking them about their day, family, what they do for a living, etc. When you approach people in this manner, they will sense that you have a genuine concern for their well-being. And in turn, they might ask you about your life, family, etc. If that is the case, you can then use that opportunity to share how your day is going with Christ in your midst, then proceed to share your faith. Avoid asking people closed-ended questions. Thus, try not to ask people if they are a "Christian", because most people will respond by saying: Yes, especially if they live in the USA. But unfortunately, most people who would say <u>YES</u> to you do not truly know what it means to be a Christian, and/or are not genuine Christians.

Hence, I recommend that you simply ask people an open-ended question such as "who is Jesus Christ to you?" That way you would then engage them in an open-ended dialogue about the "real Jesus Christ" of the Bible. I say the "real Jesus Christ" because **various cults such as the Jehovah's Witnesses and the Mormons call upon the name of Jesus, but they are referring to a different**

Jesus, and not the True Jesus Christ of the Bible as He describes Himself. So be very clear about this! There is Only One Jesus Christ, the Jesus Christ of the Christian Bible!

## Pray and Look For Opportunities to Witness

Be certain that you are praying for God to embolden you when you witness, and you are not praying and asking Him whether or not you should witness; there is a big difference in this attitude of prayer, think about it! When God has already expressed His will for us in the Bible, such as in this case [witnessing], praying and asking His response to the issue would be a wrong prayer. Rather, know that it is God's will for you to always witness, then ask Him for opportunities to do so and for the strength, through the Holy Spirit, to speak boldly for Christ. I have heard stories of Christians praying for prolonged periods of time, asking God if it would be okay to witness to their neighbor: do not do this, just go and witness! It is God's will for you to do so! Also, there are those Christians who are waiting to be led by God before witnessing; again, this is wrong: just go and witness in faith! — He has already told you so in His Word!

## Your Lifestyle Has to Be Consistent with the Talk

Remember that people are more interested in the way you live out your Christian faith, rather than what you tell them. Thus, if your lifestyle is inconsistent with godliness, you might as well not even bother to witness to anyone. This is an interesting principle: even the unbelievers can tell when a so called "Christian" is a hypocrite (i.e., saying one thing and doing the complete opposite). The unbelievers will use the same Bible Words to "shame you" in your hypocrisy. It is amazing how some unbelievers know the exact

Scripture to use in order to "shame" a Christian whose lifestyle is inconsistent with the faith. And sadly, they will make comments such as "it is because of people like you that I do not want to become a Christian." Of course this is FALSE, but the unbelievers will make such a comment.

*Even though we are not ultimately responsible for the salvation of others, we have to be careful because we have a responsibility to God, by allowing Him to work through us in reaching the unbelievers.*

<u>Bottom line</u> — do not allow your lifestyle to be a stumbling block to others (i.e., giving them an excuse to maintain a "closed" heart to the Gospel Message), rather, the Bible teaches that our lifestyles should draw others closer to God. **Even though we are not ultimately responsible for the salvation of others, we have to be careful because we have a responsibility to God, by allowing Him to work through us in reaching the unbelievers.** Hence our actions and lifestyles as Christians carry more weight than our endless "talking and preaching about the Lord Jesus."

**Learn to Accept Closed-doors**

There are times when you might be led by God to witness to someone, but their response will be: NO. If that is the case, do not coerce or manipulate others to reach a decision to accept God, that will not be God's will; and manipulating people might lead to either of these outcomes: (1) pushing them away, or (2) leading them to make a false confession to accept Christ just to impress you so that you would leave them alone. Neither of these will glorify God, so do not "push" people: **each person must perceive in their**

**heart their need for a Savior, and then submit their will, and choose to follow Jesus Christ.** As another example, there are other times when you might sense that you missed an opportunity for witnessing, and you will be disappointed. Regardless, do not be too hard on yourself; rather, repent and move on, while praying and trusting God to use someone else to witness to the person you might have missed the opportunity to share Christ with.

**Do not "Force It"**

Let your witnessing to others flow out of a genuine love and compassion for them. If you are struggling in this area, I recommend that you ask God to fill your soul with compassion for the "lost", and He will. Do not witness out of obligation; do it out of agape love. And keep in mind that you do not have to witness to everyone you come across. Most importantly, learn to sense the "right time", and take advantage of the opportunity. As mentioned earlier, the "right time" might be when someone asks you about your day, family, work, etc. Or when people are undergoing crisis, such as the death of a loved one, major losses, diseases, etc; times like these often present the opportunities for witnessing.

**Be Honest About What You Do Not Know**

If you are asked a difficult or challenging question when witnessing to someone and you do not know the answer: be honest. Never try to embellish God's Word in order to convince anyone. Doing that will limit the work of the Holy Spirit, who is the Spirit of Truth, Whose presence and power is quenched in the presence of lies. Rather, if you do not know the proper response, gently tell them you do not know, but you will research it and get back to them.

Also, remember to get their contact information to get back to the person later, if he or she will give it to you. If not, it is okay too, trust God and move on, then take the time to study and look up the answers so that you will be better prepared next time. **Be aware that you will never have all of the answers about your salvation because you are a finite being, so do not allow this to intimidate you. God can do miracles with the "little" you know.**

## You Cannot Tell What God is Doing in a Person's Heart

Please, never rule out anyone as unworthy to follow Christ, or as too "deep" into sin for God to accept them. You can never tell what God is doing in a person's heart. God can change anyone, and use anyone, even the worst sinner who ever existed! So as you witness to individuals, do not attempt to guess what is going on in their hearts based on their facial expressions, body language or even their speech. Your job is to be steadfast in witnessing as they allow you. I could give you dozens of examples in my own life in this regard. But due to a lack of space in this book, I will share two very brief examples here.

About two years ago, my office received a phone call from a very angry, bitter, and mentally sick and distraught teenager who wanted an appointment with me for her primary care medical needs, including refilling of her psychiatric drugs. She was referred to me by someone I know. Since that was the case, I did not want to turn her down, but the phone call came at the end of the day, and I was tired and looking forward to going home. Still, I decided to talk briefly to this lady over the phone, in order to ascertain how severe the situation was and to see if it could wait for another day. But while on the phone, I felt an immediate compassion for her, thus I asked her to come in and within 15 minutes, she arrived in my office. As she started to tell me her "horrible" psychiatry history and background, I quickly discerned that she had been experiencing a deep sense of abandonment and rejection. Her mother is homeless, and she had been to multiple foster homes since the age of 5. In spite of the bitterness and anger she exhibited, I sensed she was just seeking for acceptance and love. So I proceeded to ask her who Jesus was to her? Boy! she became very angry, blaming Jesus for her problems.

She was very resistant and essentially "shut down" to any discussions about Christ. My immediate reaction was to end the discussion, but I attempted to proceed. Each time I mentioned Christ, she got angrier; and I thought to myself that it was a wasted effort, thus I became quiet. After about 10 minutes of listening to her, I started to counsel her about the true meaning of love and acceptance in God's Kingdom. As I was ministering to her about God's kind of love, this young lady immediately started crying and telling me how she did not believe God loved her because of her horrible past and current circumstance.

Nonetheless, I proceeded to focus on the love of Christ; and finally, after about 75 minutes or so, she started to open up and she was calmed. By the time this lady left my office, she came to accept Christ as her Lord and Savior, and she did not request the refills of her medications. Ever since then, she has been steadily growing in Christ and she belongs to a local Bible believing church. Just like this lady in my example, do not rule out anyone as unreachable, and do not easily give-up. Had I given up on this lady, the Holy Spirit would not have had the opportunity to speak to her heart through my words. This lady did not accept to follow Christ because I did anything special: NO. I only spoke the Truth about God, and the Holy Spirit used that Truth to convict her. Likewise, you must be certain to speak the Truths about God to others if they would allow you to do so when you witness to them, regardless of the person's situation.

The other example I want to share is the very opposite from the story above. About a year ago, I had the opportunity to witness to a gentleman who was on Hospice Care (i.e., suffering from a terminal disease and given less than 1 year to live). When I met him, he was very happy to see me and commented about the fact that I was a Minister for Jesus Christ and a doctor, caring for peoples' spiritual and physical needs. So, I figured that he was open about God and thus engaged him in an open-ended dialogue. I boldly asked him if he was ready to meet Jesus, and why he was either ready or not ready for that encounter? Interestingly, he knew a lot about the Christian faith and about Jesus, but he professed to be an agnostic (i.e., a person who is unsure about the existence of God). So I engaged him into much dialogue as to why he was agnostic. We spent a very long time talking about God.

However, in spite of all of my efforts, he was not interested in accepting Jesus. I was very disappointed because I had initially sensed that he was interested and quickly assumed that he wanted to follow Jesus. After a long time discussing, he simply told me that he no longer wanted to continue the discussion: I respected his wish and stopped. But before I left his house, I asked him if I could pray for him, and he agreed, so I prayed for the Lord to open his heart.

Then I asked him if I could bring some books and other resources about Jesus to help him more, he agreed. He already owned a Bible, but he claimed he was not reading it. A few weeks later, I stopped by his house and dropped off some resources; but he was still not open to the discussion about accepting Christ.

I was very disappointed about that experience, but the Holy Spirit comforted me that it was not my fault. And up till today, I have never had another opportunity to witness to that gentleman again, so I do not know the outcome. I am trusting that, if he is still alive, he might have accepted Christ later, away from my presence; or that God might have used someone else. So this was a classic case whereby I was confident that this individual would accept Christ in front of me, but it did not happen; unlike the previous example, where I had not thought that she would be open to accepting Christ, yet she ended up accepting Jesus as her Lord and Savior! So you never know; just keep witnessing and trusting God with the results!

Also, keep in mind that while an individual may not accept to follow Christ in front of you, they may do that later, away from you. So never underestimate God's ability to use your words to penetrate a person's heart; thus, proclaiming the Truths about the Gospel Message is critical. We will only know fully, how many people we took with us to heaven, when we get there!

## Always Point People to Jesus Christ and How to Grow in the Faith

As you witness to others, remember that it is about Jesus Christ and not about your "awesome testimony." Be 100% certain to always point people to God through Christ as the sole reason and/or source of your testimony. Also, once someone accepts to follow Christ through you, make it a habit to obtain their contact information, so that you will be able to assist them in the process of learning and growing in the faith. For example, take the individual to your local church, recommend that he or she purchases a Bible and starts studying, right away. Most importantly, get the person involved in a Bible study, so that he or she can immediately start learning and growing in the Truths about true Christianity.

Please, do not lead someone to Christ without any sort of follow up. I liken this to taking a 6 month old child to the grocery store, then allowing the child to choose the right foods for him or herself: that child will not be able to do it! The child will be confused and perish! Likewise, as discussed earlier, a new Christian will perish, if he or she is not taught about the Truths of the faith.

In conclusion, when witnessing to others, we should never assume what the outcome will be. We must remember that our primary role as witnesses for Christ is to : (1) speak the truths about our testimonies; (2) share the honest Truths about God as found in His Word; and (3) trust the Holy Spirit with the final results as we abide in Him. With this in mind, let us now turn to the next page for some concluding remarks.

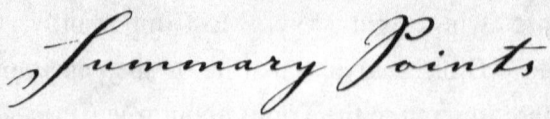

## Summary Points

- One of the primary reasons why Christians do not witness to others is because of fear of rejection;
- To be an effective witness for Christ, you must continually abide in Him, who is the source of your power;
- It is the responsibility of each Christian to witness for Christ through the power of the Holy Spirit;
- Individuals are more interested in your lifestyle as a Christian than what you tell them about Christ;
- Some basic principles and recommendations about witnessing include, but are not limited to: abiding in Christ; trusting the final outcome of your witnessing to God; being honest about your testimony; keeping in mind that it is always God's will for you to witness to others; not taking the results personally; and witnessing out of a genuine love and compassion for others, etc.

# Conclusion

The journey from the time you accept Christ as your Lord and Savior until you meet Him face to face in heaven is often filled with "twists and turns"; and major awesome surprises that will keep you "on your feet". You can be sure of this: God loves you as His beloved child , and He wants the best outcome for you each day in this journey. It may not seem like God is with you at times, but He is; this is the absolute Truth, so accept it by faith and REST!

Becoming a Christian is not about perfection. You will make many mistakes along the way. But a courageous and faithful Christian is one whose entire focus is on Christ —The author and finisher of our faith (Hebrews 12:2), while striving to mature daily.

In whatever you do, never give up on God, as He will never give up on you. Do not allow your circumstances or hardships to cause you to waver about the absolute Truths of who you have become in Christ! We walk by faith and not by sight: Focus on God and His Word, and everything else in your life will make sense and "fall in place". Remember the Lord Jesus said, as we seek first the Kingdom of God, all of our needs (spiritual, physical, emotional, etc) will be met (Matthew 6:33).

Most importantly, God's Word is powerful and has brought about lasting changes in the lives of millions of individuals, including myself, the author, since the creation of the earth. So, I highly recommend that you take some time to personally study and meditate on the Scriptures cited in this book. If you do that, based on the authority of God's Word, I guarantee that you will experience results. Then, as we are supposed to do as Christians, proceed to share your testimonies with others, in Jesus Name, AMEN!

I hope this book has equipped you with the basic understanding of what it means to become a true Christian, and stirred you to fully "excel" in your **New Identity** in Christ Jesus! Throughout this work, I have cited numerous Scriptures, hoping that you, the reader, will invest more time studying them in context for a deeper revelation; I encourage you to do that.

## Accept to Follow Jesus Christ Now!

Throughout this book, I have discussed how God wants a personal relationship with you. If you still have not accepted and received the FREE gift of salvation, this is the perfect time to do so, right now, before you close this book.

If you have been reading this book, you know exactly what to do. So right now, simply ask God to forgive ALL of your sins, then receive His Only Son, Jesus Christ, into your heart, and you will be saved!

If you still have questions regarding Salvation in Christ, I recommend that you reread chapter 1 of this book. Then, if you are sincerely ready to receive God's FREE gift to you, Jesus Christ, and you need help with doing so, simply say this prayer right now.

*Dear God, I thank you for sending your Only Son, Christ Jesus to die for all of my sins and to wipe out all of the penalties for my sins. I acknowledge I am a sinner. Please, I ask you to forgive all of my sins knowingly and unknowingly. Forgive me for not acknowledging this Truth before. Today, I believe in my heart in Your Son Christ Jesus, and in all of His claims and works. I believe He died on the cross for my sins and was raised from the dead after three days. Today, I am asking you, Jesus, to come into my life as my personal Lord and Savior and change me. From this day forward, I denounce all other false gods and idols in my life, and I have chosen you, the Only True living God. I declare by faith, that I am now a true Christian. Thank you God, in Jesus name, Amen*

## WE NEED YOUR TESTIMONY

We trust that God will use this book to draw you closer to Him. I want to hear from you. Please, feel free to contact us with your testimony of how the Lord has used this book to bring about changes in your life. However little the change might be, I will like to know, as it will be encouraging to us and to others who might benefit from your testimony.

When you send us your testimony, be sure to include your first and last name, telephone number, email and mailing address, and let us know if you want us to share your testimony with others, who might be encouraged.

**Contact Information**

Mail Your Testimony To

Dr. Ruth Tanyi Ministries, Inc
P O BOX 1806
Loma Linda, CA, 92354; USA.

Email Your Testimony To
Email: Info@DrRuthtanyi.org

# BIBLIOGRAPHY

Associated Press article "Wine Jug Bears Herod's Name," July 9 1996, http://articles.latimes.com/1996-07-09/news/mn-22431_1_wine-jug, accessed February 22, 2015.

Bruce L. Shelley, Church History in Plain Language (4th edition). Nashville: Thomas Nelson, 2013.

Charlie H. Campbell. Archaeological Evidence for the Bible. California: The Always Be Ready Apologetics Ministry, 2012.

F. F. Bruce. The Canon of Scripture. Illinois, IVP Academic, 1988.

F. F. Bruce. The New Testament Documents: Are they Reliable. Grand Rapids : William B. Eerdmans, 1981.

Flavius Josephus, The Antiquities of the Jews, 18:63-64.

Fox News "2,000-Year-Old Priestly Burial Box Is Real, Archaeologists Say," June 29th 2011, http://www.foxnews.com/scitech/2011/06/29/israeli-scholars-confirm-authenticity-2000-year-old-burial-box-belonging-to/, accessed February 10, 2015.

Gordon D. Fee and Mark L. Strauss. How to Choose a Translation For All Its Worth: A Guide to Understanding and Using Bible Versions. Grand Rapids: Zondervan, 2007.

Gordon D. Fee and Douglas Stuart. How to Read the Bible for All Its Worth. Grand Rapids: Zondervan, 2003.

Gordon D. Fee and Douglas Stuart. How to Read the Bible Book by Book: A Guided Tour. Grand Rapids: Zondervan, 2002.

Iraq and the Bible. http://www.biblearchaeology.org/post/2005/09/15/Iraq-and-the-Bible.aspx#Article, accessed March 25, 2015.

James Strong & John R. Kohlenberger 111, John. The New Strong's Expanded Exhaustive Concordance of the Bible: Red-Letter Edition. Nashville: Thomas Nelson.

J. D. Douglas & Merrill C. Tenney (editors). NIV Compact Dictionary of the Bible. Grand Rapids: Zondervan, 1989.

Josh McDowell and Bill Wilson. Evidence for the Historical Jesus: A Compelling Case for His Life and His Claims. Oregon: Harvest House Publishers, 1988.

Josh McDowell and Sean McDowell. Evidence for the Resurrection: What It Means For Your Relationship with God. California: Regal, 1996.

Lightfoot, Neil R. How We Got The Bible (3rd edition, Revised and Expanded). Grand Rapids: Baker Books, 2003.

Los Angeles Times " Biblical Pool Uncovered in Jerusalem," August 9, 2005, http://articles.latimes.com/2005/aug/09/science/sci-siloam9, accessed February 5, 2015.

https://www.merriam-webster.com/dictionary/religion.

Metzger M. Bruce. The Canon of the New Testament. Its Origin, Development and Significance. Oxford: Clarendon Press, 2009.

Siroj Sorajjakool, Mark F. Carr and Julius Nam (editors). World Religions for Healthcare Professionals. New York: Routledge, 2010.

Tanyi, RA; Berk, LS; Lee JW; Boyd, K., Arechiga, A (2011). The effects of a Psychoneuroimmunology (PNI) based lifestyle intervention in modifying the progression of depression in clinically depressed adults. International Journal of Psychiatry in Medicine, 42(2):151-66.

The Chicago Hittite Dictionary Project. https://oi.uchicago.edu/

research/projects/chicago-hittite-dictionary-project, accessed May 10th 2015.

Walter C. Kaiser Jr. The Old Testament Documents: Are they Reliable and Relevant? Illinois: IVP Academic, 2001.

Wegner Paul. The Journey from Texts to Translations: The Origin and Development of the Bible. Grand Rapids: Baker Academic, 1999.

W. E. Vine, Merrill F. Unger, William White, Jr. Vine's Complete Expository Dictionary of Old and New Testament Words. Nashville: Thomas Nelson, 1996.

## OTHER BOOKS BY DR TANYI

Answers to the Toughest 25 Questions about the "Real Jesus"

Can I Trust the Bible as God's Word? How do I Know? What Is the Evidence?

**COMING SOON!**

13 Reasons why People Get Sick! A Biblical Perspective & Remedies

Did God Really Say that? How to Overcome Doubt and Receive God's Promises: 10 Life-Changing Lessons Learned from Overcoming Metastasis Colon Cancer.

Healed by the Stripes of Jesus: A True Story of God's Unconditional Grace and Love: My Story! My Miracle! How I Overcame Metastasis Colon Cancer: You can Be Healed Too!

# AUDIO CD TEACHING LIBRARY

The Heart of True Christianity: The Gospel Message of Jesus Christ: Answers to 10 Major Questions Pertaining to Your Salvation in Christ Jesus

What Are the Gifts of the Spirit?

Holy Spirit-Led Healthy Emotions: The Fruit of the Spirit and Your Health

How to Overcome Doubt and Receive God's Promises

13 Reasons Why People Get Sick: A Biblical Perspective & Remedies

Unforgiveness and Other Toxic Emotions: How to Walk in Forgiveness

## AUDIO CD TEACHING LIBRARY

Live Above Your Fears & Overcome Sicknesses and Diseases | Be Anxious No More | Daily Habits For Your Soul

## OTHER TEACHINGS BY DR TANYI

**Discipleship Bible Teaching Series**

**Biblical Preventive Health with Dr Ruth ® Magazine**

**13 Reasons Why True Christianity is Different: A Wall Mount Poster**
*A Call to Action Poster*

Visit **Dr Ruth Tanyi Ministries YouTube Channel** and watch our FREE Devotional Teachings, Plus Other FREE Teachings at your convenience, 24/7. Subscribe to our YouTube Channel and start enjoying our Free Teachings Today.

Visit www.Drruthtanyi.org/blog and watch our FREE Devotional Teachings.

## Obtaining Ministry Resources

To get more information about the above ministry resources, please visit our Website: **www.DrRuthTanyi.org**

Contact Information
You Can also Email or Contact us:

**Dr Ruth Tanyi Ministries, Inc**
P O BOX 1806
Loma Linda, CA, 92354, USA
Email: Info@DrRuthtanyi.org

## ABOUT THE AUTHOR

**Dr. Ruth Tanyi, DrPH, NP, ACSM HFS; CNS; MA Ministry**

Dr. Ruth Tanyi is a Bible Teacher, Doctor of Preventive Care/Integrative Medicine, Board Certified Nutritionist and Exercise Physiologist. She is the founder /CEO of Dr. Ruth Tanyi Ministries, a non-denominational Christian, non-profit ministry located in San Bernardino, California, with primary focus on spreading the uncompromising Gospel of Jesus Christ; sharing God's unconditional love and grace, while concurrently teaching others how to integrate Bible-based principles with medical lifestyle practices in order to prevent and overcome diseases.

Even before being healed by God from metastasis colon cancer and other diseases in 2009, Dr Ruth felt called by God into ministry. However, since her healing and experiential knowledge and revelation of the love and grace of God, she has become an ardent student and teacher of the Word of God.

Dr Ruth's greatest desire is to tell others about God's unconditional love and grace, which she supernaturally experienced, and to teach individuals the lessons she learnt from God on how she received her healing, thereby helping others to be set free as well. Since God is no respecter of persons, Dr Ruth wants to strengthen others by reminding them that if God can heal her, He (God), can set them free as well regardless of the doctor's diagnosis or prognosis: All things are possible with God.

Dr Ruth is a public speaker and author, and offers a CD and DVD teaching library in addition to books on various topics ranging from the essential doctrines of true Christianity, to teachings on the very

*About The Author*

essential connection between God's Word and Medicine. Dr Ruth is also actively involved in the Body of Christ via her involvement with other ministries in advancing the Gospel of Jesus Christ, and in espousing the necessity of knowing God's Word. She considers herself to be a non-denominational Bible believing Christian, with a deep desire to fellowship and work with fellow brothers and sisters in Christ, regardless of denominational differences, for the common goal of advancing God's Kingdom and proclaiming the Gospel Message of Jesus Christ in these last days.

Prior to her calling into ministry, she had produced numerous TV series on lifestyle practices and disease prevention which aired throughout Southern California, and are still broadcasting through various media such as True Health Broadcasting Network, and SmartLifestyleTV, a division of LLBN Network worldwide. Her award winning TV series "Bad Sugar"® which focused on Diabetes, in addition to her other TV teachings on lifestyle and disease prevention continues to change thousands of lives.

Dr Tanyi has published numerous academic peer-reviewed journal articles and research papers, and she continues to serve as external reviewer for various International academic peer-reviewed journals. She is still pursuing her academic research in the area of lifestyle practices in preventing and overcoming depression. She has been nominated and selected in WHO IS WHO IN AMERICA and in WHO IS WHO IN Medicine and Healthcare. She is in private practice in San Bernardino California, and lives in Southern California.

For more information visit www.DrRuthTanyi.org, or to contact Dr Tanyi to speak at your event, church or non-Christian event, email her at: DrRuth@DrRuthTanyi.org, or call (909) 383 7978.

www.ingramcontent.com/pod-product-compliance
Lightning Source LLC
Chambersburg PA
CBHW020938180426
43194CB00038B/247